Hiking
Waterfalls
Kentucky

A Guide to the State's Best Waterfall Hikes

Johnny Molloy

FALCONGUIDES

GUILFORD, CONNECTICUT

An imprint of The Rowman & Littlefield Publishing Group, Inc.
4501 Forbes Blvd., Ste. 200
Lanham, MD 20706
www.rowman.com
Falcon and FalconGuides are registered trademarks and Make Adventure Your Story is a trademark of The Rowman & Littlefield Publishing Group, Inc.

Distributed by NATIONAL BOOK NETWORK

Photos by Johnny Molloy unless otherwise noted
Maps by The Rowman & Littlefield Publishing Group, Inc.

British Library Cataloguing in Publication Information available

Library of Congress Cataloging-in-Publication Data available

ISBN 978-1-4930-3787-2 (paperback)
ISBN 978-1-4930-3788-9 (e-book)

∞™ The paper used in this publication meets the minimum requirements of American National Standard for Information Sciences—Permanence of Paper for Printed Library Materials, ANSI/NISO Z39.48-1992.

Printed in the United States of America

Contents

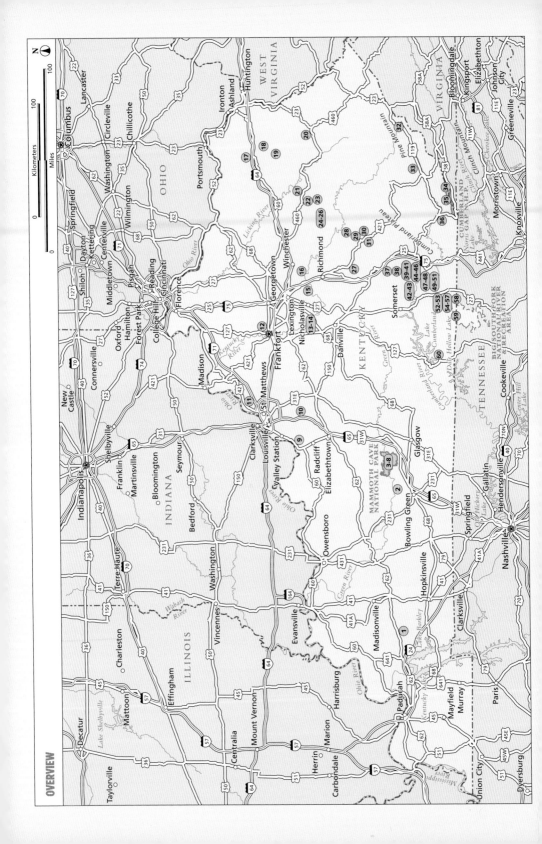

Waterfall Hikes of the Lower Cumberland Plateau

Introduction

What a pleasure it is to explore the waterfalls of Kentucky and to share them with you! Waterfalls are special—arguably the most enchanting spectacle in nature. At their most basic, they are simply falling water, yet after coming upon a waterfall, we are captivated and happily surprised at their transitory beauty.

Moreover, when combining waterfalls with hiking you construct a superlative outdoor experience. Hiking to a waterfall adds a reward at the end of the trail for your efforts. Additionally, while hiking to waterfalls you will likely see other jewels in the sparkling crown of nature.

Although simply moving water, waterfalls display a variety of characteristics—whether it is the wide, low tumble of Creation Falls in the Red River Gorge, or the powerful roar of Cumberland Falls on the Cumberland River, or the long, narrow descent of Marks Branch Falls in the Daniel Boone National Forest. Perhaps the variety of cataracts found along Pounder Branch comes to mind, or the geological fascination that is Sand Cave Falls. Maybe you think of the oft-photographed Bad Branch Falls in far eastern Kentucky, or the remarkable Saltpeter Cave Falls of western Kentucky.

There is more, for the hikes along the way to the waterfalls harbor additional rewards: Walk the hiker suspension bridge when visiting Hawk Creek Suspension Bridge Falls, soak in the spectacular waterside scenery of Dog Slaughter Creek en route to Dog Slaughter Falls, or stride atop the bluffs above Grayson Lake while visiting the waterfalls there. Admire the arch en route to Peter Branch Cascade. See the wildflowers while hiking to Raymer Hollow Falls at Mammoth Cave National Park. Each place is further enhanced by having both waterfalls and other superlative natural features we can enjoy on our hike.

Some of you may already have a favorite Kentucky waterfall. Or maybe you are looking for new waterfalls to visit. In this guide, sixty hikes will lead you to over a hundred named waterfalls! Among these, even the most experienced Kentucky waterfaller will discover new destinations. Anyone who has gone to a waterfall multiple times understands that waterfalls change with circumstances and seasons—this is a function of rain and time of year. For example, in spring you can see the white plunge of Laurel Gorge Falls in Elliott County, but that waterfall gushing in spring can slow to a trickle in autumn. However, a drenching summer thunderstorm may morph Tioga Falls into a brown roiling froth. Of course, the changing seasons frame the waterfalls differently month to month. The muted tones of winter's leafless hardwoods or a snowscape form a setting dissimilar to the colorful leaves of autumn or the shady forest of summer.

Using this guide you can explore over a hundred named waterfalls (plus other unnamed cataracts) stretched all across the Bluegrass State. The hikes range from quarter-mile jaunts to 9-mile treks.

Let's face it: In our rush-rush electronic universe, we are hurriedly looking for an authority, "someone who knows," to help us pursue our goal of hiking to Kentucky's waterfalls. This is my approach: Imagine you and me relaxing around a campfire, and you ask about the best waterfall hikes in Kentucky. I tell you as one friend would tell another, rather than reading like a dry, dull textbook. Kentucky's waterfalls are too captivating for that! Yet this guide conveys concise, organized information to help busy people make the most of their limited and precious outdoor recreation time, and provides an opportunity to experience the best waterfall hikes that can be had in the Bluegrass State.

While contemplating the waterfall hikes in this guide, the cataracts of Cumberland Falls State Park come to mind first. The popular Cumberland Falls stands out since it is the Bluegrass State's most powerful cataract, where the Cumberland River stretches 125 feet wide before crashing 67 feet in a roar of whitewater. Not only does it shine in the daytime, but it is also famed for its nocturnal "moonbow" where the light of the moon shining on the cataract creates a show, purportedly one of only two moonbows on the planet. Eagle Falls makes its 40-foot curtain dive into a boulder-lined plunge pool before flowing into the Cumberland River. Lesser-known Eagle Creek Cascade creates a sheet of white just upstream of Eagle Falls. Other cataracts at Cumberland Falls State Park include the slender spillers that are Rock House Falls, Blue Bend Falls, and Anvil Falls.

Other waterfalls are also protected in Kentucky's parks and forests. Arch Falls actually flows through a natural arch before tumbling from a vertical cliff line. Seldom-visited Dardy Falls makes a curtain plunge into a remote gorge at the Big South Fork National River & Recreation Area, while easily reached and frequently visited Broke Leg Falls spills in stages before making a dramatic dive from a high ledge, creating a variety of looks within one grand pour-over. You can visit the dramatic falls of Glade Branch near Paintsville Lake, or head to Natural Bridge State Park to see the falls on the Sand Gap Trail. Walk the interconnected system of nature trails to view Yahoo Falls—Kentucky's highest cataract—from multiple angles. Visit the strange and unique cataracts near Smoky Bridge, another natural arch, at Carter Caves State Park. Moreover, we have to mention the bevy of waterfalls found in the Cane Creek Wildlife Management Area highlighted by Vanhook Falls!

Kentucky's ample public lands are repositories for not only human and natural history, but also mountains, streams, wildlife, and waterfalls. Hike the wildflower-rich backcountry at Mammoth Cave National Park to see Bent Tree Falls, or walk to the slender spiller at the historic entrance to Mammoth Cave itself. Check out the dramatic drop of Tioga Falls near Louisville, or visit the falls at the preserved Shaker Village near Harrodsburg. Enjoy natural Kentucky and a fine waterfall at Raven Run Sanctuary. Admire Kentucky's most westerly hike-to cascade at the Jones-Keeney Wildlife Management Area.

A look at the waterfall locator map shows no cataracts in far western Kentucky. Why is that? It is simply a function of geology and geography. A lack of vertical variation as well as little resistant rock strata have prevented the waterfall-creating process from occurring.

How fortunate we are to have these preserved lands laced with trails that lead to varied waterfalls! The foresight of creating parks, forests, and preserves that protect waterfalls and building trails within them benefits us greatly, lending opportunities to experience the aquatic splendor that runs through the Bluegrass. These destinations also harbor the natural beauty for which Kentucky is known, from wilderness cataracts to waterfalls flowing through deep gorges to urban falls. May the hikes presented in this book help you appreciate the fantastic and varied waterfalls of Kentucky. Enjoy!

Helpful Hints for Photographing Waterfalls

Since all the hikes in this guide take us to waterfalls, it is only natural that many of us like to photograph these cascades, flumes, and cataracts of Kentucky. I photograph every waterfall I visit, preserving the collection on my computer and printing and framing some of my favorites. These are not all quality photographs—just snapshots to preserve a memory, as folks often do with their smartphones.

Not every photograph I take of a waterfall is great. Getting an excellent waterfall shot takes time, effort, and a little luck. For the best shots, you need a tripod, a digital camera with manual settings, and early morning or late afternoon light. Capturing the personality of a waterfall may mean several visits during different times of the year.

Here are a few hints that may help you become a better waterfall photographer:

Tripod. You need a sturdy tripod because you cannot hold a camera sufficiently steady when using slow shutter speeds. Be sure the tripod is compact and lightweight so you will be willing to carry it with you no matter how long the waterfall hike. Small models with telescoping legs are available. Set your camera and use a timer, reducing shake caused by pressing the shutter button.

ISO speed. The ISO setting on most modern digital cameras is designed to approximate the ISO speed (image sensor speed) of a chosen film and corresponding camera setting used in a traditional film camera. The lowest ISO number you will find on a digital camera, usually 80 but sometimes lower, is generally the preferred setting for shooting waterfalls. This number will yield the greatest detail, sharpness, effects, and color accuracy.

Shutter speed. Slow shutter speeds give a sense of movement. The movement of flowing water is completely stopped at $\frac{1}{2000}$ second. The fastest water will soften starting at $\frac{1}{60}$ second. At $\frac{1}{15}$ second, water movement will be clearly seen, but not be completely blurred. Most waterfall photographs are shot at $\frac{1}{8}$ second or slower to produce a soft quality. After a while you will find the shutter speed you like most, although the flow rate and speed of the waterfall will dictate your shutter speed.

Time of day. Midday sun creates harsh lighting and shadows. Visit a waterfall at daybreak or an hour before sunset, and use the wonderful quality of the light. Cloudy days afford additional photo opportunities.

Exposure. The white water of a falls will often cause underexposure of your shot, making the water gray and the foliage slightly dark. The beauty of digital cameras is being able to see what you just shot and adjust aperture, shutter speed, or ISO setting.

Perspective. Waterfall photographs need a reference to indicate their size. To give a feeling of depth and space, use foreground elements such as trees, rocks, and people. Try to frame the waterfall.

Position. Shoot from the top, bottom, or side of the falls. Treat the waterfall like a piece of architecture. Be creative while shooting the waterfall from different perspectives.

People. The high reflectance of water tends to underexpose people in a waterfall photograph. Position people considering proper lighting for both them and the waterfall.

Rainbows. If you are lucky enough to find a rainbow at the end of a waterfall, take as many pictures as you can. Shoot at different settings, then delete the least worthy pictures back at home on your computer.

Watch the horizon. Horizon lines should be level and in general not placed in the center of the composition. In the image area, look for wasted space, light and dark areas, and distracting elements.

The above tips will increase your chances for a spectacular waterfall photograph, making a lasting memory of your Kentucky waterfall hike.

How to Use This Guide

Take a close enough look and you will find that this guide contains just about every-thing you will ever need to choose, plan for, enjoy, and survive a waterfall hike in Kentucky. Stuffed with useful area information, *Hiking Waterfalls in Kentucky* features sixty mapped and cued hikes leading to over a hundred named waterfalls, grouped together geographically. The following is an outline of the book's major components.

Each hike starts with a short **summary** of the hike's highlights. These quick over-views give you a taste of the hiking adventures and the waterfalls to be visited. You'll learn about the trail terrain and what surprises each route has to offer.

Following the overview, you will find the **hike specs**—quick, nitty-gritty details of not only the waterfall but also the hike to it:

Waterfall height: This is how far the waterfall drops from top to bottom.

Waterfall beauty: This is a 1 to 5 number, 5 being the most beautiful waterfall.

Distance: The total distance of the recommended route—one-way for a loop hike or the round-trip on an out-and-back or lollipop hike. Options are additional.

Difficulty: Each hike has been assigned a level of difficulty: easy, moderate, or difficult. The rating system was developed from several sources and personal experi-ence. These levels are meant to be a guideline only and may prove easier or harder for different people depending on ability and physical fitness. An easy waterfall hike will generally cover 3 miles or less total trip distance, with minimal elevation gain and a paved or smooth-surfaced dirt trail. A moderate waterfall hike will cover up to 7 miles total trip distance in one day, with moderate elevation gain and potentially rough ter-rain. A difficult hike may cover more than 10 miles total trip distance in one day, have strenuous elevation gains, and/or have rough or rocky terrain.

Hiking time: The approximate average time it will take to cover the route. It is based on the total distance, elevation gain, and condition and difficulty of the trail. Your fitness level will also affect your time.

Trail surface: General information about what to expect underfoot.

Other trail users: Such as horseback riders, mountain bikers, etc.

Canine compatibility: Know the trail regulations before you take your dog hiking with you. Dogs are not allowed on several waterfall hikes in this book.

Land status: City park, state park or forest, national park or forest, etc.

Fees and permits: Whether you need to carry any money with you for park entrance fees and permits.

Maps: This is a list of other maps to supplement the maps in this book. USGS maps are the best source for accurate topographical information, but the local park map may show trails that are more recent. Use both.

Trail contact: This is the location, phone number, and website for the local land manager in charge of the trails within the selected hike. Get trail access information before you head out, or contact the land manager after your visit if you see problems with trail erosion, damage, or misuse.

The **Finding the trailhead** section gives you dependable driving directions to where you'll want to park. This also includes GPS trailhead coordinates, which you can plug into your device and then navigate to the trailhead. **The Hike** is the meat of the chapter. Detailed and honest, it is a carefully researched impression of the waterfall, the hike, and interesting things you may see along the way, both natural and human. Under **Miles and Directions,** mileage cues identify all turns and trail name changes, as well as points of interest.

A detailed and expertly crafted map is included with each hike and is derived from GPS tracks created while on the waterfall hike.

How to Use the Maps

Overview map: This map shows the location of each hike in the area by hike number.

Route map: This is your primary guide to each hike. It shows the waterfalls, all of the accessible roads and trails, points of interest, water, landmarks, and geographical features. It also distinguishes trails from roads and paved roads from unpaved roads. The selected route is highlighted, and directional arrows point the way.

Trail Finder

To get our readers started on the hikes that best suit their interests and abilities, we include this simple trail finder that categorizes each hike into a helpful list. Your hikes can fall under more than one category.

Hike #	Hike Name	Best Hikes to Tall Waterfalls	Best Hikes to Secluded Waterfalls	Best Waterfall Hikes for Swimming	Best Waterfall Hikes for Children	Best Waterfall Hikes for Nature Lovers	Best Waterfall Hikes for Backpackers
1	Saltpeter Cave Falls	•				•	
2	Shanty Hollow Lake Falls	•				•	
3	Cascades of the McCoy Hollow Trail		•	•			•
4	Cascades of the First Creek Trail		•			•	•
5	Wildcat Hollow Cascade		•			•	•
6	Collie Ridge Campsite Falls		•			•	•
7	Raymer Hollow Falls	•	•			•	•
8	Falls of Buffalo Creek, Miles-Davis Falls	•	•			•	•
9	Tioga Falls	•			•		
10	Cascades of Rock Run				•	•	
11	Cascades of Harrods Creek Park				•	•	
12	Hurst Falls	•			•	•	
13	Fulling Mill Falls				•	•	

Hike #	Hike Name	Best Hikes to Tall Waterfalls	Best Hikes to Secluded Waterfalls	Best Waterfall Hikes for Swimming	Best Waterfall Hikes for Children	Best Waterfall Hikes for Nature Lovers	Best Waterfall Hikes for Backpackers
14	Waterfall of Shaker Landing	•			•	•	
15	Evans Mill Falls				•	•	
16	Falls of the John Holder Trail		•	•	•		
17	Smoky Bridge Falls				•	•	
18	Falls of Grayson Lake State Park	•		•	•	•	
19	Laurel Gorge Falls	•			•	•	
20	Falls of Glade Branch	•	•		•	•	
21	Broke Leg Falls	•			•		
22	Copperas Falls	•	•			•	•
23	Creation Falls, Turtle Falls				•	•	•
24	Upper Whittleton Falls		•		•		•
25	Sand Gap Trail Falls		•			•	
26	Waterfall of Whittleton Arch					•	•
27	Anglin Falls	•			•	•	
28	Alcorn Branch Falls		•				•
29	Turkey Foot Cascade				•	•	
30	McCammon Branch Falls	•			•	•	
31	Flat Lick Falls	•		•	•	•	

Hike #	Hike Name	Best Hikes to Tall Waterfalls	Best Hikes to Secluded Waterfalls	Best Waterfall Hikes for Swimming	Best Waterfall Hikes for Children	Best Waterfall Hikes for Nature Lovers	Best Waterfall Hikes for Backpackers
32	Bad Branch Falls	•	•				
33	Gabes Branch Falls		•	•	•		
34	Sand Cave Falls		•			•	•
35	Falls of Shillalah Creek		•		•	•	
36	Honeymoon Falls, Divorce Falls				•	•	
37	Hawk Creek Suspension Bridge Falls	•	•			•	•
38	Big Dog Falls		•	•	•		
39	Vanhook Cascade, Vanhook Falls	•	•			•	•
40	Falls of Pounder Branch, Plus Vanhook Falls	•	•		•	•	•
41	Falls of Bee Rock				•	•	
42	Arch Falls, Bear Creek Falls	•		•		•	•
43	Peter Branch Cascade		•	•			•
44	Lakeside South Cascade				•	•	•
45	Ned Branch Falls		•		•	•	•
46	Falls of the Scuttle Hole	•			•	•	
47	Cascades of Bark Camp Creek		•	•		•	•

Hike #	Hike Name	Best Hikes to Tall Waterfalls	Best Hikes to Secluded Waterfalls	Best Waterfall Hikes for Swimming	Best Waterfall Hikes for Children	Best Waterfall Hikes for Nature Lovers	Best Waterfall Hikes for Backpackers
48	Star Creek Falls, Dog Slaughter Falls	•	•	•			•
49	Waterfalls of the Cumberland River Gorge	•				•	•
50	Blue Bend Falls		•		•		
51	Eagle Falls, Cumberland Falls, Eagle Creek Cascade	•			•	•	
52	Yahoo Falls, Roaring Rocks Cataract	•			•	•	
53	Falls of Jones Branch, Yahoo Falls	•	•			•	•
54	Julia Lynn Falls, Princess Falls		•	•	•		•
55	Princess Falls, Lick Creek Falls, Lower Lick Creek Falls	•	•			•	•
56	Blue Heron Falls, Upper Blue Heron Falls	•	•		•		
57	Dick Gap Falls, Big Spring Falls		•			•	•
58	Dardy Falls		•		•		•
59	Marks Branch Falls	•	•			•	•
60	Seventy Six Falls	•			•		

MAP LEGEND

Municipal

≡75≡ Interstate Highway

≡421≡ US Highway

≡835≡ State Road

≡457≡ County/Forest Road

├──┼──┤ Railroad

· · · · · · · State Boundary

Trails

- - - - - - Featured Trail

- - - - - - Trail

Water Features

Lake/Reservoir

River/Creek

Intermittent Stream

Waterfall

Rapid

Spring

Land Management

National Park/Forest/
Recreation Area

National Wilderness

State/Local Park/
Wildlife Area/Preserve

Symbols

∧ Arch/Cave

Boat Ramp

Bridge

▲ Campground

⊛ Capital

† Cemetery

•—• Gate

Lodging

🅿 Parking

Picnic Area

■ Point of Interest/Structure

Ranger Station

Restrooms

Stairs

Tower

○ Town

① Trailhead

Viewpoint/Overlook

Visitor/Information Center

Waterfall Hikes of Western and Central Kentucky

1 Saltpeter Cave Falls

You will be astounded at this most westerly waterfall hike in Kentucky. Here, in the Jones-Keeney Wildlife Management Area, a stream rolls off a rugged rock formation for 70 free-falling feet, crashing into a plunge pool and rock cathedral similar to those found in far eastern Kentucky. The walk itself is short. First, you make an easy walk then reach a short but steep journey down rocks, roots, and vegetation to reach the bottom of the cataract. However, once at the base of the falls, you can admire it from 360 degrees, including from inside the rock shelter that is Saltpeter Cave.

Waterfall height: 70 feet
Waterfall beauty: 5
Distance: 1-mile out-and-back
Difficulty: Easy; does have short, steep scramble
Hiking time: About 0.5 hour
Trail surface: Natural
Other trail users: None
Canine compatibility: Leashed pets allowed

Land status: State wildlife management area
Fees and permits: None
Maps: Jones-Keeney WMA; USGS Olney, Dawson Springs
Trail contact: Kentucky Department of Fish and Wildlife Resources, #1 Sportsman's Ln., Frankfort 40601; (800) 858-1549; www.fw.ky.gov

Finding the trailhead: From exit 92 on I-69 near Dawson Springs, take KY 109 south toward Dawson Springs and follow it for 1.8 miles to turn right on US 62 west. Drive for 4.2 more miles, passing through the town of Dawson Springs along the way, then make the sharp left uphill turn onto Archery Club Road. Follow it for 0.9 mile to the yellow gate on your right. Park here. If you go just a little farther on the road, it will dead-end at Hunter Cemetery. GPS: N37° 8.706' / W87° 45.085'

The Hike

Saltpeter Cave Falls is located within the confines of Jones-Keeney Wildlife Management Area (WMA), holding the distinction of being Kentucky's oldest publicly held hunting ground. Located near Dawson Springs, the WMA was purchased back in 1931 by—you guessed it—Joe Jones and B. L. Keeney, who were members of the Kentucky Game and Fish Commission, forerunners of today's Kentucky Department of Fish and Wildlife Resources. Jones and Keeney subsequently donated their parcel to the commonwealth.

Today the 2,055-acre plot is home not only to wildlife but also to some surprisingly rugged rock formations and a waterfall, part of the greater Dawson Cliffs, also known as Hunter Bluff. Here a tributary of East Fork flows from uplands off a precipice, spilling 70 feet into a pool, behind which stands Saltpeter Cave, a rock shelter. Judging by the name, potassium nitrate, aka "saltpeter" or "nitre," was once extracted from the shelter. Saltpeter was important to pioneer Kentuckians, since it

Saltpeter Cave Falls crashes into its plunge pool after a thunderstorm.

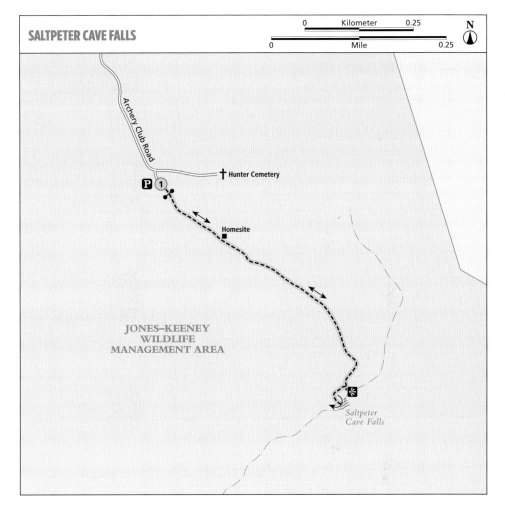

SALTPETER CAVE FALLS

was necessary in making gunpowder. The bluff above the cave—the one over which Saltpeter Falls makes its dive—is an excellent perch, and you will see that the falls dive from a pair of perched "horns" that add uniqueness to this pour-over.

The walk first takes you along a level area, once a homesite and now covered with spreading perennial flowers in spring. The track traces an old road with many fallen pines, yet hikers make their way down the track then reach the unnamed tributary of East Fork. Here you drop into scrubby brush and emerge at the cliff of Saltpeter Falls. Walk out on the rock to see the "horns" of the falls. From here a well-used path of sorts takes you steeply down rock, roots, and brush to the base of the cataract. It's a simple matter to explore the waterfall from all sides, as well as the rock shelter.

It is hard to believe a waterfall this dramatic and tall is hidden away in western Kentucky—see it for yourself. Other treasures such as an arch and more cliffs await someone willing to explore further at Jones-Keeney WMA.

Miles and Directions

0.0 Leave the parking area and pass around the yellow pole gate. Begin following an old road. Note the extensive perennial flowers.

0.4 Split right, descending through pines and scrubby woods. Reach the top of Saltpeter Cave Falls. Enjoy the view and descend a steep track.

0.5 Reach the bottom of Saltpeter Cave Falls. Explore the waterfall from all angles before backtracking to the trailhead.

1.0 Arrive back at the trailhead, completing the waterfall hike.

2 Shanty Hollow Lake Falls

You will be surprised by this beautiful waterfall at a state fishing lake. Mostly known for its angling possibilities, Shanty Hollow Lake also features some scenic shoreline. Here a tributary of upper Clay Lick Creek cuts through a stone gorge, recalling the Cumberland Plateau far to the east. The hike first leads along the lakeshore, turning up the embayment of Clay Lick Creek, then follows the tributary as it wanders beneath bluffs, cliff lines, and big boulders to end at the cliff where Shanty Hollow Lake makes its dive.

Waterfall height: 45 feet
Waterfall beauty: 4
Distance: 1.4-mile out-and-back
Difficulty: Easy
Hiking time: About 0.8 hour
Trail surface: Natural
Other trail users: None
Canine compatibility: Leashed pets allowed

Land status: State lake
Fees and permits: None
Map: USGS Reedyville
Trail contact: Kentucky Department of Fish and Wildlife Resources, #1 Sportsman's Ln., Frankfort 40601; (800) 858-1549; www.fw.ky .gov

Finding the trailhead: From Bowling Green, take KY 185 north/Gordon Avenue for 8.5 miles to turn right onto KY 1037. Follow it east for 3.5 miles, then turn right onto KY 1592 and follow it for 1 mile to its dead end at Shanty Hollow Lake. The trail starts in the southeast corner of the parking area. Take note not to block the upper lot during weekdays, as it is a school bus turnaround. GPS: N37° 8.690' / W86° 23.021'

The Hike

Shanty Hollow Lake comes in at 114 acres and offers quality angling for largemouth bass, channel catfish, and bream. It also has a surprisingly gorgeous parcel of land with a high waterfall as the centerpiece of a geologically rich cove. Locally known, Shanty Hollow Lake Falls attracts plenty of visitors—and the hike to it is short and sweet. In fact, the hike is busy enough to where multiple paths braid through the boulder gardens and bluffs found en route to the falls. Yet it is impossible to get lost, so make the most of your adventure and explore your way through the interwoven paths. But as all roads lead to Rome, all trails here lead between the trailhead and Shanty Hollow Lake Falls.

Upon reaching Shanty Hollow Lake Falls—by the way on the top 10 all-time Kentucky waterfall names list—you will dead-end at a semicircular stone cathedral overhanging a circular, boulder-bordered plunge pool—a classic Kentucky cataract. Nearby, stone bluffs run down the valley of the watercourse, with more boulders and rock houses in the area, all begging examination. It is a primeval setting, and one you

The stream of Shanty Hollow Lake Falls carves this mini slot canyon.

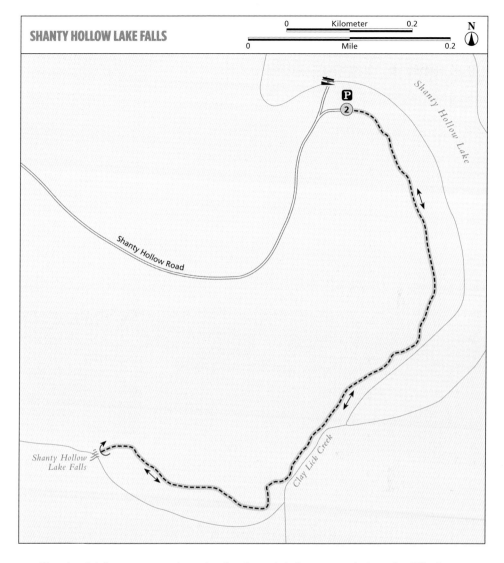

will enjoy. Make sure to explore the slender, mini slot canyon below the falls. Do not climb above the falls; reckless waterfallers get hurt here on a regular basis.

Miles and Directions

0.0 From the parking area, take the hiking trail leading from the southeast corner of the upper parking area. Pass around a metal and boulder barrier. Shanty Hollow Lake is off to your left, and boulders rise to your right as the Clay Lick embayment continues to narrow. Wildflowers are prevalent in spring.

0.3 Curve southwesterly into Clay Lick Creek. The trail starts to split apart with some braids along the cliff line up top, others along the stream below, and still others winding amid boulders.

0.5 Turn into the stream of Shanty Hollow Falls. Walls of the gorge house rock shelters. Enjoy the creek and the geological beauty.

0.7 Reach Shanty Hollow Lake Falls, pirouetting 45 feet from a rock border. The falls can be enjoyed from 180 degrees. Explore other geological wonderments, including the mini slot canyon just downstream from the falls. Backtrack to the trailhead.

1.4 Arrive back at the trailhead, completing the waterfall hike.

3 Cascades of the McCoy Hollow Trail

This hike begins at Temple Hill, the most remote trailhead in Mammoth Cave National Park. The waterfall exercise travels deep in the valley of the Green River, along bluffs and flats, turning into tributaries of the Green, where some enticing cascades can be found, including two that could serve as small swimming holes. Along the way you can enjoy deep-woods beauty and remoteness deserving of national park protection.

Waterfall height: In order, 16 feet, 5 feet, 7 feet, 5 feet

Waterfall beauty: 3

Distance: 6-mile out-and-back

Difficulty: Moderate; has one downhill that requires return uphill

Hiking time: About 3 hours

Trail surface: Natural

Other trail users: Equestrians

Canine compatibility: Leashed pets allowed

Land status: National park

Fees and permits: None

Maps: Mammoth Cave National Park; USGS Rhoda

Trail contact: Mammoth Cave National Park, PO Box 7, Mammoth Cave 42259; (270) 758-2180; www.nps.gov/maca

Finding the trailhead: From exit 48 on I-65 at Park City, take KY 255 north for 2.4 miles to KY 70. Turn left on KY 70 west for 2.5 miles, then stay right on Mammoth Cave Parkway and follow it for 2.3 miles to a four-way intersection. Here, turn left on Green River Ferry Road. After driving 1.3 miles, take the Green River Ferry across the Green River. Once across, continue driving for 5.7 more miles to KY 1827. Turn left onto KY 1827 and follow it for 1.1 miles. Turn left onto Ollie Road and follow it for 2.7 miles to Houchins Ferry Road. Make another left turn here, following Houchins Ferry Road for 3.3 miles to reach the Temple Hill trailhead on your left. GPS: N37° 13.127' / W86° 13.344'

The Hike

The McCoy Hollow Trail runs in and out of small valleys that are open by the Green River and tighten up away from the river. It is in the valleys where the cascades of McCoy Hollow are found, including Kettle Falls and McCoy Hollow Cascade, with its attendant pool. Bluffs and rock features rise above the streams, adding geological beauty.

Along the way you will see three primary waterfalls. The first hollow, where Three Springs Campsite lies, is home to sleek and slender Kettle Falls as well as a minor cascade just downstream at the trail crossing. Kettle Falls rolls down a mossy slope before diving from a ledge. The second hollow has a straightforward 7-foot overhung ledge drop into a pool that far outstrips the size of the stream creating the cataract. The noise of this pour-over will alert you to its presence. The final hollow—the actual McCoy Hollow—produces the final waterfall, McCoy Hollow Cascade. Here

This cascade in McCoy Hollow creates an outsized plunge pool.

a curved shelf creates a slide into which the stream flows, forming another relatively deep pool, bordered by a gravel bar.

And it is a fine hike to these falling waters of white. Being in the depths of the Green River valley creates a sense of remoteness, an adventure to the back of beyond. I highly recommend this hike for mid-spring, when the flowers are blooming and the trees are exploding with neon green leaves that seem to be growing before your very eyes. The water will be flowing better then, too. Overnighting at the Three Springs Campsite will further enhance the adventure.

The hike first drops off Temple Hill toward the Green River, the only extended elevation change of the adventure, then the river comes into view for the first time. Bluffs rise in majesty before you turn into the first hollow to see Kettle Falls. After Kettle Falls and the spring crossings, the path follows the hollow back downstream. Enjoy more looks down to the cedar-and-hardwood-covered flats along the Green River.

The path curves into another hollow, passing another waterfall. If the stream is flowing at all, you will hear this pour-over. The recovery pool is surprisingly deep for such a small stream. The McCoy Hollow Trail then repeats its pattern, curving around the head of this hollow and returning downstream. The path passes the waterfall a second time.

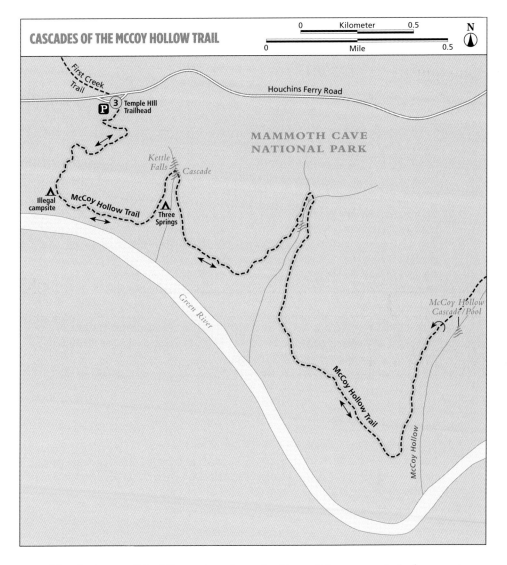

The final part of the hike cruises along the Green River yet again before turning into McCoy Hollow. Rock outcrops enhance the beauty of the mini-gorge. Keep your eyes peeled on the stream below and you will see this final 5-foot angled rush of water—McCoy Hollow Cascade—fill a bluish recovery pool. This pool is a good place to enjoy falling water, still water, and the preserved nature that is Mammoth Cave National Park.

Miles and Directions

0.0 The McCoy Hollow Trail leaves the Temple Hill trailhead, descending easterly in hickory-oak woodlands with an understory of beech on an increasingly sloped hillside. The path turns into a steep hollow, cutting a watery path to the Green River.

0.6 Reach an illegal campsite on a semi-level shelf above the Green River. The path makes a sharp left, heading east, and the Green River comes into view on your right. An impressive bluff with overhanging rock borders the trail to your left. This and other bluffs recall the cliff lines and rock shelters of eastern Kentucky.

0.9 Curve away from the Green River and into a feeder branch hollow to intersect the spur trail to the Three Springs backcountry campsite. The Three Springs camp is set in an attractive flat alongside the feeder branch.

1.0 The trail leads you just above a low, wide cascade at a point where three streams come together, downstream of Kettle Falls. Kettle Falls can be found about 100 feet upstream from this trail crossing. Look to the northwest of the McCoy Hollow Trail where the trail crosses the main stream. When the leaves are off the trees, you can see Kettle Falls from the path. Look for an angled falls flowing over moss-covered stone then dropping from a rock rim.

1.4 The trail turns left into the next hollow.

1.6 Come to another cascade. It is close and audible from the trail but difficult to reach, as the slope is steep here. A careful scramble will take you to the overhung shelf from which this stream falls, creating a surprisingly deep pool.

1.7 Rock-hop the stream of the previous falls, plus a feeder branch, then turn back out toward the Green River.

2.1 Return to the Green River.

2.6 Turn into McCoy Hollow.

3.0 Reach McCoy Hollow Cascade and pool. It is well off the trail below, but worth the scramble. The slope is less than that of the previous cataract at 1.6 miles, making access easier. Here the stream filters wide over a mossy stone slab into a deep plunge pool. Backtrack to the trailhead.

6.0 Arrive back at the trailhead, completing the waterfall hike.

4 Cascades of the First Creek Trail

This hike not only leads you to a pair of respectable spillers, but also takes you by some of the more dramatic trailside scenery in Mammoth Cave National Park. First, cruise old roads, soaking in some evidence of pre-park dwellers, then drop to view a delicate veil-type spiller glittering over a small rock house. From there, pass rock outcrops, cacti, and hemlocks far above the Nolin River, gaining views. Descend into bottoms of the Nolin River, where you will find a two-tiered streamer pouring over a mossy rim.

Waterfall height: In order, 8 feet, 10 feet
Waterfall beauty: 3
Distance: 7.6-mile out-and-back
Difficulty: Moderate; does have some hills at the end
Hiking time: About 4.5 hours
Trail surface: Natural, some gravel
Other trail users: Equestrians

Canine compatibility: Leashed pets allowed
Land status: National park
Fees and permits: None
Maps: Mammoth Cave National Park; USGS Rhoda
Trail contact: Mammoth Cave National Park, PO Box 7, Mammoth Cave 42259; (270) 758-2180; www.nps.gov/maca

Finding the trailhead: From exit 48 on I-65 at Park City, take KY 255 north for 2.4 miles to KY 70. Turn left on KY 70 west for 2.5 miles, then stay right on Mammoth Cave Parkway and follow it for 2.3 miles to a four-way intersection. Here, turn left on Green River Ferry Road. After driving 1.3 miles, take the Green River Ferry across the Green River. Once across, continue driving for 5.7 more miles to KY 1827. Turn left onto KY 1827 and follow it for 1.1 miles. Turn left onto Ollie Road and follow it for 2.7 miles to Houchins Ferry Road. Make another left turn here, following Houchins Ferry Road for 0.1 mile to reach the First Creek trailhead on your right. GPS: N37° 14.644' / W86° 11.452'

The Hike

This hike offers a bit of everything en route to a pair of cascades: pre-park history, geological wonders, flora, views, wildflowers, streams, and a river. The First Creek Trail first travels an old road (muddy in places during waterfall season), then follows a ridge running westward. The first cascade comes as a surprise after walking over 2 miles in dry uplands. A short, abrupt descent leads you to a shower-like, low-flow waterfall dropping 8 feet over a rock rim. The rock is carved out beneath the rim, forming a small, wet shelter. This delicate dropper is no aquatic show of force, rather a simple spiller of beauty. The rock outcroppings around it enhance the scenery, and sitting boulders beg a rest.

From this first pour-over, the path descends to a moist mini-gorge; hemlock trees thrive in the cool, shady environment. Soon you'll turn away from the gorge and traverse a linear, sloped rock slab that proves difficult to navigate. Note the change in vegetation here, as the south-facing slope harbors mountain laurel and chestnut oaks that enjoy drier situations than hemlock. A keen eye will also spot prickly pear cactus, another dry-site species very unusual for these parts. In just a short span, this hike displays Mammoth Cave National Park's rich biodiversity—from hemlocks to cacti—that makes this park so special above the ground as well as below.

The path joins the top of the ridge, which now becomes narrow and rocky. Steep bluffs drop off to your right, and occasional views open into Second Creek below. Notice the hemlock trees here, too, that grow just below the rock face on the north side of the ridge.

From there you pass fine views of the Nolin River and a spur to the confluence of Second Creek and the river. The First Creek Trail then rolls through the ash-covered bottomland of the Nolin River. To your right is the river bottomland; a bluff rises to your left. Straight-trunked tulip trees, sycamores, and maples add to the forest. Ahead, to your right, look for piled rocks amid the woods before coming to a chimney and other metal relics marking an old homesite.

This two-tiered spiller can be found in the Nolin River bottoms.

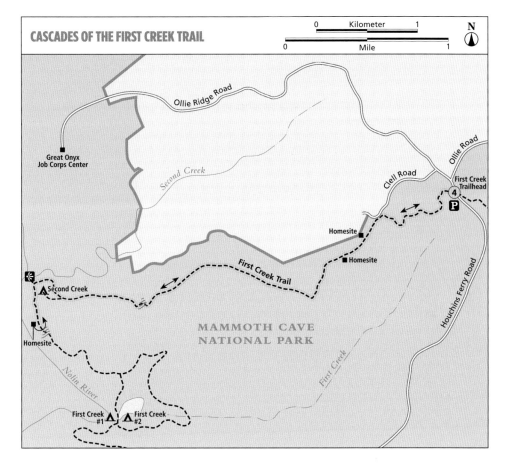

0   Kilometer   1

0   Mile   1

N

Ollie Ridge Road

Great Onyx
Job Corps Center

Second Creek

Ollie Road

Clell Road

First Creek
Trailhead

4

P

Homesite

Homesite

Second Creek

Houchins Ferry Road

First Creek Trail

MAMMOTH CAVE
NATIONAL PARK

First Creek

Homesite

Nolin River

First Creek
#1

First Creek
#2

Beyond the homesite, cross a streamlet to find the second waterfall, a 10-footer dropping over a rock formation upstream, within sight of the trail. The second falls flows from a hollow to then widen and dance down a ferny, mossy, stone face in two tiers before bouncing its way over the trail then slowing in the Nolin River bottoms.

Neither of the two cataracts along this hike have a name, but both of them can be called fine destinations in a national park that is a pride of Kentucky.

Miles and Directions

0.0 The First Creek Trail leaves the First Creek trailhead from the lower end of the teardrop-shaped parking area. Do not confuse this with the Wet Prong Trail, which leaves east from the bottom end of the parking area, near the trailhead kiosk. The First Creek Trail leaves west from the parking loop and dips to a draw that runs to the First Creek drainage, to your left (south). Pass a second branch, then climb toward the park border among oak-dominated woods.

0.6 Come to a gate on the park boundary line. Here the First Creek Trail joins old Clell Road, heading southwest, shaded by Virginia pines, dogwoods, and oaks. The trail mostly straddles the ridgeline dividing First and Second Creeks.

0.7 The old road passes a homesite on the right marked by persistent yuccas, planted by the forgotten settler who cleared this now-forested country.

1.1 Pass another homesite.

1.4 The trail makes an abrupt right turn yet stays along the ridgeline, undulating a bit, passing flats.

2.6 Reach the first cascade after a short drop. Here a low-flow stream forms a shower-like 8-foot fall over a rock shelter. Boulders make good relaxing spots. After resting, break through a bluff below, following a stream through a cleft in the rocks before curving into the Second Creek valley. Enjoy glances into the Nolin River gorge. Walk among hemlocks and atop bare naked rock.

3.2 Intersect the spur trail left to a Second Creek backcountry campsite. Keep descending into moister terrain beyond the spur trail. Second Creek comes into view on your right. The hillside is steep here as the path circles the Second Creek campsite uphill. Enjoy looks at Second Creek.

3.5 Pass a spur trail leading right to a view of the Nolin River. The trail continues down to a campsite at the confluence of Second Creek and the Nolin River.

3.8 Reach the second cascade, a 10-foot two-tier dropper, to the left of the trail, after passing a homesite on the right of the trail. This waterfall is visible from the trail, with a short user-created spur leading to the pour-over. Backtrack to the trailhead.

7.6 Arrive back at the trailhead, completing the waterfall hike.

5 Wildcat Hollow Cascade

This Mammoth Cave National Park waterfall adventure starts in the preserve's northwest corner, where it then drops into the attractive Wet Prong Buffalo Creek valley. The hike then wanders down the vale, turning into Wildcat Hollow, a slender slit through which a clear stream courses, eventually to dance off a trailside ledge then make a widening slide.

Waterfall height: 8 feet
Waterfall beauty: 3
Distance: 5.6-mile out-and-back
Difficulty: Moderate
Hiking time: About 3 hours
Trail surface: Natural, some gravel
Other trail users: Equestrians
Canine compatibility: Leashed pets allowed

Land status: National park
Fees and permits: None
Maps: Mammoth Cave National Park; USGS Rhoda
Trail contact: Mammoth Cave National Park, PO Box 7, Mammoth Cave 42259; (270) 758-2180; www.nps.gov/maca

Finding the trailhead: From exit 48 on I-65 at Park City, take KY 255 north for 2.4 miles to KY 70. Turn left on KY 70 west for 2.5 miles, then stay right on Mammoth Cave Parkway and follow it for 2.3 miles to a four-way intersection. Here, turn left on Green River Ferry Road. After driving 1.3 miles, take the Green River Ferry across the Green River. Once across, continue driving for 5.7 more miles to KY 1827. Turn left onto KY 1827 and follow it for 1.1 miles. Turn left onto Ollie Road and follow it for 2.7 miles to Houchins Ferry Road. Make another left turn here, following Houchins Ferry Road for 0.1 mile to reach the First Creek trailhead on your right. GPS: N37° 14.644' / W86° 11.452'

The Hike

Wildcat Hollow Cascade is a modest but proud spiller located along the Wet Prong Trail. This 8-foot pour-over is easy to spot, since the trail curves right around the falls, deep in Wildcat Hollow. Its unusual form is the cataract's most noteworthy feature. Just below the trail it makes a standard ledge drop over layered limestone, then it fans out, widening lavalike over slick rock before slipping from a little lip into a pool and flowing on down a stone-bluff-lined mini-gorge. Most passersby give it a top-down glance, since the walls of the creek below the falls defy easy approach. However, determined waterfallers can enjoy a face-on view, looking upstream. One possibility is to work your way directly down the cascade using caution. Find another route if the water is high.

The hike to Wildcat Hollow Cascade is straightforward. (*Note:* Equestrians use this trail with regularity—expect to deal with muddy spots during the waterfall season.) You start on a ridge dividing Wet Prong Buffalo Creek from First Creek, both tributaries of the Green River, the famed Kentucky waterway coursing through the

Wildcat Hollow Cascade can be found just below the trail.

heart of Mammoth Cave National Park. Along the ridge you pass through what were once the fields of settlers, before the area grew up with pines, pioneering the forest. In their shade grow the future kings of the area: the maples, oaks, and hickories. You will see many fallen pines now. More will tumble over time; in a generation or two, very few pines will be left. This is known as forest succession.

After passing a trail junction, you will turn into the Wet Prong valley. This beautiful bluff-bordered branch of the Green River flows year-round amid a lush woodland of beech and magnolia trees, with oaks finding their place higher up the valley. Wildflowers grow rampant in spring. The best time to undertake this hike is winter through early spring to enjoy the cascade and the more than sixty species of wildflowers that grace Mammoth Cave National Park.

The hike passes a homesite, traversing a rock-lined old road before turning back out to the main Wet Prong valley. Mountain laurel borders the trail—watch for its pinkish white blooms in early May. Small spring branches gurgle across the trail. You soon turn into Wildcat Hollow. A clear stream sings over rocks at its base, above which rise cliff lines. You will cross this tributary of Wet Prong just above Wildcat Hollow Cascade. This tumbler first drops off a rock ledge then fans out atop a wide rock before slowing in a pool. Overhanging rock houses border the stream here. The flat

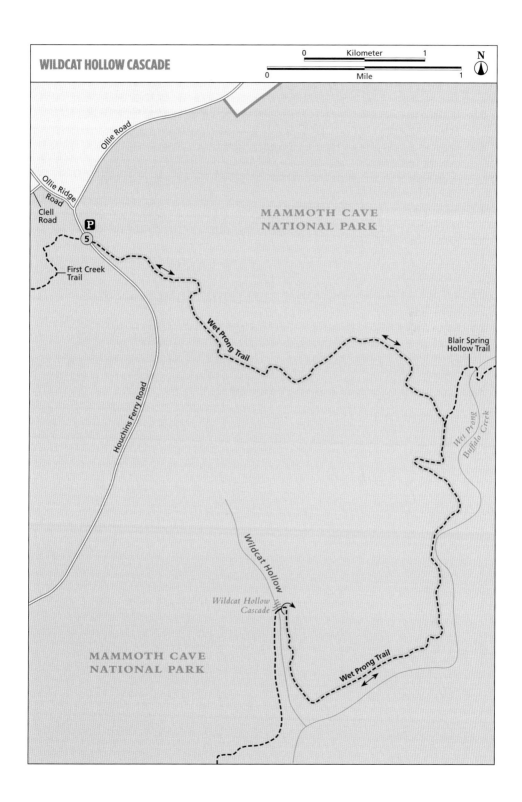

0   Kilometer   1

0   Mile   1

N

Ollie Road

Ollie Ridge Road

Clell Road

P

5

MAMMOTH CAVE
NATIONAL PARK

First Creek Trail

Wet Prong Trail

Blair Spring
Hollow Trail

Houchins Ferry Road

Wet Prong
Buffalo Creek

Wildcat Hollow

Wildcat Hollow
Cascade

Wet Prong Trail

MAMMOTH CAVE
NATIONAL PARK

on the far side of the stream makes for a fine picnic spot, where you can best determine your approach to the falls should you desire a face-on view.

Miles and Directions

0.0   The Wet Prong Trail leaves the First Creek trailhead from the east side of Houchins Ferry Road, heading southeast, through a forest transitioning from pines to hardwoods.

0.6   Reach an old trail junction. Horse hitching posts are located in the level area. This was once the beginning of the now-abandoned Wet Prong Loop. The signed Wet Prong Trail keeps easterly on a ridgeline. White oaks dominate the ridge, which forms a divide between branches of Wet Prong.

1.4   Reach a bona fide trail intersection on a slope. Here the Blair Spring Hollow Trail leaves left to cross Wet Prong and climb to Collie Ridge. Stay right with the Wet Prong Trail, heading down the Wet Prong valley.

1.5   Pass an old homesite. The trail is lined with a rock wall to your right. Curve into and out of a small hollow.

2.5   Turn right into Wildcat Hollow. The stream of the cascade flows below through a slender mini-canyon.

2.8   Reach Wildcat Hollow Cascade at the trail crossing of the stream flowing through Wildcat Hollow. Here the watercourse narrows to jump off a ledge then fan outward at an angle before slowing in a pool. Note the gorge walls below the 8-foot cascade. Backtrack to the trailhead.

5.6   Arrive back at the trailhead, completing the waterfall hike.

6 Collie Ridge Campsite Falls

This waterfall lies in the heart of the Mammoth Cave National Park backcountry and is a solid hike to reach the cataract, no matter from what trailhead you start. Our hike takes the easiest route, using the upland Collie Ridge Trail its entire length. The track passes perhaps more evidence of pre-park residents than any other trail in the park. The final segment of the hike descends into lowlands to reach Collie Ridge campsite, where a spring emerges from the hillside, immediately fashioning a waterfall, then runs over rocks to reach a slender ledge drop directly beside the campsite before flowing on to meet Wet Prong Buffalo Creek.

Waterfall height: In order, 8 feet, 5 feet
Waterfall beauty: 4
Distance: 9.2-mile out-and-back
Difficulty: Moderate despite the mileage
Hiking time: About 4.5 hours
Trail surface: Gravel, natural
Other trail users: Equestrians
Canine compatibility: Leashed pets allowed

Land status: National park
Fees and permits: None
Maps: Mammoth Cave National Park; USGS Rhoda
Trail contact: Mammoth Cave National Park, PO Box 7, Mammoth Cave 42259; (270) 758-2180; www.nps.gov/maca

Finding the trailhead: From exit 48 on I-65 at Park City, take KY 255 north for 2.4 miles to KY 70. Turn left on KY 70 west for 2.5 miles, then stay right on Mammoth Cave Parkway and follow it for 2.3 miles to a four-way intersection. Here, turn left on Green River Ferry Road. After driving 1.3 miles, take the Green River Ferry across the Green River. Once across, continue driving for 5.7 more miles to KY 1827. Turn left onto KY 1827 and follow it for 1.1 miles. Turn left onto Ollie Road and proceed 0.4 mile to the Lincoln trailhead on your left. GPS: N37° 15.329' / W86° 9.509'

The Hike

Collie Ridge Campsite Falls is yet another example of the fascinating result of the honeycombed karst system below the surface of Mammoth Cave National Park, for the waterfall emerges from a hill and wastes no time to immediately form a curtain-drop cataract before flowing to execute a classic free fall from a stone rim. Although neither part of Collie Ridge Campsite Falls is tall, they are still worthy of inclusion in this guide.

Furthermore, Collie Ridge campsite is a recommended overnight destination for backpackers who like to pitch their tent in the back of beyond and work for their solitude. A backcountry permit is required for overnight stays at Mammoth Cave National Park, and can be obtained at the national park visitor center. Finally, if the rain has been heavy and the trails are especially sloppy (almost all the trails in the Mammoth Cave backcountry are shared with equestrians; the horses can muck up

This waterfall is a welcome sight for backcountry campers at Collie Ridge.

the trails), the Collie Ridge Trail is graveled throughout its length and delivers foot-friendly conditions.

The Collie Ridge Trail traverses a crest dividing the Wet and Dry Prongs of Buffalo Creek, bisecting the heart of the Mammoth Cave National Park backcountry. It is heavily used, and includes a spur path connecting to a park-permitted equestrian outfitter. The path leaves the Lincoln trailhead and works its way south, then southwest, along an old roadbed to end not far from the Green River. The Collie Ridge Trail has a gentle grade through most of its length, with very few steep sections. Since it runs along the ridge, a backbone trail if you will, multiple trail junctions are encountered, all of which are clearly signed. After relishing this track from end to end, you will be rewarded with another waterfall enhancing the aboveground world of Mammoth Cave National Park.

Miles and Directions

0.0 Leave the Lincoln trailhead on a narrow path that is the Collie Ridge Trail. Descend through a hardwood forest dotted with pines. Traverse a dry drainage.

0.3 Reach a wide roadbed. Turn right (south) and you are now on the historic roadbed that runs along Collie Ridge. Continue a downgrade on a much wider track, saddling alongside upper Dry Prong Buffalo Creek.

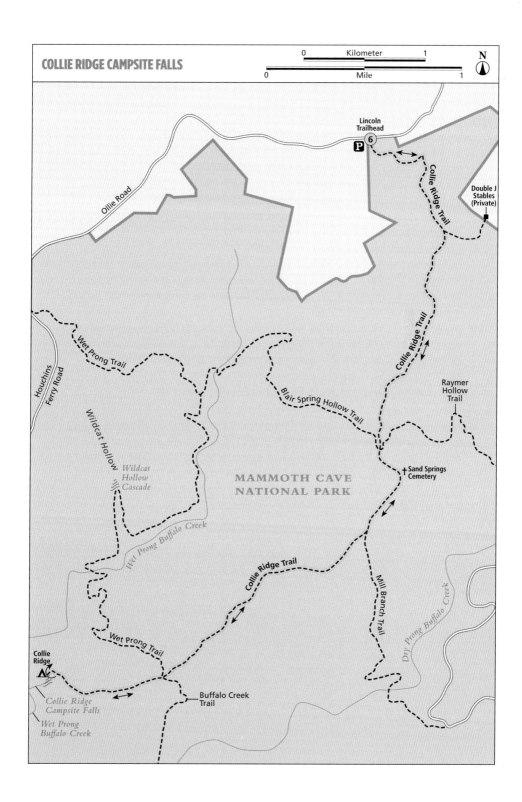

COLLIE RIDGE CAMPSITE FALLS

0 Kilometer 1

0 Mile 1

N

Lincoln Trailhead
P 6
Collie Ridge Trail
Double J Stables (Private)
Ollie Road
Collie Ridge Trail
Wet Prong Trail
Raymer Hollow Trail
Houchins Ferry Road
Blair Spring Hollow Trail
Wildcat Hollow
Wildcat Hollow Cascade
MAMMOTH CAVE NATIONAL PARK
† Sand Springs Cemetery
Wet Prong Buffalo Creek
Collie Ridge Trail
Mill Branch Trail
Dry Prong Buffalo Creek
Wet Prong Trail
Collie Ridge △
Collie Ridge Campsite Falls
Wet Prong Buffalo Creek
Buffalo Creek Trail

0.8 Come to a trail junction. Here a spur path leads left and uphill to Double J Stables, a horse rental and equestrian camp facility. The Collie Ridge Trail continues south, crossing over the uppermost Dry Prong—here it may actually be flowing. Make a moderate but steady ascent from the creek, leveling out in an open area in tall woods.

1.3 Reach a high point, and roll along Collie Ridge.

2.0 Come to another intersection, with horse hitching posts. Here the Blair Spring Hollow Trail leaves right and travels 1.8 miles to the Wet Prong Trail. The Raymer Hollow Trail leaves left 6.1 miles to the Mill Branch Trail (and Raymer Hollow Falls along the way), then another mile to Maple Springs Loop. Keep straight on the Collie Ridge Trail.

2.1 Come to Sand Springs Cemetery. Here you'll find quite a few primitive stones serving as markers. Curve back to the southwest, making a rocky descent to a gap. As you climb out of the gap, look left below the trail for a large rock overhang, similar to those in eastern Kentucky.

2.5 Intersect the Mill Branch Trail, which heads left for 1.9 miles to meet the Raymer Hollow Trail. Stay with the Collie Ridge Trail, dividing the watersheds in a southwesterly direction. Homesites are prevalent along this part of the trail. Look for large trees beside the trail—these are often indicators of homesites. Open rock slabs spill over the trail bed in places, and the path dips into shallow gaps.

3.9 The Collie Ridge Trail ends at a trail junction. Here the Wet Prong Trail leaves right and travels 0.9 mile to the McCoy Hollow Trail, while the Buffalo Creek Trail heads left for 2 miles to meet the Dry Prong Trail. Stay straight with the spur trail leading to the Collie Ridge backcountry campsite.

4.1 Pass horse hitching posts. From here the trail narrows and begins descending toward Wet Prong.

4.6 Reach the Collie Ridge campsite after a final short but steep drop. The level bench houses a tent pad, fire ring, lantern post, and horse hitching posts. The falls are to your left. On the steepest part of the hill, the upper 8-foot cataract emerges from the hillside. The second falls is very near the campsite, making its 5-foot drop from a stone lip, and is the water source for the campsite. Backtrack to the trailhead.

9.2 Arrive back at the trailhead, completing the waterfall hike.

7 Raymer Hollow Falls

Raymer Hollow Falls is the perennial favorite and most beloved trailside cataract in all of Mammoth Cave National Park. The 22-foot spring-fed spiller forms a mantle of white as it drops over a trailside ledge near Dry Prong Buffalo Creek. The trek to this icon first follows wide and easy Collie Ridge before dipping to Raymer Hollow and Dry Prong, where the cataract can be viewed after a crossing of Dry Prong, normally wet at this juncture.

Waterfall height: 22 feet
Waterfall beauty: 4
Distance: 7.6-mile out-and-back
Difficulty: Moderate to difficult
Hiking time: About 3.5 hours
Trail surface: Gravel, natural
Other trail users: Equestrians
Canine compatibility: Leashed pets allowed

Land status: National park
Fees and permits: None
Maps: Mammoth Cave National Park; USGS Rhoda
Trail contact: Mammoth Cave National Park, PO Box 7, Mammoth Cave 42259; (270) 758-2180; www.nps.gov/maca

Finding the trailhead: From exit 48 on I-65 at Park City, take KY 255 north for 2.4 miles to KY 70. Turn left on KY 70 west for 2.5 miles, then stay right on Mammoth Cave Parkway and follow it for 2.3 miles to a four-way intersection. Here, turn left on Green River Ferry Road. After driving 1.3 miles, take the Green River Ferry across the Green River. Once across, continue driving for 5.7 more miles to KY 1827. Turn left onto KY 1827 and follow it for 1.1 miles. Turn left onto Ollie Road and proceed 0.4 mile to the Lincoln trailhead on your left. GPS: N37° 15.329' / W86° 9.509'

The Hike

I still remember the first time I laid eyes on Raymer Hollow Falls nearly twenty years ago. I was surprised at how such a strong-flowing waterfall could emerge from a spring then tumble down a ledge. In addition, the waterfall wasn't even on a creek! At that time I had a less-than-complete understanding of the underground plumbing system that is Mammoth Cave National Park. Here, rain filters into the ground, gathers in underground passages, emerges in springs, and continues deeper into the Mammoth Cave system, always moving, and always eroding limestone to create additional passages. Elsewhere, aboveground streams dry up and emerge down valley. And so it goes.

In the case of Raymer Hollow Falls, a spring emerges from the hillside above Dry Prong Buffalo Creek, then pours over a layered limestone shelf before making a vertical free fall. It then flows on to feed Dry Prong Buffalo Creek soon after.

Raymer Hollow Falls is Mammoth Cave National Park's most acclaimed cataract.

Your conduit to Raymer Falls is first Collie Ridge, where an old road turned trail makes for an easy wide passage. Collie Ridge was one of the most heavily settled areas in what became Mammoth Cave National Park. Homesite evidence is commonplace. The old road has been graveled and improved since that time, making the walk easier. (*Note:* You will be sharing the trails here with horses and they can muck things up, despite the park's efforts at keeping the pathways in good shape.)

You will leave Collie Ridge after joining the Raymer Hollow Trail, working your way down the east slope of Collie Ridge into tributaries of Dry Prong. During waterfall season—winter through spring—these tributaries will be flowing. The downward gradient is mild, and you are close to Raymer Hollow Falls upon passing the spur trail to the Raymer Hollow campsite, set on a bluff above Dry Prong.

The final part of the trek leads down along bluff-bordered Dry Prong to the bottomland, where a creek crossing awaits. Despite the name, Dry Prong is perennially wet in its upper watershed. It the water is up, you may have to ford. However, your reward awaits just across the stream. A short spur leads to tall Raymer Hollow Falls, spilling in 22 feet of aquatic glory. Many a hiker and equestrian take the short spur to the cataract. The waterfalls, Dry Prong, and the stone-pocked vale fashion a national park–level scene that will confirm Raymer Hollow Falls as Mammoth Cave National Park's most acclaimed waterfall.

Miles and Directions

0.0   Leave the Lincoln trailhead on a narrow path that is the Collie Ridge Trail. Descend through a hardwood forest dotted with pines. Traverse a dry drainage.

0.3   Reach a wide roadbed. Turn right (south) and you are now on the historic roadbed that ran along Collie Ridge. Continue a downgrade on a much wider track, saddling alongside upper Dry Prong Buffalo Creek.

0.8   Come to a trail junction. Here a spur path leads left and uphill to Double J Stables, a horse rental and equestrian camp facility. The Collie Ridge Trail continues south, crossing over the uppermost Dry Prong—here it may actually be flowing. Make a moderate but steady ascent from the creek, leveling out in tall woods.

1.3   Reach a high point, and roll along Collie Ridge.

2.0   Come to another intersection, with horse hitching posts. Head left on the Raymer Hollow Trail as it begins a gently graded excursion down to Dry Prong. The gravel track first leads northeast.

2.3   The Raymer Hollow Trail descends in earnest, then crosses several creeklets. You stay well above the stream of Raymer Hollow below.

3.0   Circle around an old homesite.

3.4   The spur trail to the Raymer Hollow campsite leaves left. Stay straight with the Raymer Hollow Trail. Sporadic bluffs rise to your right.

3.6   Drop into the bottoms of Dry Prong.

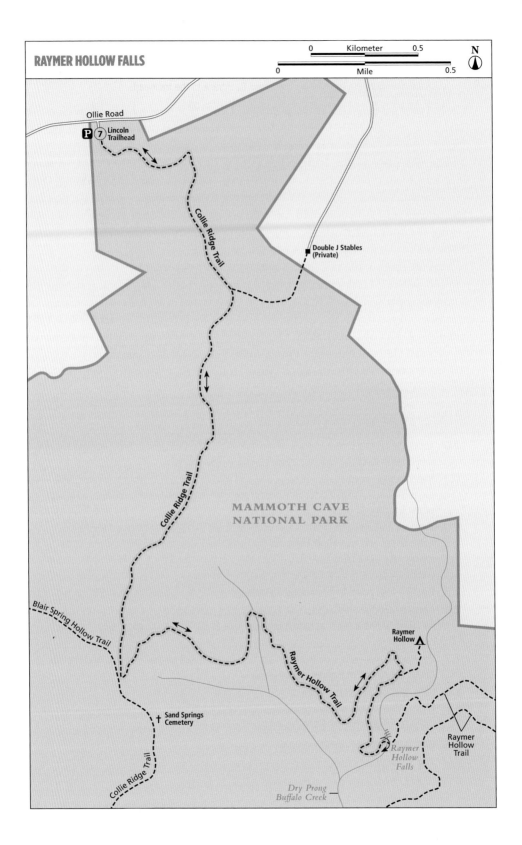

RAYMER HOLLOW FALLS

0   Kilometer   0.5
0   Mile   0.5

N

Ollie Road

P 7 Lincoln Trailhead

Collie Ridge Trail

Double J Stables (Private)

Collie Ridge Trail

MAMMOTH CAVE
NATIONAL PARK

Blair Spring Hollow Trail

Raymer Hollow Trail

Raymer Hollow

† Sand Springs Cemetery

Collie Ridge Trail

Raymer Hollow Trail

Raymer Hollow Falls

Dry Prong
Buffalo Creek

3.8 Make the crossing of Dry Prong. Raymer Hollow Falls makes its 22-foot maneuver across the stream, fed by a spring which in turn feeds Dry Prong. After crossing the creek, it is but a short stroll to the base of the pour-over. Backtrack to the trailhead.

7.6 Arrive back at the trailhead, completing the waterfall hike.

8 Falls of the Buffalo Creek Trail, Miles-Davis Falls

This hike takes you through a formerly settled part of Mammoth Cave National Park to several intriguing and varied waterfalls. The Buffalo Creek Trail leads past a pair of warm-up falls, one a spring that emerges as a waterfall, then passes a waterfall that ends in a sink. Next, the hike swings past a slender cataract spilling from atop a bluff. Tall Miles-Davis Falls, the final cataract, provides the denouement as it dramatically tumbles in sweeping stages.

Waterfall height: In order, 5 feet, 10 feet, 6 feet, 25 feet, 55 feet
Waterfall beauty: 5
Distance: 7.4-mile out-and-back
Difficulty: Moderate; does have short bush-whack segment
Hiking time: About 4.5 hours
Trail surface: Natural
Other trail users: Equestrians on most trails

Canine compatibility: Leashed pets allowed
Land status: National park
Fees and permits: None
Maps: Mammoth Cave National Park; USGS Rhoda
Trail contact: Mammoth Cave National Park, PO Box 7, Mammoth Cave 42259; (270) 758-2180; www.nps.gov/maca

Finding the trailhead: From exit 48 on I-65 at Park City, take KY 255 north for 2.4 miles to KY 70. Turn left on KY 70 west for 2.5 miles, then stay right on Mammoth Cave Parkway and follow it for 2.3 miles to a four-way intersection. Here, turn left on Green River Ferry Road and drive 1.3 miles to take the Green River Ferry across the Green River. Once across, continue driving for 2.2 miles to Maple Springs Loop. Turn left and follow Maple Springs Loop 0.9 mile to the trailhead on your right. The signed Buffalo Creek Trail leaves left, west from the trailhead. GPS: N37° 12.333' / W86° 8.358'

The Hike

If the water is up, you will be in for a variety of waterfalls, displaying the aquatic possibilities of cataracts in Mammoth Cave National Park. You will first come to Bison Falls, a straightforward ledge fall. Below it spills Xterra Falls, a spring-fed cataract that emerges from a hillside, stair-stepping over angled ledges before dropping the balance of its 10-foot descent over rock rim. Bison Falls can be seen and heard from the trail, but you must work your way about 100 yards downstream to find Xterra Falls, flowing down the north side of the creek.

Next comes the most unusual falls—when it is flowing—Bent Tree Falls. This seasonal cascade flows across the trail then follows its stone bed, making a strange U-turn before dropping about 6 feet over a ledge to disappear into a sinkhole, feeding the world's longest mapped cave system that is this national park. Down-trail you will

This tier of Miles-Davis Falls forms a delicate curtain.

reach Bluffs Falls, a narrow rivulet threading 25 feet over a protruding rock lip. Finally, a 0.3-mile bushwhack leads you to Miles-Davis Falls, so termed for the nearby cemetery of the same name. This 55-foot multistage highlight first falls about 15 feet over a rock edge in curtain fashion before flowing a bit to tumble in three ever-widening descents, creating a magical spot seen by few park visitors.

And the hike itself isn't too bad either. The Buffalo Creek Trail uses pre-park roads in its westward quest, passing old homesites along the way. Its unusual turns are owed to the fact that the road once skirted the property lines of settlers who lived at what became Mammoth Cave National Park. In many places, the long-used track has cut a deep bed into the once-tilled land, now regrown to forest.

The hike has little in elevation change until it modestly drops to the Bluffs Campsite and Bluffs Falls. The off-trail segment from Bluffs Falls to Miles-Davis Falls stays along the same elevation contour line, making this last part a matter of working your way through brushy vegetation at times. Like all waterfall hikes at Mammoth Cave, this endeavor is best enjoyed from winter through early spring, while the water is flowing and you have the added benefit of being able to more easily make your way to Miles-Davis Falls.

While here, consider overnighting at the Bluffs Campsite. The backcountry camp is equipped with a fire ring, tent pad, and lantern post, and is set amid big boulders and imposing cliff lines. Get your water from Bluffs Falls. Note that a backcountry permit is required for overnight stays. Permits are available at the Mammoth Cave visitor center.

Miles and Directions

0.0 The Buffalo Creek Trail leads from the southwest part of the Maple Springs trailhead, near the restrooms, tracing a gravel path westerly. After just a short distance the Sal Hollow Trail leaves left, while the Buffalo Creek Trail curves right to soon join old Buffalo Road near a metal pole gate. Head left, westbound again. Cedars and hardwoods shade the southwesterly tacking track.

1.1 Intersect the Turnhole Bend Trail on your left, which heads 1.8 miles to the Turnhole Bend backcountry campsite. To your right, the Dry Prong Trail leads 2.3 miles to again meet the Buffalo Creek Trail. Stay straight with the Buffalo Creek Trail, then curve right, northerly, still on the old road.

1.3 Come to 5-foot Bison Falls, to the left of the trail. When flowing, the curtain spiller is close enough to be heard. Prior to Bison Falls, the stream of the cataract flows over a naked rock slab. This streambed forms Sal Hollow and eventually feeds the Green River. To see Xterra Falls, continue downstream below Bison Falls about 100 yards and look for the 10-foot falls making its dash and dive after emerging from the north side of the vale.

1.6 The Buffalo Creek Trail first curves north only to make a hard left, turning westbound. It now stays on the ridgeline to the north of Sal Hollow.

2.1 Come to Bent Tree Falls and Sinkhole just to the left of the path. A streambed empties into the sink. If you peer down, you can see the former roof of the sink, which collapsed from undercutting moisture as it seeped into a small fissure in the ground. Finally the weight of

FALLS OF BUFFALO CREEK, MILES–DAVIS FALLS

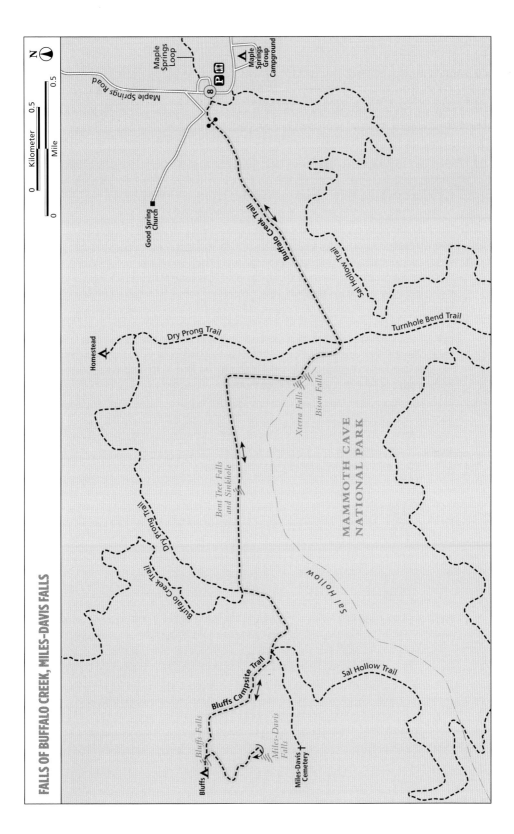

the rock and soil over the hole became too much to bear, causing the cave-in. If flowing (and not just dripping), this is a fascinating fall, with the stream's dash across the trail curving 180 degrees into the sink before disappearing 6 feet over a ledge.

2.4 After making a hard left turn, the Buffalo Creek Trail intersects the Sal Hollow Trail. At this point the Buffalo Creek Trail splits right as a narrower path. However, we stay straight, southbound on the old road, which has now become the Sal Hollow Trail. Continue easy, mostly level hiking.

2.7 Come to a four-way intersection. Here, head right onto the Bluffs Campsite Trail, while the Miles-Davis Cemetery Trail keeps straight. The balance of the Sal Hollow Trail heads left 7.8 miles back to the Maple Springs trailhead. Turn right on the Bluffs Campsite Trail (no horses allowed) and travel westerly on a singletrack path in woods.

2.9 The Bluffs Campsite Trail descends in earnest. Watch carefully, as old settler roads can lead you astray.

3.3 Reach slender Bluffs Falls, spilling 25 feet from an overhanging cliff line. Here the Bluffs Campsite Trail continues a short distance to the Bluffs Campsite. Now, to reach Miles-Davis Falls, leave southeast from Bluffs Falls, crossing the stream forming the hollow below. Do not follow the hollow downstream; rather, continue along the same elevation contour line of the bluffs over which Bluffs Falls dives. Curve southwest, making your way through woods mixed with brush, then turn back southeast into the next hollow south. Large, building-block boulders accompany the route. If flowing decently, you will hear (and see if the leaves are off the trees) the cataract pouring across the chasm of this hollow in multiple glorious tiers. Work your way toward the falls.

3.7 Reach Miles-Davis Falls. The highest fall drops about 17 feet from a sheer bluff, then flows on to the next three drops, cascading in curtain-like stair-step fashion, widening upon descent. Admire the cataract but respect the resource and try not to churn up the ground around the spring-fed pour-over. Backtrack to the trailhead.

7.4 Arrive back at the trailhead, completing the waterfall hike.

Waterfall Hikes of North-Central Kentucky

9 Tioga Falls

This huge 100-plus-foot cataract falls in stages from a hillside spring on Fort Knox Military Reservation. A marked and maintained trail open to the public leads you to this aquatic wonder. Parts of the path follow the Muldraugh Road, a stage road from the early 1800s. Once at the falls, signs warn hikers from climbing the multistage white walls of water. Honor the regulations of the military reservation and you will not get hurt, as have so many visitors to Tioga Falls down through the decades.

Waterfall height: 115 feet
Waterfall beauty: 5
Distance: 2-mile out-and-back
Difficulty: Easy; does have a few hills
Hiking time: About 1.1 hours
Trail surface: Natural, a little bit of road
Other trail users: None
Canine compatibility: Leashed pets allowed

Land status: United States military reservation
Fees and permits: None
Maps: Tioga Falls National Recreation Trail; USGS Fort Knox
Trail contact: Radcliff/Fort Knox Tourism & Convention Commission, PO Box 845, 562 A1 North Dixie, Radcliff 40159; (270) 352-1204; www.radclifftourism.org

Finding the trailhead: From exit 1 on KY 841/Gene Snyder Freeway south of downtown Louisville, take US 31W south for 9.5 miles and turn left on KY 835/Louisville and Nashville Turnpike. Follow KY 835 south for 0.8 mile to reach the trailhead at a three-way road intersection, below a high railroad trestle. The parking area is signed. GPS: N37° 58.131' / W85° 57.663'

The Hike

Located in northern Kentucky in the Ohio River valley, in an area with a much lesser concentration of waterfalls than on eastern Kentucky's Cumberland Plateau, Tioga Falls is yet one of the highest, most impressive waterfalls in the entire Bluegrass State, and that is saying a lot. Dropping over 100 feet in two primary stages, Tioga Falls bursts forth from a hillside. It then stair-steps down a high, mostly vertical stone wall and gathers again to widen down a slide before plunging in a final vertical curtain descent, then flows past trail's end. The Tioga Falls Trail, your route to this thriller of a spiller, traces a historic wagon road part of its route, adding another layer of allure for this path.

One important thing to know: This hike takes place on the property of Fort Knox. Please adhere closely to trail regulations. Unfortunately, waterfall visitors have been climbing upon and around the falls, then getting injured and worse, forcing the military reservation to erect unsightly signs and barriers around the falls. In the past, the trail has even been closed. It has since reopened, but is currently shorter than its original loop design. The trail is also subject to temporary closure if the army is using the area for military exercises. Despite the warnings, you are welcome to visit Tioga

Tioga Falls can be a rip-roaring spiller in wintertime.

Falls and also check out the Bridges to the Past Trail. It starts at the same trailhead and follows the old route of the L & N Turnpike, crossing some of the oldest standing stone bridges in the entire Commonwealth of Kentucky.

The hike to Tioga Falls starts beneath a high trestle of the Paducah & Louisville Railroad. You will be crossing that track later. For now, pass under the archway delineating the Tioga Falls Trail and quickly reach a stream, the outflow of Poplar Spring, another upwelling in these hills overlooking the Ohio River. A hiker bridge takes you over the stream to head west, only to briefly join Railroad Trestle Road. The road leads past an unusual parcel of private property. A brick structure, once a 1930s Southern Bell Telephone Company relay station, is now reincarnated (at least part of it) as a residence.

This private property is the reason for the short walk along the road, for beyond the curious home the hike rejoins the natural surface trail on a sharp climb to reach the tracks of the Paducah & Louisville Railroad. Here, make sure to look north across the Ohio River valley, reaching into Indiana and as far as the clarity of the sky allows. In the fore, the hike leads you across the tracks of the still-active railroad, now following the old Muldraugh Road, another wagon track that opened up early Kentucky. As you work around a bend, look for the leveling rock work that has kept this track in use to this day, albeit as a hiking trail.

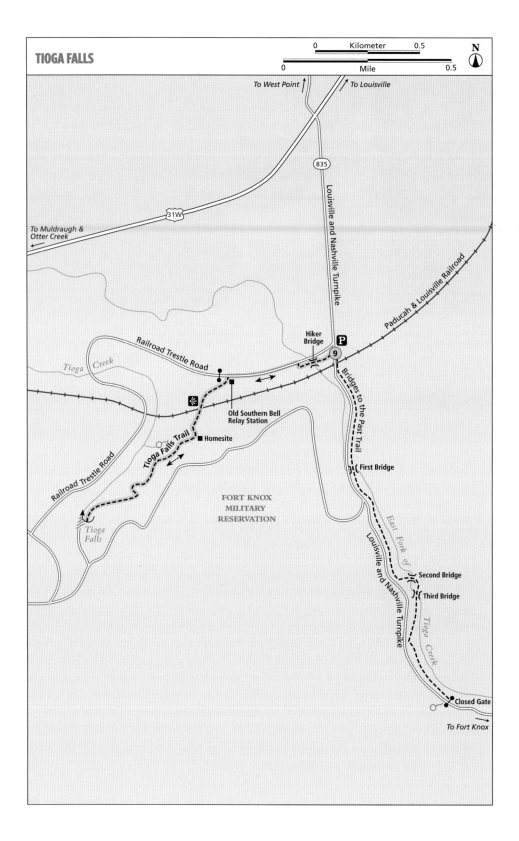

TIOGA FALLS

Kilometer
0   0.5

Mile
0   0.5

N

To West Point

To Louisville

835

31W

To Muldraugh &
Otter Creek

Tioga Creek

Railroad Trestle Road

Louisville and Nashville Turnpike

Paducah & Louisville Railroad

Hiker
Bridge

P

9

Old Southern Bell
Relay Station

Bridges to the Past Trail

Tioga Falls Trail

■ Homesite

Railroad Trestle Road

FORT KNOX
MILITARY
RESERVATION

First Bridge

Tioga
Falls

East Fork of

Louisville and Nashville Turnpike

Second Bridge

Third Bridge

Tioga Creek

Closed Gate

To Fort Knox

The trail passes well above a spring and 40-foot waterfall below, on an ultra-steep slope. Before long the water song of Tioga Falls echoes in the valley. Turn a corner and there you are. Here, Tioga Falls makes its spectacular set of drops, seemingly out of place in this part of Kentucky. Yet there is the waterfall in all its 100-foot-plus glory. As mentioned, many a visitor has yelled "Hey y'all! Watch this!" then proceeded to climb the falls and along its super-steep slopes, eventually tumbling into an injury. Some make it back to the trailhead under their own power, while others are carried out on a stretcher. Remember this—the numerous accidents have resulted in the barriers and signage at the falls, marring the scene a bit and making the incredible cataract more difficult to legally photograph.

Miles and Directions

0.0 From the trailhead, join the Tioga Falls Trail to soon reach the creek of Poplar Spring. Cross the stream on a hiker bridge, heading west.

0.1 The trail abruptly turns right to meet Railroad Trestle Road. Upon reaching the road, turn left, continuing westerly.

0.4 After passing the old Southern Bell Telephone relay station, leave left from Railroad Trestle Road, rising steeply on a natural surface path.

0.5 Come to the Paducah & Louisville Railroad. Before crossing the tracks, look back to the north for a panoramic view of the Ohio River valley stretching into the Hoosier State. Cross the railroad tracks and join the old Muldraugh Road as it wanders through high hills. Look for extensive rock work on the downside of the old wagon road.

0.6 Pass an old homesite on your left. Look for still-blooming perennial flowers and squared-off spots. As you continue down the trail, listen for a spring bursting forth and creating a waterfall well below on the ultra-steep hillside.

1.0 Come to Tioga Falls and the official end of the trail. Here, to your left, the outflow of Tioga Spring creates a 100-foot-plus-high multistage cataract. Do not climb the falls. The trail once continued past to other falls in the distance but is now closed. Honor military reservation regulations. Backtrack to the trailhead.

2.0 Arrive back at the trailhead, completing the waterfall hike.

10 Cascades of Rock Run

This little trek at fabled Bernheim Forest takes you past a series of quaint cataracts in the Rock Run watershed. Your loop hike first takes you to a crossing of Rock Run, where you walk a bit upstream to find a wide, low pour-over on the creek. Continue on hillsides above the stream to find a few more spillers, wet-weather tributaries of Rock Run. While here, combine this short hike with a trip to the forest and arboretum visitor center as well as other trails.

Waterfall height: In order, 3 feet, 8 feet, 4 feet, 7 feet
Waterfall beauty: 3
Distance: 0.5-mile lollipop
Difficulty: Easy walking; potentially difficult creek crossing
Hiking time: About 0.4 hour
Trail surface: Natural
Other trail users: None
Canine compatibility: Leashed pets allowed

Land status: Private arboretum, open to the public
Fees and permits: Fee required on weekends; weekdays are free
Maps: Bernheim Forest Trail Map; USGS Fort Knox
Trail contact: Bernheim Arboretum and Research Forest, 2075 Clermont Rd., Clermont 40110; (502) 955-8512; www.bernheim.org

Finding the trailhead: From exit 112 on I-65 south of Shepherdsville, take KY 245 south for 0.9 mile and turn right into Bernheim Forest. Follow the signs for the visitor center. Obtain information and a trail map at the visitor center, then take Forest Hill Drive for 0.7 mile to the Rock Run Trail, on your left. Trailhead parking is on the right. GPS: N37° 54.7512' / W85° 38.8895'

The Hike

Bernheim Forest is an important asset to the Commonwealth of Kentucky. The private research forest and arboretum's motto is "connecting people with nature"—and that it does. Although modestly endowed with falling water, the preserve contains over 15,000 acres of native upland hardwood forest as well as a collection of 8,000 varieties of trees, shrubs, and other plants. Therefore, it is a combination of natural woodland and laid-out gardens.

This sizable tract of land came to be through the philanthropy of a German immigrant by the name of Isaac W. Bernheim, who migrated to the United States shortly after the Civil War. The 20-year-old wandered the Northeast making a living as a salesman before finding his way to the Bluegrass State. Once in Kentucky, he got into the bourbon-making business and grew an empire. The capitalist was very grateful to his adopted state of Kentucky and his adopted country. As a memorial he financially supported statues of American heroes such as Abraham Lincoln, Thomas Jefferson, and Henry Clay for public display.

This delicate faucet-like spiller pours into Rock Run.

In 1929 the distiller of bourbon purchased what was to become Bernheim Forest. The land was in poor condition, having been logged over and mined for iron ore. Nevertheless, Mr. Bernheim determined to provide a preserve where hard-working citizens could escape to nature and eye-pleasing gardens. The famed landscape architecture firm of Frederick Law Olmsted (which designed New York's Central Park, among other parks) went to work building lakes and roads and designing the gardens.

Mr. Bernheim appreciated seeing his vision come to be. Alas, he passed away in 1945, five years before the forest opened to the public in July 1950. Nevertheless, his vision of a place connecting people with nature has endured. The forest, located south of Louisville, attracts over 250,000 visitors annually.

Truth be known, very few visitors come here for waterfalls. However, Rock Run does feature cascades in season, primarily from winter through mid-spring. The stream drains hills of the forest, including the hilltop upon which a nearly century-old fire tower stands (another must-visit while at Bernheim Forest).

Rock Run is a tributary of Long Lick Creek, flowing outside the boundaries of Bernheim Forest and itself a tributary of the Salt River, which in turn feeds the Ohio River. Although spring-fed, Rock Run can nearly run dry during the high summer and fall. Early spring is an excellent time to visit, as the cascades will be flowing and the Rock Run watershed will be rich with wildflowers. In fact, in the early days of Bernheim Forest, the valley of Rock Run was used to cultivate wildflowers.

The hike is a simple loop. You will leave the trailhead then split left, dropping down to Rock Run. If the water is up, the cascades will be flowing but this crossing will be more difficult, perhaps even a wet ford. After crossing Rock Run, make your way upstream a short distance to view the sole spiller on Rock Run. Here the stream makes a wide but low curtain of white, bordered by layered rock bluffs. This is the only cascade of note on Rock Run. The other waterfalls are on tributaries flowing into Rock Run, and will be the first to dry up as the warm season progresses.

The hike leads along the hills above Rock Run, crossing these little tributaries, themselves tumbling in small drops over layered rock. After a quarter-mile you return to Rock Run, making a second crossing. Neither crossing is easy if the water is up, which is the only time waterfall seekers will be on the trail. As you make your way across Rock Run, look across the creek at two cascades flowing down seasonal drainages. One of the two spillers makes a ledge drop just before feeding the waters of Rock Run.

Beyond the crossing, make your way back upstream on a slope. The singletrack path leads just above a final cataract, this one decanting 7 feet in a strand over a little stone bluff. You have to get below the trail to gain a head-on view of this one.

THE FATHER OF AMERICAN LANDSCAPE ARCHITECTURE

The firm that designed the gardens and forests, roads, and lakes of Bernheim Forest was founded by none other than Frederick Law Olmstead. Olmstead was born in Hartford, Connecticut, but soon left home, exploring different places and methods of employ, from farmer to sailor. He attended multiple schools, and later worked as a newspaper correspondent and publisher. Nevertheless, in 1857, at age 35, Olmstead found himself superintendent of New York's Central Park. He and partner Calvert Vauxhad implemented their winning park development plan that included winding paths, scenic views, and large green spaces, many features that we see in today's parks throughout the country.

Central Park established Olmstead as a man who could enhance outdoor space to be both attractive and functional. He lent his skills throughout the country, from preserving Yosemite Valley in California to landscaping the 1893 Chicago's World's Fair to designing the grounds of the US Capitol. Olmstead eventually moved to Boston, where his notable accomplishment was creating the Emerald Necklace, the chain of nine parks ringing the city.

Using precepts developed under Olmstead's direction, his firm designed Bernheim Forest, creating one more parcel upon which the long hand of Frederick Law Olmstead touched the landscape of the United States, including right here in Kentucky.

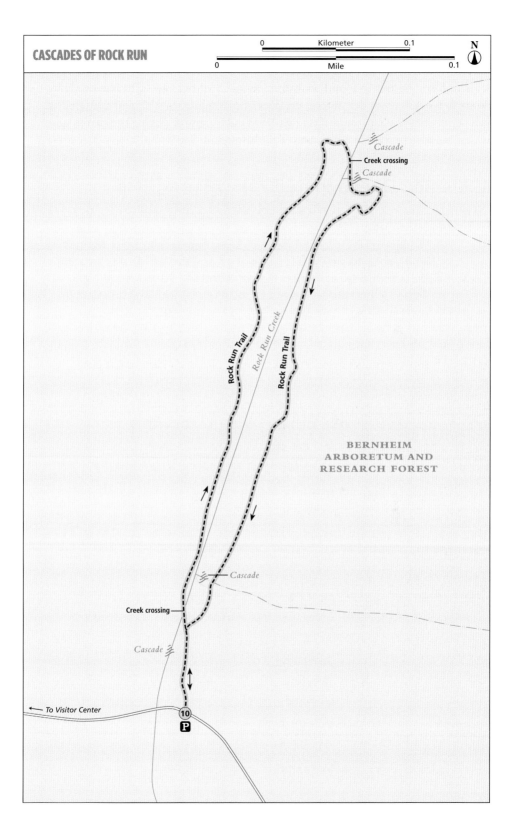

CASCADES OF ROCK RUN

Kilometer
0   0.1

Mile
0   0.1

N

Cascade

Creek crossing

Cascade

Rock Run Trail

Rock Run Creek

Rock Run Trail

BERNHEIM
ARBORETUM AND
RESEARCH FOREST

Cascade

Creek crossing

Cascade

To Visitor Center

10

P

The walk is soon over and you are back at the trailhead. But your adventure at Bernheim should be just beginning. The forest presents over 40 miles of trails through which to explore this kid- and adult-friendly outdoor treasure of Kentucky. Other things to see and do include fishing the lakes, checking out the children's play garden, viewing the art displays, eating at the visitor center cafe, and making the canopy tree walk. Consider becoming a member of the arboretum and forest, keeping alive the legacy of Isaac Bernheim.

Miles and Directions

0.0 Leave north from the signed Rock Run trailhead. Soon come to a split in the loop. Head left, quickly dropping to cross Rock Run. When the falls are running, this may be a wet ford. After crossing, work your way upstream to view the cascade on Rock Run, then resume the trail downstream.

0.3 Make the second crossing of Rock Run. Here you can see two tributaries descending in cascades, one of which delivers its main drop just before reaching Rock Run. Continue the trail upstream, looking for wildflowers and admiring singing shoals on Rock Run.

0.5 Arrive back at the trailhead, after finding a final cataract, this one spilling narrowly over a small rock bluff.

11 Cascades of Harrods Creek Park

Explore this dandy little preserve to find a few wet-weather spillers tucked between Harrods Creek and a subdivision. The hillside park occupies a slender swath of sloped land, drained by little streams that form a few falls running during winter and spring and after heavy rains. Though the walk to the cataracts is short, you can easily extend your hike by looping along the balance of these trails.

Waterfall height: In order, 15 feet, 10 feet, 3 feet
Waterfall beauty: 3
Distance: 0.5-mile out-and-back
Difficulty: Easy
Hiking time: About 0.5 hour
Trail surface: Natural
Other trail users: None
Canine compatibility: Leashed pets allowed

Land status: City park
Fees and permits: None
Maps: Harrods Creek Park; USGS Anchorage
Trail contact: City of Prospect, 9200 US 42, Prospect 40059; (502) 228-1121; www.prospectky.us/government/parks-and-recreation-committee/harrods-creek-park

Finding the trailhead: From exit 9B on I-71 northeast of downtown Louisville, take KY 841/Gene Snyder Freeway 1.4 miles to exit 37, Prospect. From there, join US 42 east and follow it for 2 miles to Hunting Creek Drive, a subdivision entrance road. Turn right and follow Hunting Creek Drive for 0.8 mile, then keep straight at a traffic circle, joining Deep Creek Drive. Stay with Deep Creek Drive for 0.2 mile to Montero Drive. Turn left and follow Montero Drive a short distance to reach Harrods Creek Park on your right. Do not turn into the park and use the lot for the preserve; rather, park on Montero Drive where the Blue Trail begins. GPS: N38° 20.510' / W85° 36.011'

The Hike

It is a pleasant little surprise to find a few cascades here in the shadows of Louisville, northeast of downtown. Here you will find Harrods Creek Park, a linear slice of green situated between the Hunting Creek subdivision and Harrods Creek, just a few miles upstream from where Harrods Creek empties into the Ohio River. In fact, this stretch of Harrods Creek is close enough to the Ohio that the park was partly submerged during the flooding of the river back in 2018. A layer of mud was left after the waters receded, leaving the flats along Harrods Creek a mess. Nevertheless, the park has recovered well and is a good addition to the prospects of Prospect, Kentucky.

As a waterfall enthusiast, however, you will find the drive to the park somewhat strange and unusual, since you enter a subdivision to reach the park, as opposed to a wildland where waterfalls are often found. Better the park is here than not at all. The 105-acre preserve occupies the hills and flats along Harrods Creek and includes a total of 4 miles of hiking trails. You will likely see deer on your trek here, as they are quite used to people. Furthermore, it is not difficult to discern that the local deer are

Early spring is a good time to find waterfalls at Harrods Creek Park.

being fed by residents and park visitors, as they less-than-shyly hang out, waiting to see if you are going to feed them. Don't do it. Wild animals that become dependent on human food are no better off than a human junkie addicted to drugs.

The park also has a kayak/canoe launch for those who want to paddle sanguine Harrods Creek. Anglers will be bank fishing in season, holding cane poles overhanging the creek, watching the bobber for when a bream, bass, or catfish takes the bait. Birders also can be found here, clad in their pith helmets, knee-length khakis, knee-high socks, binoculars, and bird books. Wildflowers from toothwort to trillium can be found here in spring.

The park, however, is mostly about hiking the trails. Moreover, most visitors do not come to Harrods Creek Park for the cascades, for the spillers are seasonal, pouring forth from mid-winter through spring and following summer thunderstorms. By autumn most of the streams here have all but dried up, save for Harrods Creek. However, if the water is right, you are in the greater Louisville area, and you need to hear and see some falling water, come view the cascades at Harrods Creek Park.

The hike starts at the upper end of the Blue Trail, on Montero Drive. If you start at the parking lot inside the park, you will miss the uppermost cascades. After parking on Montero Drive, follow the Blue Trail downhill on a rocky, rooty track. An unnamed feeder branch of Harrods Creek flows in stages to your left, creating little falls, cascades, and long slides. Unfortunately, since the stream drains the streets and houses above, a little trash makes its way into the watercourse—but don't let that deter you. Continuing down you get good looks at the spills from a bluff above the creek before dropping more to cross the stream.

Just beyond the stream crossing, a side trail links to the parking area. Beyond the intersection the trail bridges another tributary. If the water is flowing, you will clearly hear cascades. From there it is but a short upstream scramble to a series of cascades, slowly widening until the seasonal watercourse makes a final descent over a 6-foot-wide ledge. While this is no Cumberland Falls, it is a delight and pleasant surprise. From there, continue on the Blue Trail, intersecting the Orange Trail. The Orange Trail takes you along the bluff to a swing where you can overlook Harrods Creek. This is a fine place to relax, but you can also walk down the tributary toward Harrods Creek and find a short ledge drop. You will also find a grassy track running alongside Harrods Creek that is also used by walkers.

The hike is short, so consider making a loop through the park for additional exercise and scenic pleasure. Just watch out for those birders with their pith helmets and binoculars, staring up at the trees!

Miles and Directions

0.0 From Montero Drive, follow the Blue Trail downhill, quickly sidling alongside a stream draining Hunting Creek subdivision. Note the cataracts, cascades, and slides along the stream—when it is flowing well.

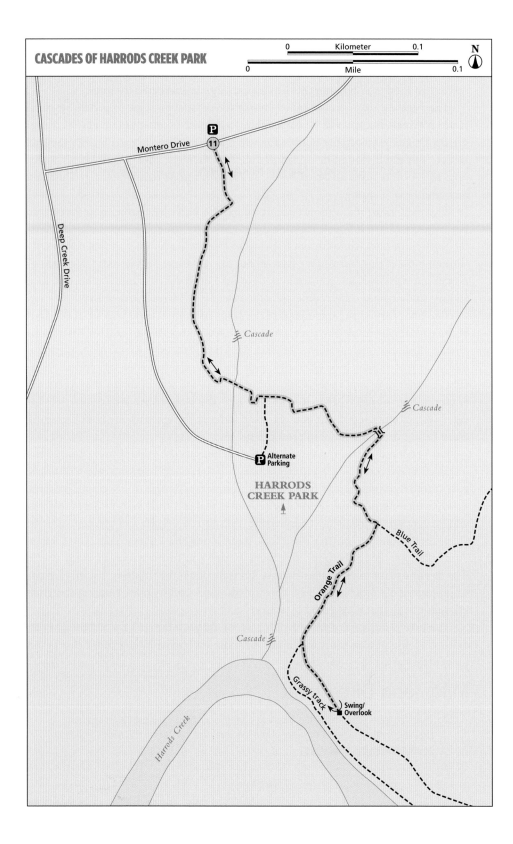

0.1 Rock-hop the creek and quickly come to a spur trail leading to the parking area inside the preserve. Continue on the Blue Trail.

0.2 Reach a wooden hiker bridge over a smaller tributary. At the bridge, walk up the creek about 20 yards to find a stair-step cascade.

0.3 Meet and join the Orange Trail, as the Blue Trail heads left. Follow the Orange Trail along a bluff to a swing and overlook of the sometimes-flooded flats of Harrods Creek. You can walk down to the flat and find another little spiller dropping a few feet over a stone ledge. Backtrack or make a loop through the park combining the Blue, Orange, Red, and Green Trails.

0.6 Arrive back at the trailhead on Montero Drive, completing the waterfall walk.

12 Hurst Falls

This hike at Frankfort's Cove Spring Park combines waterfalls and history. First, view easily accessible Hurst Falls, then make a circuit through the park, passing wet-weather cascades along tributaries flowing from the adjacent hills. Along the way you can see stone walls of a dam that held back the waters of Cove Spring, creating the first public water supply west of the Appalachian Mountains.

Waterfall height: In order, 20 feet, 4 feet, 16 feet, 22 feet
Waterfall beauty: 4
Distance: 1.3-mile loop
Difficulty: Easy
Hiking time: About 0.8 hour
Trail surface: Natural, a little asphalt
Other trail users: None

Canine compatibility: Leashed pets allowed
Land status: City park
Fees and permits: None
Maps: Cove Springs Park; USGS Frankfort East
Trail contact: Frankfort Parks & Rec, 800 Louisville Rd., Frankfort 40601; (502) 875-8575; www.frankfortparksandrec.com

Finding the trailhead: From exit 58 on I-64 near Frankfort, take US 60 west/Versailles Road for 4 miles (along the way it becomes US 421 but you stay on Versailles Road), then take the ramp for US 127 north, Owenton. Get off the ramp and turn left on US 127 north, then follow it for less than 0.1 mile and turn right onto Cove Spring Road, entering the park. Quickly veer left and follow the main park road to its dead end at the trailhead. GPS: N38° 13.1107' / W84° 50.8917'

The Hike

What is now Cove Spring Park—where this waterfall hike takes place—has undergone many a transformation over the past 200-plus years. Located just outside the heart of Frankfort, Kentucky's capital city, the reliable waters of Cove Spring have played a part in Kentucky history. Before Daniel Boone and company made their way to the Bluegrass, buffalo and aboriginal Kentuckians sought out Cove Spring for its pure and constant flow. The spring and the nearby ford of the Kentucky River were way stops for men and animals traversing the heart of the Bluegrass, following the dusty and muddy trails first created by the wandering buffalo.

By the 1750s white men were pushing through what became Frankfort, battling the Indians who called the area home. In 1780 a fellow named Stephen Frank was killed at the shallow crossing of the Kentucky River, skirmishing the Shawnee. The spot became known as Frank's Ford. Meanwhile, wily James Wilkinson persuaded the Virginia legislature to grant 100 acres near Frank's Ford to develop a town, an outpost of civilization and buffer against the Indians.

Remember, what is now Kentucky was part of Virginia at the time. However, when Kentucky became the fifteenth state back in 1792, the little town of "Frankfort" beat out Lexington to become the state's capital. The settlement at the confluence of Benson Creek and the Kentucky River grew, establishing not only the capitol building but also the state penitentiary right there in town, at the corner of High and Mero Streets.

By 1800 the city sought the clean and reliable Cove Spring to supply the capital with water. A dam was built downstream of Cove Spring, using heavy limestone block rising nearly 30 feet from end to end across a downstream hollow. The waters of Cove Spring were soon backed up. Then a fellow named Richard Throckmorton figured out a way to get that good water to the fine citizens of Frankfort. He constructed a system of interconnected hollowed-out cedar logs, moving water to the town and the prison. The prison needed water for the inmates who were kept there. The prisoners worked on site, and were leased as convict labor for area businesses and farms.

Hurst Falls stair-steps 20 feet into a pool.

The first public supply on the west side of the mountains helped Frankfort grow, but the Frankfort Water Company, as it was known, was continuously fraught with problems. In the 1880s iron pipes were used to transport the aqua at Cove Spring. However, water pressure and supply problems continued to plague the waterworks at Cove Spring, creating an epidemic of lawsuits.

The dam remained in place until the 1980s, when it was breached. Later, Cove Spring Park was established by the city. In 2006 the City of Frankfort commenced restoring the park streams inundated by the old dam. The banks were reshaped—less channel-like and shallower and curved, re-creating natural flow conditions so when floods occurred the waters did not erode the banks and deepen the stream.

Interestingly, part of this hike takes you across what was the bottom of the water retention pond for over a century and a half. The pond overflow tower still stands near the old dam. As you walk through this refurbished meadow, see how changes are taking place as the streamside becomes vegetated once again.

Now how about the waterfalls here? Hurst Falls is easily the park's signature cataract, and the walk to view it can be measured in feet. During dry times, only Hurst Falls will be flowing. However, during wetter times, from winter through early spring and after storms, Cove Spring Park features other cascades. The preserve's trail system leads past these spillers.

Upon leaving the parking area, you will immediately head for the sight and sound of Hurst Falls, a spiller dropping 20 feet from a stone wall into a shallow pond and then into Cove Spring Branch, the main waterway of the park. From there you walk to and above the old waterworks dam, passing a 4-foot curtain-drop cataract on Cove Spring Branch. This is an artificial spiller, part of the stream restoration process, oxygenating the water to improve aquatic wildlife habitat.

You then turn into a tributary of Cove Spring Branch, joining the Holly Trail. The pathway runs parallel to the tributary, which contains a host of comely stair-step cascades that are quite camera-friendly when moving. Most of the singular stair-step drops are but a foot or two; however, the continuous nature of the cascades makes them quite a sight for a Bluegrass waterfall enthusiast wanting to see some tumbling waters on their home turf.

The hike then takes you by a concreted-in spring and onward to the uplands, where cedar and hickory reign among the limestone outcrops. Look for curious trailside benches made of native stone. By now you have figured out that if the waterfalls are flowing, the trail is going to be sloppy. You then find yourself descending along another tributary featuring noisy cascades—and scads of Virginia bluebells in the spring. However, the best spillers in this watershed are found where this tributary and another seasonal branch come together at the base of the hollow. The elevated view from the trail will impress, as these cascades also form a long stair-step of white, lurching over layered limestone.

Next, you return to Cove Spring Branch, where you can make the optional side trip to Cove Spring, tucked away in its own hollow. Finally, the hike opens onto a

Long cascades like this can be found at Cove Spring Park.

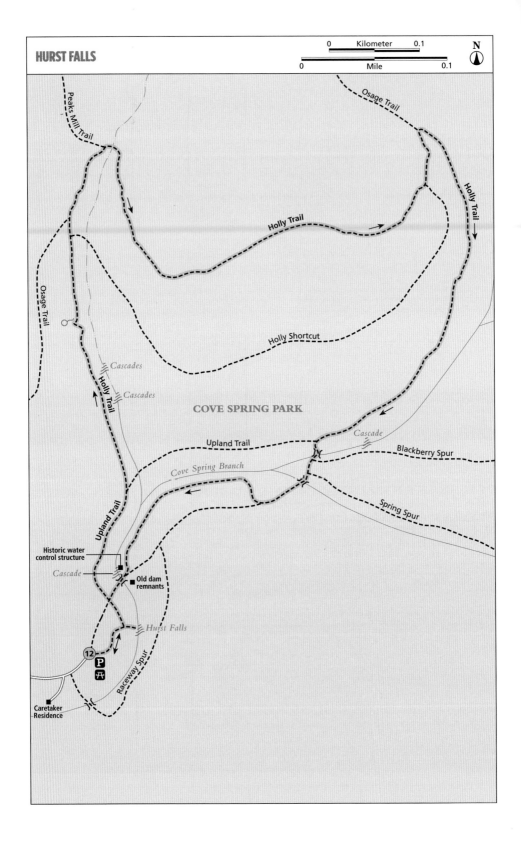

HURST FALLS

0   Kilometer   0.1
0   Mile   0.1

N

Peaks Mill Trail

Osage Trail

Holly Trail

Osage Trail

Holly Trail

Holly Shortcut

Cascades

Holly Trail

Cascades

COVE SPRING PARK

Upland Trail

Cascade

Blackberry Spur

Cove Spring Branch

Spring Spur

Upland Trail

Historic water
control structure

Cascade

Old dam
remnants

Hurst Falls

12

P

Raceway Spur

Caretaker
Residence

meadow, the restored area once underwater and covered higher than a man's head in silt. The transformation is impressive. Check out the naturalized shoals and pools of Cove Spring Branch and the stone tower of the water overflow structure, a rock edifice dating back to early Frankfort. And finally, you return to the trailhead for a second look at Hurst Falls. A picnic shelter adds dining possibilities as a fitting reward for your waterfall hike here at Franklin's historic Cove Spring Park.

Miles and Directions

0.0 From the trailhead, walk toward Hurst Falls, visible from the parking area. A little bridge takes you across Cove Spring Branch to the 20-foot cavalcade of white, dropping in stages over a mostly vertical rock bluff. An observation deck brings you directly to the falls and the little man-made pool below it. From Hurst Falls, walk toward wooden steps climbing near the old dam site to view a 4-foot curtain fall. Climb the stairs, beginning the Upland Trail.

0.1 Head left on the Holly Trail after rising above the old dam site. Look for cascades along the tributary beside which the Holly Trail leads.

0.3 Pass a circular concrete-lined spring to the left of the trail. Keep ascending.

0.4 Keep straight beyond intersections with the Holly Shortcut and the Osage Trail to intersect the Peaks Mill Trail. Stay right here, still on the Holly Trail, stepping over the streambed of the tributary along which you have been walking. Cruise cedar woods on a hillside.

0.7 Stay on the Holly Trail as you intersect the other end of the Holly Shortcut. Just ahead, intersect the other end of the Osage Trail. Here, turn right, descending a hollow where a noisy tributary is cutting downward, still on the Holly Trail.

0.9 Reach the lower end of the hollow where two tributaries come together. Here, when the leaves are off the trees, you can observe a long stair-step cascade, picturesquely pouring over layers of rock.

1.0 Come to the other end of the Upland Trail. Stay left here, crossing a trail bridge, and meet the Blackberry Spur and Spring Spur. Here is your chance to take the Spring Spur to visit historic Cove Spring, the source of all the hullabaloo in these parts. Ahead, cross the outflow of Cove Spring on a bridge, then pass through the restored meadow on an asphalt path.

1.2 Walk by the dam remains and the standing water overflow tower.

1.3 Arrive back at trailhead near Hurst Falls, completing the waterfall hike.

13 Fulling Mill Falls

This unusual waterfall hike to an unusual waterfall takes place at the historic Shaker Village near Harrodsburg. Mostly known for their period structures, crafts, lodging, and dining, they also have over 37 miles of trails exploring 3,000-plus acres of land. This hike passes historic structures then joins the Shawnee Run Trail where you find Fulling Mill Falls, a cataract pouring from a hillside above Shawnee Run, where a wool processing mill once stood. Be apprised this waterfall hike does require one creek crossing, which at higher flows will be a ford. While here, allow time to explore the grounds and learn about the Shaker Village. You will not be able to pass it up.

Waterfall height: 18 feet
Waterfall beauty: 4
Distance: 1.6-mile out-and-back
Difficulty: Easy; does have one potential ford
Hiking time: About 0.9 hour
Trail surface: Some paved, natural
Other trail users: None
Canine compatibility: Pets not allowed on trails departing from Centre or West trailhead

Land status: Private preserve, open to public
Fees and permits: None required for hiking trails
Maps: The Trails of Shaker Village; USGS Harrodsburg
Trail contact: Shaker Village, 3501 Lexington Rd., Harrodsburg 40330; (800) 734-5611; www.shakervillageky.org

Finding the trailhead: From the intersection of New Circle Road and US 68 on the southwest side of Lexington, take US 68 west for 21 miles to reach the right turn to Shaker Village. From the entrance, drive just a short distance to the welcome center, where you sign a waiver to hike on the private property. It is required. From there, follow the signs to the West Lot trailhead, parking near the trailhead kiosk and not in the conference parking area. GPS: N37° 49.6014' / W84° 45.4220'

The Hike

Regardless of what you might have heard, American communal living did not start in our era with the 1960s hippies. The Shakers, given the name because of their shaking vibrations during Christian religious ceremonies, had come over from England, arriving in America before it became a country. The Shakers spread through early America, arriving in central Kentucky in 1805. Here they founded one of twenty-one nationwide villages and named their community Pleasant Hill.

Within two decades, nearly 500 Shakers held 4,500 acres on this agglomerated tract bordering the Kentucky River. The Shakers constructed over 260 structures on the property, of which 34 buildings still stand and are the heart of the Shaker Village. Known for their hard work and simple living—and celibacy—Shaker farm and finished products began being shipped down the Kentucky River and throughout the commonwealth. Their farming, furniture making, and other business endeavors

Fulling Mill Falls emerges from a cave then feeds Shawnee Run.

brought admiration from the community, though their unwillingness to side with the Union or the Confederacy during the Civil War vexed their neighbors. However, after the war the Shaker community at Pleasant Hill began a slow downhill trend, falling into debt, losing membership, and attracting few new converts. A century after their arrival at Pleasant Hill, the Shakers had ended their run as a religious society. Their vows of celibacy may have hastened their end.

The last twelve living members sold their land in exchange for care until they passed away. This transpired, and Pleasant Hill became populated by secular citizens. Things changed in 1961, when an organization known as the Shaker Village of Pleasant Hill was founded with the mission to restore the property. It took time, but buildings were purchased and structures were restored to their early appearance. Utility lines were buried, and US 68 was routed outside the enclave, giving it the yesteryear aura.

Today the land has become a multipurpose destination where you can discover history, dine, lodge, take a boat ride on the Kentucky River, and even hike to waterfalls. Other endeavors include viewing living history demonstrations, undertaking guided tours of all types, and visiting a historic farm replete with animals used in the Shakers' heyday. Outdoorsy undertakings utilize the preserve and center on the trail system. There is a lot to see here at the Shaker Village.

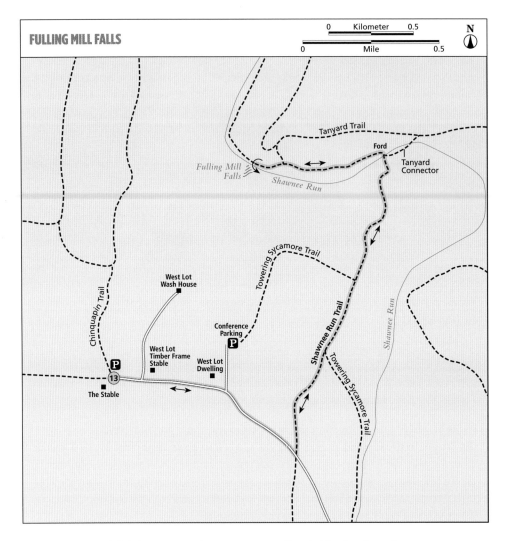

Our waterfall hike starts at the West Lot trailhead. Absolutely make sure to go to the visitor center first and sign the waiver. There is no charge to hike here, and we should cooperate to keep the trails open and free. The beginning of the hike can be confusing. For starters, from the trailhead you backtrack on the road you drove in on rather than instantly depart on a path. The road takes you by the West Lot Timber Frame Stable, built in 1830, then the West Lot Dwelling, built in 1828.

Beyond here walk a little bit farther through a grassy area, still on the road, and then hang a left to join the Shawnee Run Trail. This path takes you down to Shawnee Run, a gurgling stream flowing through the heart of the property. It is here where you must cross Shawnee Run. At higher flows this will be a certain ford; however, in summertime you could perhaps rock-hop. Then it is but a short walk to Fulling Mill Falls.

This is an interesting cataract. First off, it is not on Shawnee Run but is rather a spring bursting forth from a hillside directly above the creek, then flows into Shawnee Run. This spring emerges then drops in stair-step fashion, giving its waters to Shawnee Run. The waterfall widens and is then divided in the middle by remnants of the fulling mill, widening further. The mill, built by the Shakers, used the waterpower of the spring to process woolens.

Only the foundations of the two-story stone mill remain, and you will stand atop this foundation when admiring Fulling Mill Falls. It is easy to step in Shawnee Run for a closer look at Fulling Mill Falls, a waterfall that will not run dry, even when other stream falls have slackened to trickles.

Miles and Directions

0.0 Depart from the West Lot trailhead after not having parked in the conference parking area. Follow the paved road back east, the way you came, passing first the West Lot Timber Frame Stable, then the attractive West Lot Dwelling. Continue on the paved road, curving south.

0.2 Reach the signed Shawnee Run Trail in a grassy area. Head left, northbound, on a grassy track.

0.3 Come to a trail intersection. Here the Towering Sycamore Trail leaves right for Shawnee Run. Keep straight with the Shawnee Run Trail.

0.4 Come to another intersection. Here an arm of the Towering Sycamore Trail heads left through meadows to reach the conference parking area. Continue straight with the Shawnee Run Trail, descending toward Shawnee Run. Ahead, cut through an old gate.

0.6 Reach Shawnee Run and a trail intersection. Here a connector to the Tanyard Trail leaves right. Stay left with the Shawnee Run Trail, making the ford over Shawnee Run.

0.8 Come to Fulling Mill Falls after passing another connector to the Tanyard Trail. Here a bench and interpretive information enhance the scene. Across Shawnee Run, Fulling Mill Falls pours from a spring opening then widens as it bounces down limestone ledges to merge with Shawnee Run. It is a scenic and oft-photographed spiller. Backtrack to the trailhead.

1.6 Arrive back at the trailhead, completing the waterfall hike at Shaker Village.

14 Waterfall of Shaker Landing

You'll find this waterfall spilling from the Kentucky River Palisades, sheer bluffs above the Kentucky River, stretching for nearly 100 miles. Here at historic Shaker Landing, the pouring water tumbles over 60 feet from the palisades in multiple stages, eventually to feed the Kentucky River. Start the hike at the Shaker Village, passing preserved structures from yesteryear, and join the River Road Trail, a nearly two-century-old track. Enjoy expansive views, then reach Shaker Landing and the alluring waterfall.

Waterfall height: 60 feet
Waterfall beauty: 5
Distance: 3.4-mile out-and-back
Difficulty: Easy to moderate
Hiking time: About 1.8 hours
Trail surface: Some paved, natural
Other trail users: None
Canine compatibility: Leashed dogs allowed

Land status: Private preserve, open to public
Fees and permits: None required for hiking trails
Maps: The Trails of Shaker Village; USGS Wilmore
Trail contact: Shaker Village, 3501 Lexington Rd., Harrodsburg 40330; (800) 734-5611; www.shakervillageky.org

Finding the trailhead: From the intersection of New Circle Road and US 68 on the southwest side of Lexington, take US 68 west for 21 miles to reach the right turn to Shaker Village. From the entrance, drive just a short distance to the welcome center, where you sign a waiver to hike on the private property. It is required. From there, follow the signs to the East Lot trailhead, parking near the trailhead kiosk north. GPS: N37° 49.186' / W84° 44.131'

The Hike

Three Shaker missionaries, part of a Christian sect originating in England, arrived in this part of Kentucky back in 1805, seeking converts. It wasn't long before they grouped with new believers and organized, developing a community they dubbed Pleasant Hill. The Shakers, named for their moving fervor during religious services, determined to make a living using the resources on their collectively acquired 4,000 or so acres, part of which included the confluence of Cedar Branch and the Kentucky River. The hollow created by Cedar Branch allowed a potential passage from the upland Bluegrass, where the expanding community of Pleasant Hill stood, down to the river from which the palisades of the Kentucky River rose.

These palisades, sheer bluffs escalating majestically from moving river waters, while quite scenic from our point of view, impeded river access. Two centuries back, the Kentucky River was a vital transportation and trade link connecting the commonwealth to the outside world. In 1826 the Shakers laid out River Road, where burgeoning Pleasant Hill would link to what came to be known as Shaker Landing

This tall waterfall pours from the Kentucky River Palisades.

on the river. Down this road the industrious, utilitarian Shakers sent quality products from brooms to barrels to be loaded onto flatboats and sent downriver for trade.

Trade brought money and communication to the Shakers. They continued growing and building before entering a period of decline, until a century later the Shakers were no more. However, they left a legacy on the land, preserved today as the Shaker Village of Pleasant Hill. The period buildings and lifeways of that time are encapsulated here, attracting thousands of visitors each year to dine, lodge, and enjoy the crafts and cultural pursuits as well as the 37 miles of trails lacing the terrain.

Visiting the Shaker Village and adding a waterfall hike is a fine way to spend a day in the Bluegrass. Using the trails here you can cobble together a rewarding historic waterfall hike. After first going to the welcome center and signing the required waiver, drive to the East Lot trailhead (along the way you will pass many of the Shaker buildings, tempting a visit). A short road walk leads you back on the road you came in on to then head east, crossing US 68. From there join River Road—usually gated during the colder, wetter season when the waterfall of Shaker Landing is flowing— and walk the road a bit before joining the River Road Trail, the path tracing the 1826 Kentucky River access laid out by the Shakers.

Think of wagons and mules hauling goods up and down the road, as you follow the footsteps of travelers and visitors and residents. This attractive path allows views into the gorge of the Kentucky River, where you can gaze out to High Bridge, an 1877 railroad span crossing the river. When the water is flowing you will also see a few ephemeral waterfalls spilling toward the Kentucky River. The trek leads down to flats along the river, where you rejoin the newer River Road, used by modern-day visitors driving down to Shaker Landing to take a ride on the *Dixie Belle* riverboat, cruising the Kentucky River and seeing the palisades from the water.

You then reach Shaker Landing, where stone foundations of buildings recall the past. The still-standing Timber Frame Stable kept horses for the stagecoach running through the Shaker Village and beyond. From there, join the Palisades Trail. It leads you to the waterfall of Shaker Landing, a tall affair with multiple stages over layered limestone. The first drop is well back from the trail. The stream then gathers to spill a second time in a more angled fashion. The third major descent is more curtain-like and spills at your feet before dropping a bit more then flowing in winding fashion to give its waters to the Kentucky River. The cataract can be quite showy from winter through spring, when it is typically flowing adequately.

The sheer bluffs of the Kentucky River Palisades rising astride the waterfall are arguably the most intriguing aspect of the falls, lending perspective to the dancing cataract. While here, make the short loop on the north end of the Palisades Trail to admire the cliffs and explore the flats beside the waterway. In the warm season you could even incorporate a riverboat ride. The narrated cruises last around an hour.

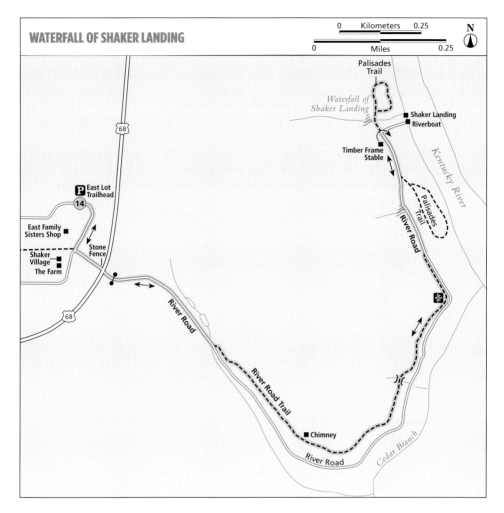

Miles and Directions

0.0 From the East Lot trailhead, backtrack on the road that you drove in on.

0.1 Head left, easterly, toward US 68 on a grassy track between fences. If you were to go right, westerly, you would head into the heart of the Shaker Village. However, walk easterly and soon come to a stone fence with a built-in stone stile, cross the fence, and then cross US 68 to join paved River Road.

0.2 Pass a gate on River Road. This gate is closed more often during the cold season. Walk along River Road heading downhill.

0.5 Leave left from River Road after passing a pair of small ponds. Join the River Road Trail, the historic track used by the Shakers to link their village of Pleasant Hill to the Kentucky River. Vegetation lines the track. Hike through a mix of woods and fields.

0.7 Pass by a stone chimney of a forgotten cabin. The land begins to drop off sharply below.

1.0 Use a metal hiker bridge to cross a low-flow tributary that makes about an 8-foot fall above the trail. Views begin to open of the river gorge.

1.2 Open onto an outcrop with an excellent view. High Bridge crosses the gorge, and you can see down below to the confluence of Cedar Branch and the Kentucky River.

1.3 Metal stairs lead you down from the River Road Trail to the current River Road. Join River Road, passing a very high but very low-flow waterfall to your left.

1.5 Walk by the Timber Frame Stable from 1866. You are now in the greater Shaker Landing. This is the parking area for riverboat riders, so do not be alarmed if you see lots of cars. Note the stone foundations of other nearby buildings, including the old warehouse and a dwelling, but the stable is the only standing building down here.

1.6 Come to the waterfall of Shaker Landing after leaving the riverboat area and walking the Palisades Trail just a short distance. Here you see the multitiered cataract tumbling over layered limestone flanked by a very steep hill and the rising Kentucky River Palisades. What a sight!

1.7 Backtrack after walking the little northern loop of the Palisades Trail, checking out the bluffs above and the nearby flats as well as the river. You can return to the trailhead using a combination of River Road and the River Road Trail or just River Road. If using only River Road, exercise caution but also note a couple of seasonal waterfalls spilling near the road.

3.4 Arrive back at the trailhead, completing the waterfall hike at Shaker Village.

15 Evans Mill Falls

This loop hike takes you not only to Evans Mill Falls, a two-pronged cataract at the confluence of Raven Run and a tributary, but also to a rewarding overlook of the Kentucky River as well as other highlights—all taking place at popular Raven Run Nature Sanctuary, located outside Lexington. When the water is up, you will see still other waterfalls. Nevertheless, no matter the time of year, you will be rewarded with scenic and historical points of interest here at Raven Run Nature Sanctuary. Winter and spring are recommended visitation times for maximum waterfall flows.

Waterfall height: In order, 6 feet, 25 feet, 20 feet, 25 feet
Waterfall beauty: 4
Distance: 3.5-mile lollipop
Difficulty: Moderate
Hiking time: About 2 hours
Trail surface: Mostly natural
Other trail users: None
Canine compatibility: No dogs allowed
Land status: Nature sanctuary
Fees and permits: None. Hours: Apr: 9 a.m. to 6 p.m.; trails close at 5:30 p.m. May: 9 a.m. to 7 p.m.; trails close at 6:30 p.m. June–Aug: 9 a.m. to 8 p.m.; trails close at 7:30 p.m. Sept: 9 a.m. to 7 p.m.; trails close at 6:30 p.m. Oct: 9 a.m. to 6 p.m.; trails close at 5:30 p.m. Nov–Mar: 9 a.m. to 5 p.m.; trails close at 4:30 p.m.
Maps: Raven Run Nature Sanctuary; USGS Coletown
Trail contact: Raven Run Nature Sanctuary, 3885 Raven Run Way, Lexington 40515; (859) 272-6105; www.ravenrun.org

Finding the trailhead: From exit 104 on I-75 just southeast of Lexington, take KY 418 west for 2.4 miles to US 25/Old Richmond Road. Turn left and follow Old Richmond Road south for 3.3 miles to KY 1975/Jacks Creek Pike. Turn right and follow Jacks Creek Pike for 2.5 miles, then turn left, staying with Jacks Creek Pike. After 1.3 miles, stay straight with Jacks Creek Pike, joining KY 1976 as KY 1975 goes right. Continue for 1.4 more miles on KY 1976/Jacks Creek Pike and turn left onto Raven Run Way. Follow Raven Run Way for 0.3 mile to its dead end at the visitor parking area for Raven Run Sanctuary. GPS: N37° 53.246' / W84° 23.828'

The Hike

Raven Run Sanctuary is a special preserve run by the Lexington parks department. Once an 800-acre working farm first established in 1790, what has become Raven Run Nature Sanctuary was actively farmed until the 1930s, when the land was left fallow, growing over into the forest we see today. The land and buildings were acquired by the City of Lexington. The city, along with a philanthropic outfit known as Friends of Raven Run, built a fine nature center (add time to check out the visitor center before your hike if possible) that is the heartbeat of the parcel, located on a tract important for not only human history but also natural history.

Evans Mill Falls is a highlight of Raven Run Sanctuary.

The former farm site, situated high in the Bluegrass, is cut by steep creeks leading down to the Kentucky River and its magnificent palisades. The site therefore encompasses a biologically diverse array of uplands and the gorges cut by Chandler Creek and Raven Run, as well as the bluffs and lowlands along the Kentucky River.

Raven Run Sanctuary is a popular destination for hikers and nature lovers, and for waterfall aficionados—in season. From the visitor parking area you first follow a concrete sidewalk-like trail to the nature center, where you can get oriented, view the center's indoor displays, and grab a trail map. Make sure to sign in before your hike. It is required.

The trail system here at Raven Run Sanctuary is a network of interconnected color-coded paths. Luckily, most trail intersections are marked with a letter—for example, intersection C—allowing you to easily find your place on the preserve trail map. The Red Trail is undoubtedly the most popular path, as it passes several highlights. Our waterfall hike traces much of the Red Trail.

After leaving the visitor center, you work your way through a facilities area that was part of the old farm, including the barn. You then join the Red Trail, entering full-blown woods (part of the sanctuary is open meadows, especially the uplands). The Red Trail leads past stone fences built over two centuries ago. Look for little arched passages at the bottom of the fence in places. These openings were created to let water pass through the fence where natural drainages channeled storm runoff. These arches are not only scenic but also functional!

You then come to Chandler Creek, a pretty stream cutting its way through to feed the Kentucky River below. Here you will find an eye-pleasing 6-foot slide cascade and also the historical farm limekiln. The farm owners had to produce their own lime to make mortar for building and improve soil by making it less acidic. Here, limestone was heated to upwards of 1,000 degrees, creating calcium oxide, commonly known as lime.

The Red Trail takes you to the overlook of the Kentucky River. Note the bluffs, the famed Kentucky River Palisades that stretch for almost 100 miles along the waterway. Chandler Creek is falling below but is on private property. This is a popular area for taking breaks, so expect folks hanging around the overlook. Soak in the view yourself before resuming the circuit.

The next part of the hike takes you into the Raven Run valley, along the wildflower-rich north slope of the vale. Here you will bridge a wet-weather stream which if flowing will reward visitors with a top-down view of a 25-foot waterfall pouring from the ledge below. The bridge allows you to safely stand atop the spiller. Unfortunately, this stream is but a trickle more often than not.

The hike delves deeper into the Raven Run valley, and before long you are at the site of the Evans gristmill and the waterfalls there. Just upstream, Raven Run and an unnamed tributary converge. Just above their convergence both streams begin falling, forming falls that continue falling after they meet. Above them bluffs of Raven Run rise in splendor—and just downstream a wet-weather tributary of Raven Run tumbles from these bluffs, creating a bonus waterfall. ***Note:*** In a dry autumn you will be lucky water is flowing anywhere at all.

In addition, you won't miss the remains of the mill built by Peter Evans. The squared-off foundation is just below the observation deck. This is a place to linger. After enjoying Evans Mill Falls, continue the loop. It will take you out of the woods and into tree-bordered meadows, where cattle once grazed back in the farming days. Despite a plethora of trail intersections, multiple signs guide you back to the nature center, completing the historical waterfall adventure.

Miles and Directions

0.0 Leave the visitor parking area and follow a winding concrete path toward the nature center.

0.1 Reach the nature center.

0.2 Come to a four-way trail intersection. Turn right here on the Red Trail toward the overlook. Begin descending a well-used path in woods, and shortly come alongside a stone fence. Cedar trees are common.

0.5 The trail and the parallel stone fence make a hard right.

0.6 Come to Chandler Creek and intersection A. Take a right here to view a 6-foot slide cascade just upstream as well as the old limekiln. Resume the loop.

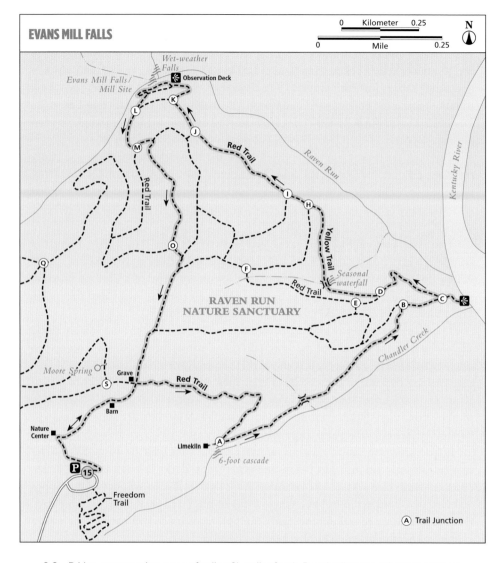

0   Kilometer   0.25

0   Mile   0.25

N

Wet-weather Falls

Evans Mill Falls / Mill Site

Observation Deck

K

L

J

M

Red Trail

Raven Run

Kentucky River

Red Trail

I

H

O

Yellow Trail

Q

F

Seasonal waterfall

Red Trail

E

D

C

B

RAVEN RUN NATURE SANCTUARY

Chandler Creek

Moore Spring

Grave

S

Red Trail

Barn

Nature Center

Limekiln

A

6-foot cascade

P 15

Freedom Trail

Ⓐ Trail Junction

0.9 Bridge a wet-weather stream feeding Chandler Creek. Boardwalks pass other wet areas as Chandler Creek falls well below you.

1.1 Reach intersection B. Head right here, staying with the Red Trail. Descend the nose of a ridge.

1.2 Reach intersection C. Turn right here and shortly reach the outcrops and overlook of the Kentucky River. You can see some of the tall bluffs, known as the Kentucky River Palisades, to the north. Below and to your right, you can hear spilling water as Chandler Creek tumbles into the river. These falls are off-limits as they are off sanctuary property. Backtrack to intersection C.

1.3 Arrive back at intersection C. Continue on the Red Trail, heading away from the Kentucky River in a rich wildflower area.

1.6 Reach intersection D. Here, split right to join the Yellow Trail. Cruise a cool north slope in a rich wildflower area featuring trillium and Dutchman's-breeches.

1.7 Reach the trail bridge over a wet-weather cascading creek. Here a 25-foot waterfall spills from a stone rim just below the bridge, allowing a top-down view when it is flowing, which it is usually not doing.

1.9 Come to intersection H. Stay right here, quickly reaching and passing through intersection I. Stay right with the Red Trail.

2.2 Hike under a power line and come to intersection J while still under the power line. Here a spur heads left. Stay straight with the Red Trail, reentering woods.

2.3 Meet intersection K. Head right here for the Evans gristmill. At this point you can hear Raven Run running. Circle down to the stream and stay on the trail closest to Raven Run. It will take you by Evans Mill Falls and above the confluence of two streams. Also check out the view from the observation platform.

2.5 Reach intersection L. Stay straight here, climbing from Raven Run.

2.6 Come to intersection M. Head left here, leaving the Red Trail and soon leaving the woods. Ahead, reach another intersection. Stay right and ascend into meadows.

2.9 Meet intersection O in meadows. Continue on a wide grassy track toward the nature center.

3.2 Return to the four-way intersection where you were at hike's beginning. Backtrack to the nature center.

3.4 Reach the nature center. Continue backtracking.

3.5 Arrive back at the trailhead, completing the waterfall hike.

16 Waterfall of the John Holder Trail

Visit a fun little waterfall at a historic Kentucky state nature preserve located near the Kentucky River. Lower Howard's Creek Nature & Heritage Preserve is the setting for this waterfall hike. First, walk imposing bluffs well above Lower Howard Creek, passing the pre–Civil War Robert Martin house foundations, then drop to Lower Howard Creek, shrouded in exquisite limestone cliffs. After walking a bit along the creek, turn into a crystalline tributary stream where a slide cascade pours into an inviting triangular pool. You can extend the adventure by continuing on the John Holder Trail to see historic sites from early settlement days.

Waterfall height: 20 feet
Waterfall beauty: 4
Distance: 1-mile out-and-back
Difficulty: Easy
Hiking time: About 0.7 hour
Trail surface: Natural
Other trail users: None
Canine compatibility: Pets not allowed

Land status: State nature preserve
Fees and permits: None
Maps: Lower Howard's Creek Nature & Heritage Preserve; USGS Ford
Trail contact: Kentucky State Nature Preserves Commission, 801 Teton Trail, Frankfort 40601; (502) 573-2886; www.naturepreserves.ky.gov

Finding the trailhead: From exit 95 on I-75 just north of Richmond, take KY 627 north for 6 miles and turn right on KY 1924 south, just after bridging the Kentucky River. From there follow KY 1924 for 0.1 mile, then turn right again on KY 418 west/Athens-Boonesborough Road and follow it for 1.1 miles to Halls Restaurant and the Lower Howard's Creek Preserve parking area on your right. GPS: N37° 55.1226' / W84° 16.3748'

The Hike

This waterfall hike takes place in a historic area of Kentucky, where Lower Howard Creek empties into the Kentucky River. Fort Boonesborough—where Daniel himself first decided to settle here in Kentuck'—is just about a mile distant. In 2001 the Commonwealth of Kentucky realized the natural and historical significance of this area and dedicated this preserve. Not only do rare and endangered flora call it home, but it's also where settlers built homes, roads, water-powered mills, and a landing on the Kentucky River.

Ol' John Holder was the kingpin hereabouts after establishing a way station where Lower Howard Creek flowed into the Kentucky River. Holder was but a mile from Fort Boonesborough but also along the Salt Springs Trace, a road linking Fort Boonesborough to nearby saltworks. His spot was a hub and here he constructed a backwoods "empire," complete with a trading post, boatyard, tavern, river ferry, and landing, where travelers floated on goods-loaded flatboats from here all the way to

This waterfall is bordered by slick walls. Exercise caution.

New Orleans via the Kentucky, Ohio, and Mississippi Rivers. They then sold their boats for lumber and walked back via the famed Natchez Trace.

We can gain glimpses of that time, as well as a good look at a fine cascade, here at Lower Howard's Creek Nature & Heritage Preserve. The waterfall attracts visitors not only for its flowing beauty but also for the translucent pool into which it pours. Figuratively and literally speaking, it is a cool little area, up a small side creek where you find a break in the bluffs rising above Lower Howard Creek. The unnamed side creek—where the waterfall is found—has bluffs of its own forming slick walls around the pool of the waterfall. The spiller bubbles down an angled slide, regroups, then makes the second bigger slide into the triangular plunge pool that attracts summertime stream splashers. Be apprised the rocks and walls around the waterfall are very slick. Exercise caution.

While having water fun we can also engage in historical study. You will leave the trailhead on the John Holder Trail, traveling the 1775-era Salt Springs Trace to pass remains of Lisletown then visit the aforementioned Robert Martin House. You then come to the Old Ford. To go to the falls you do not cross Lower Howard Creek here, but walk a low ledge upstream then turn into the next creek on your right. However, if you want more historical study, make the ford and continue the John Holder Trail on a narrow spit of land between two extreme bends of Lower Howard Creek. Here

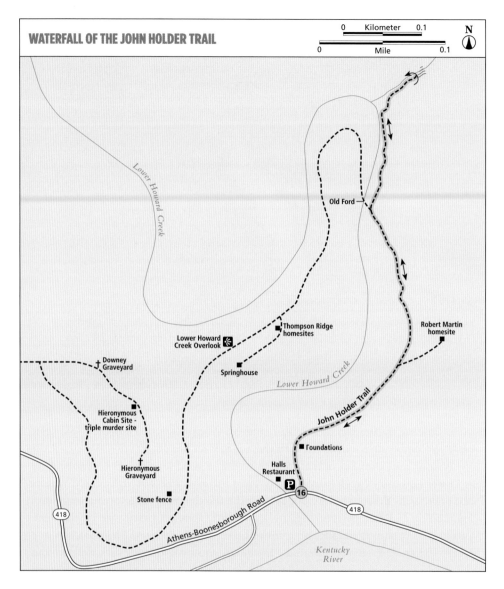

you will find multiple old homesites and graveyards from the 1800s, stone fences, springhouses, and the eerie cabin site of a 1939 triple murder . . . The preserve is closed from sundown to sunrise, so if the regulation does not deter you, maybe the triple murder site will keep you from coming to the preserve after dark.

The preserve contains 338 acres to explore. Lower Howard Creek has been designated a Kentucky Exceptional Waterway. You will be impressed with the bluffs and the stream pools, as well as the rapids. Overall, Lower Howard Creek is a special parcel of Kentucky, where human and natural history—along with a waterfall—are on display. Treat the well-visited place for what it is—a preserve.

Miles and Directions

0.0 Leave from the parking lot shared by Halls Restaurant and the preserve on the John Holder Trail. Climb the gravel path under a power line clearing, immediately coming to home foundations on your right, part of the old Lisletown. Level out on the wide trail on a steep bluff. Lower Howard Creek is visible below, coursing down a gorge in pools and shoals. Note the escaped ivy from homesites running along the trail.

0.2 Come to a split in the trail. Here a spur leads right up to the Robert Martin homesite, where a two-room log house was built in 1856. Visit the homesite, then continue on the John Holder Trail. Pass several bridged wet-weather streamlets coursing from layered limestone on the hillside to your right. This is a rich wildflower area. Cedars are abundant as well.

0.4 Come to the Old Ford, where the trail, tracing historic roads, crosses Lower Howard Creek at a wide and shallow spot. For more historical study, you can ford the creek and continue the path. However, to see the waterfall, stay on the right bank of Lower Howard Creek and walk along the low streamside ledge. Parts of this ledge will be wet from dripping limestone above. When Lower Howard Creek is flooded, this ledge will be underwater and the falls will be inaccessible.

0.5 Turn right into the unnamed stream valley where the watercourse has created a break in the bluffs of Lower Howard Creek. Work your way up the creek on gravel bars and rocks until you reach the 20-foot slide cataract and pool. It is a popular dipping spot in the summer. Backtrack to the trailhead.

1.0 Arrive back at the trailhead, completing the hike.

Waterfall Hikes of Eastern Kentucky

17 Smoky Bridge Falls

Check out a pair of very unusual waterfalls at Carter Caves State Resort Park, a geological wonder unto itself. It is but a short walk to Smoky Bridge, a huge natural arch. Here you peer into the circular passageway under Smoky Arch, and on an adjacent stone wall, a waterfall emerges from a crevice, surging from pure rock. Nearby, a seasonal stream stair-steps its way down layers of rocks, adding more aquatic beauty to the state park–worthy scene.

Waterfall height: In order, 7 feet, 15 feet
Waterfall beauty: 4
Distance: 0.2-mile out-and-back
Difficulty: Easy
Hiking time: About 0.3 hour
Trail surface: Concrete, natural
Other trail users: None
Canine compatibility: Leashed pets allowed

Land status: State park
Fees and permits: None
Maps: Carter Caves State Resort Park; USGS Olive Hill
Trail contact: Carter Caves State Resort Park, 344 Caveland Dr., Olive Hill 41164; (606) 286-4411; http://parks.ky.gov/parks

Finding the trailhead: From exit 161 on I-64 east of Olive Hill, take US 60 east for 1.3 miles to KY 182. Turn left and follow KY 182 for 2.7 miles to the left turn into Carter Caves State Resort Park. Follow the signs to the park pool, parking in the large lot below the pool. You will pass the park visitor center on the way. It is a good idea to stop at the visitor center for maps and information. GPS: N38° 22.146' / W83° 7.535'

The Hike

Carter Caves State Resort Park—as its name implies—is located in karst country, a land where the aboveground and underground plumbing system creates a compelling interaction of land and water both above and below the surface. For waterfall fans like us, it presents a double-edged sword.

One of the falls on this hike is undoubtedly a result of this interrelationship between land and water, for it emerges from a crack in a wall and wastes no time in becoming a waterfall, instantaneously plummeting from the crevice onto the ground below. This is a resurgence of an underground stream. The other waterfall is more traditional in the sense that it flows down a valley over layered rock, stratified stone over which the water cascades its way to Smoky Bridge. Both the waters from the crevice waterfall and the traditional waterfall flow to end in a sink, disappearing into the underworld before making their way into nearby Smoky Valley Lake.

The downside of this complicated plumbing system is that these waterfalls frequently run dry, so you have to catch them flowing in winter and spring or after heavy rains. Most of the streams in Carter Caves State Resort Park are ephemeral,

This waterfall disappears into a sink at Carter Caves State Resort Park.

running above the ground only part of the year. In autumn and during dry summers, you may be hard-pressed to find any water flowing anywhere aboveground.

Interestingly, Carter Caves State Resort Park, with over twenty caves within its boundaries, does have an underground waterfall. This park also has the greatest concentration of caves in Kentucky, and that is saying a lot considering that Kentucky is home to Mammoth Cave, with the largest known cave system on the planet. Here at Carter Caves you can take the Cascade Cave Tour year-round to see the underground waterfall. Once privately owned and operated, Cascade Cave has been shown on tours for almost one hundred years. The tour travels approximately two-thirds of a mile and involves 225 steps along the way. You will first visit the reflecting pool in the Lake Room, and then see the geological sights of the Cathedral Room. The Hanging Gardens of King Solomon and the Counterfeiter's Room are two other curiosities. The tour culminates with the visit to 30-foot-high Cascade Waterfall. The Cascade Cave Tour lasts about 75 minutes and the fee is reasonable. Check the park website for tour times.

You can also take the X Cave tour, and learn how the cavern took on its unusual name. This tour is shorter and easier. Along the way you will view Turkey Rock, the Pipe Organ, and the largest formation in the park—Giant Column. No waterfalls, though.

Our aboveground adventure takes the fishing access trail then diverges to concrete steps leading to the base of Smoky Bridge and the sinkhole that lies at its base.

If the falls are flowing, you will hear them en route. The crevice falls will immediately catch your eye as it pours directly from a bluff. The other waterfall will be dropping down a rock hollow of layered strata, dancing down to end in a small pool.

While here, not only walk under Smoky Bridge to see the waterfalls but also walk atop the geological curiosity. Smoky Bridge is a 200-foot long, 45-foot-wide, and 35-foot-high arch of limestone. The "bridge" part of the arch, known as the lintel, is about 40 feet thick. Smoky Bridge is often reported as being the largest arch in Kentucky.

In addition to the unusual spillers near Smoky Bridge, the park features 26 miles of hiking trails, exploring phenomena high and low, including other natural bridges, rock houses, wildflowers, and old homesites. Backpackers can get a permit and overnight in the backcountry. Park trails link to the paths at Tygarts State Forest, effectively expanding the wild area. You can rappel or rock climb with a permit.

More tame pastimes include overnighting at the park campground (open year-round), the rustic lodge, or a cottage. You can even dine here at Tierney's Cavern Restaurant. This hike starts near the park pool, where you can relax waterside, or head

The waterfall at the lower left pours from a rock wall near Smoky Bridge.

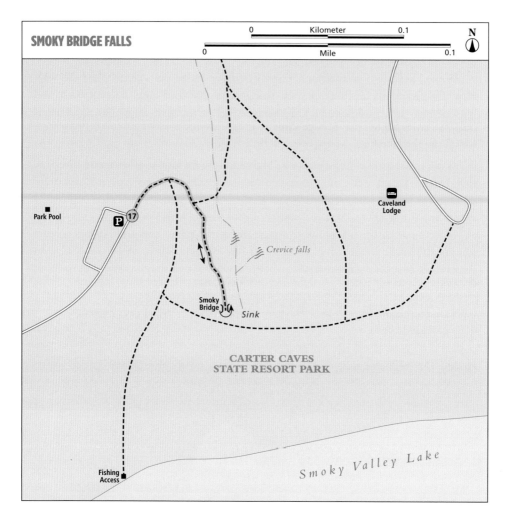

out to alluring Smoky Valley Lake and fish or paddle. Play golf or go horseback riding. Simply put, there is a lot to do here at Carter Caves State Resort Park—including waterfall hiking.

Miles and Directions

0.0 From the corner of the parking area in the lot below the park swimming pool, take the fishing access using concrete steps. Quickly reach a trail intersection. Here the fishing access trail goes right, as does as a trail to the park lodge. You, however, stay left and descend toward the bottom of Smoky Bridge. Take concrete steps.

0.1 Reach the base of Smoky Bridge, a natural arch. The passageway beneath the arch and a sink stand to your right. Leave the concrete steps and go left to view the crevice falls as well as the other stair-step cascade. Backtrack to the trailhead.

0.2 Arrive back at the trailhead, completing the waterfall hike.

18 Falls of Grayson Lake State Park

Make a loop hike featuring three cataracts, including the star of the show, 60-foot Lick Falls. Set at fine Grayson Lake State Park, you will ramble through rolling woods before first reaching Lick Falls dashing in segments through a mini-gorge to make a final plummet from a stone ledge directly into Grayson Lake. From there, work your way along the lakeshore where you will find 15-foot Buckeye Branch Falls, also tumbling into the impoundment from a more modest rim. Your third and final spiller is Bowling Branch Cascade, a long slide that also slips into Grayson Lake.

Waterfall height: In order, 60 feet, 15 feet, 20 feet
Waterfall beauty: 4
Distance: 3-mile loop
Difficulty: Easy to moderate
Hiking time: About 1.5 hours
Trail surface: Natural
Other trail users: None

Canine compatibility: Leashed pets allowed
Land status: State park
Fees and permits: None
Maps: Grayson Lake State Park; USGS Bruin
Trail contact: Grayson Lake State Park, 314 Grayson Lake Park Rd., Olive Hill 41164; (606) 474-9727; http://parks.ky.gov/parks

Finding the trailhead: From exit 172 on I-64 at Grayson, take KY 7 south for 7 miles to turn right onto Grayson Lake State Park Road (you will also see a sign for the park golf course). Follow the main park road and the signs to the park campground. If the campground is open, pass the campground entrance station and take the first acute right just beyond the entrance station to park near the basketball court. If the campground is closed and gated, park just outside the campground entrance station then walk a short distance to the trailhead. GPS: N38° 12.082' / W83° 1.760'

The Hike

Although Cumberland Falls gets the waterfall accolades among Kentucky state parks, Grayson Lake ought to get at least an honorable mention, if not more. See, this eastern Kentucky preserve not only rivals Cumberland Falls for scenery, but also will give it a run for the money when it comes to waterfalls. For Grayson Park has three scenic spillers, one of which is deservedly well known—Lick Falls, a 60-foot diving wall of white that spills into Grayson Lake. Most often seen by boaters tooling around the lake, hikers get to see the upper part of this falls that boaters cannot see, but cannot fully enjoy the bottom-up view from the lake, due to the sandstone cliffs from which Lick Falls makes its final tumble.

In addition to thrilling Lick Falls, you also get to view lesser-heralded Buckeye Branch Falls. This cataract makes a 15-foot drop off a stone ledge into a secluded cove of Grayson Lake. The final waterfall—Bowling Branch Cascade—delivers yet another

Bowling Branch Cascade scenically slides into Grayson Lake.

type of pour-over as it makes a widening slide toward the impoundment before releasing in a final vertical downgrade.

The hike between the waterfalls is fun and scenic, too. The blazed, well-marked and maintained Lick Falls Overlook Trail leaves the park campground and wanders west through woods, crossing streams between hills before sidling alongside Lick Branch. You then come down the creek and reach the upper part of Lick Falls as it cuts through rock in splashy phases before its final plunge from the gorge rim. Fortunately we can enjoy the upper falls, but unfortunately landlubbers cannot get the face-on view no matter where they go or how much they lean out from the cliff line by the falls, so don't try. However, when cruising along the cliff line down from Lick Creek Falls—if the streams are high—you will hear and see another waterfall spilling 40 feet into the same cove across the gorge. So enjoy this wet-weather falls and the upper part of Lick Falls, then move on.

You will enjoy what lies ahead. Here the Lick Falls Overlook Trail wanders along the rim of the gorge above Lake Grayson, allowing for numerous and nearly continuous winter views of the impoundment and the hills that rise above, as well as the sandstone walls that seem to go on for miles along the shore. In the winter and spring, you will hear other waterfalls making their dives into the still water of the impoundment.

FALLS OF GRAYSON LAKE STATE PARK

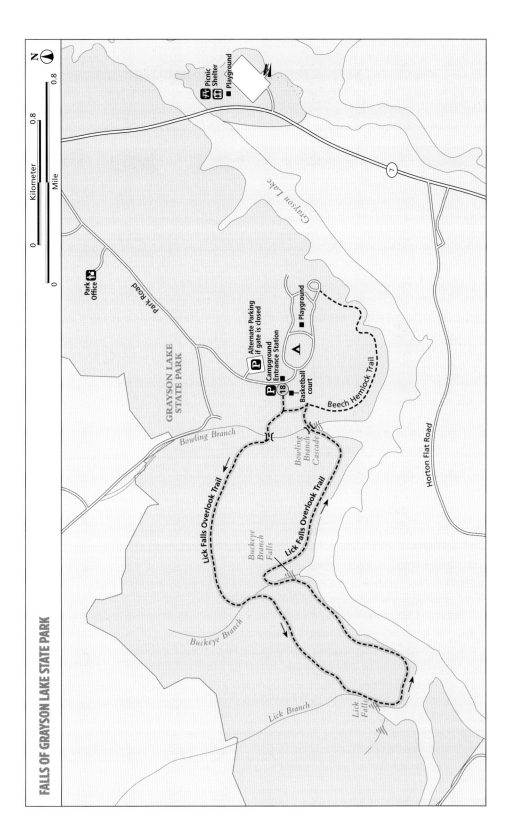

N

Kilometer
0   0.8   0.8

Mile
0   0.8

Park Office

GRAYSON LAKE STATE PARK

Park Road

Alternate Parking if gate is closed

Campground Entrance Station

Playground

18

Basketball court

Bowling Branch

Beech Hemlock Trail

Bowling Branch Cascade

Lick Falls Overlook Trail

Buckeye Branch Falls

Buckeye Branch

Lick Falls Overlook Trail

Lick Branch

Lick Falls

Grayson Lake

Picnic Shelter

Playground

Horton Flat Road

7

Ahead you will find Buckeye Branch Falls. Since it is below the trail, expect to scramble to it. Then once more you are walking the edge of the gorge above the lake, simply an enjoyable endeavor. After that, the trail takes you directly above Bowling Branch Cascade, so it is easy to view and maneuver around this pour-over for a photo.

The final part of the hike leads away from the lake and back to the trailhead. While here, consider enhancing your hiking adventure with boating, paddling, fishing, camping, or picnicking. It would be cool to see these waterfalls by both land and water.

Miles and Directions

0.0 From the signed trailhead near the park campground and basketball court, take the Lick Falls Overlook Trail westerly into woods, with open terrain on either side of the wooded strip.

0.1 Reach a trail intersection. Stay with the Lick Falls Overlook Trail as it keeps straight. Your return route comes in from the left, and an old country road goes right. The blazes lead you to Bowling Branch—cross it on a wooden hiker bridge. Hike among oaks and other hardwoods, and watch for an old stone fence from the days when this was a farm.

0.2 Cross a golf cart path. This segment of the hike is near holes 7 and 8 of the park golf course. Ahead, roll through hills.

0.7 Pass through a former farmland still growing over with brush and younger trees.

0.8 Cross small Buckeye Branch.

1.3 Come to Lick Creek after descending on an eroded track. Here the old roadbed you have picked up fords Lick Creek, but the official Lick Falls Overlook Trail stays on the left bank as a singletrack path, traversing through mountain laurel and rhododendron.

1.4 Reach the upper part of Lick Falls. Here the cataract makes an initial slide over smooth rock then fans out, sliding to a plunge pool below. It then makes another run over smooth rock before the final rush into Grayson Lake. The trail then keeps along the rim of the gorge and opens onto the main body of long, narrow Grayson Lake. Watery views open.

1.7 Pass a very low-flow waterslide that only runs during wetter times. Continue along the perched shoreline in woods.

2.0 Turn into the embayment of Buckeye Branch.

2.1 Hike above Buckeye Branch Falls. To get the best look at the pour-over, circle around Buckeye Branch and approach the spiller from the other side. You will still have to descend to get a face-on view of Buckeye Branch Falls. Turn back out to the main body of the lake.

2.6 Turn up the Bowling Branch arm of the lake.

2.7 Reach the hiker bridge crossing Bowling Branch. Bowling Branch Cascade makes its slide fall below the bridge into Grayson Lake. You can get a face-on look without much difficulty. Ascend from Bowling Branch.

2.8 Reach a trail intersection. Here the Beech Hemlock Trail leaves right while we go left, still making the loop.

2.9 Complete the loop portion of the hike after crossing a golf cart path. Turn right, backtracking toward the campground.

3.0 Arrive back at the trailhead, completing the waterfall hike.

19 Laurel Gorge Falls

Laurel Gorge Cultural Heritage Center, located on Laurel Creek in the uppermost reaches of Grayson Lake in eastern Kentucky, is home to a 90-foot-tall waterfall, nature trails, and a cultural repository documenting life in this parcel of the Bluegrass State. So when coming here, take time to walk through the cultural center as well as visit the waterfall and walk the rewarding nature trails.

Waterfall height: 90 feet
Waterfall beauty: 4
Distance: 1-mile lollipop loop
Difficulty: Easy
Hiking time: About 0.6 hour
Trail surface: Boardwalks, natural
Other trail users: None
Canine compatibility: Leashed pets allowed
Land status: Army Corps of Engineers property

Fees and permits: None. Hours: Mon–Sat noon to 5 p.m., Sun 1 to 4 p.m.
Maps: Trail map available at cultural center; USGS Isonville
Trail contact: Laurel Gorge Cultural Heritage Center, Laurel Curves Road, Old Route 32 and 7, Sandy Hook; (606) 738-5543; www .elliottcounty.ky.gov

Finding the trailhead: From the intersection of KY 32 and KY 7 in Sandy Hook, take KY 7 north for 3.1 miles, then turn right on Laurel Curves Road. Follow it for 0.2 mile, then veer right onto the Laurel Gorge Cultural Heritage Center entrance road and follow it a short distance to its dead end at the center building. GPS: N38° 7.1305' / W83° 6.4118'

The Hike

Back in the early 1990s, a local resident and Elliott County politician by the name of Rocky Adkins was looking to bring more people to visit what he thought was one of the prettiest parcels of the Bluegrass State. He thought about the gorge of Laurel Creek, which he had explored while fishing. That land was part of the uppermost reaches of Grayson Lake and owned by the US Army Corps of Engineers. Adkins then worked through countless meetings with a host of public and private entities to come out on the other end twelve years later with what has become the Laurel Gorge Cultural Heritage Center, a place to enjoy the natural beauty and historical significance of Elliott County.

You too will find this place a great way to spend a morning or afternoon. Walk the forest-bordered trails featuring long wheelchair-accessible boardwalks as well as more-challenging paths by which you can reach 90-foot Laurel Gorge Falls, a grand spiller when the water is running bold. Here a tributary of Laurel Creek reaches the rim of the gorge then recklessly dives from a sheer cliff into rocks below, splattering in front of a rock house then gathering to give its waters to Laurel Creek and Grayson Lake. This is a seasonal spiller and can reduce to a lame drip-line by autumn.

A well-timed hike and a little luck may result in seeing a rainbow in Laurel Gorge Falls.

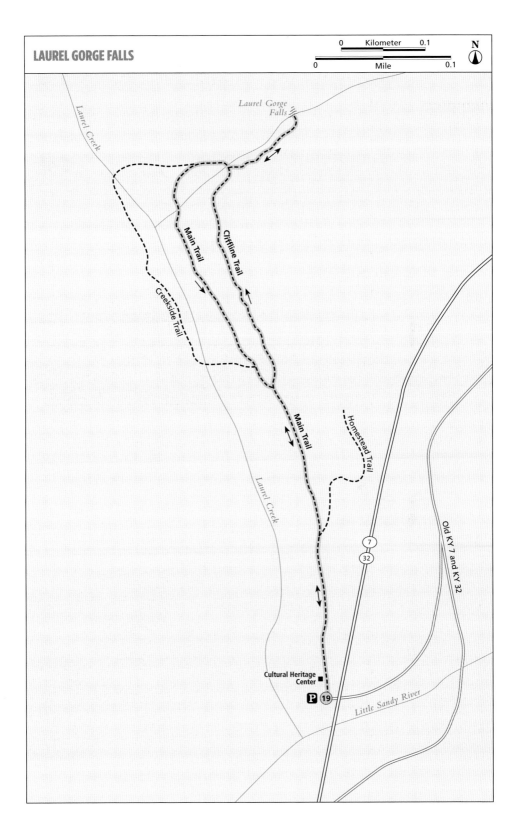

Kilometer

Mile

N

Laurel Gorge
Falls

Laurel Creek

Main Trail

Cliffline Trail

Creekside Trail

Main Trail

Homestead Trail

Laurel Creek

7

32

Old KY 7 and KY 32

Cultural Heritage
Center

P 19

Little Sandy River

However, in winter and spring you will be impressed by its height, high enough to be blown about when the breezes are stiff. The entirety of the Laurel Gorge extends for 12 miles and is 1,200 feet wide at its widest, with 300-foot-high cliffs rising from the water.

You will be impressed by the cultural center as well. Here you can examine historical displays that take you from the time of aboriginal Kentuckians to our current period. The displays especially focus on the lifeways of Appalachian mountaineers and a forgotten yet nostalgic period of state history. The cultural center also hosts guided walks for birders, wildflower enthusiasts, and history buffs. They offer a picnic shelter and picnic tables, so make an afternoon of it. They also host school and other groups. Call ahead as well as note the special opening and closing times to make the most of your Laurel Gorge Cultural Heritage Center experience.

Miles and Directions

0.0 From the parking area next to the Laurel Gorge Cultural Heritage Center, walk to the right of the building as you face the entrance then keep straight, passing the building, and begin the Main Trail. Quickly pass the Homestead Trail, leaving uphill to your right. Keep on the Main Trail as it traverses the first of many boardwalks. The upper embayment of Laurel Creek is down and to your left, while the gorge rises to your right.

0.2 The boardwalk you are on makes a split. Head right with the Cliffline Trail, going toward a dripping cliff line. The boardwalk soon ends and you are undulating at the base of the cliff line, pocked with rock houses. Ahead, squeeze between a gargantuan boulder and the cliff line.

0.4 Come to a trail intersection. Stay right toward Laurel Gorge Falls, and continue along the high cliff line.

0.5 Come to the developed overlook of Laurel Gorge Falls. Here, gain an ideal view of the 90-foot spray of white from about midpoint. You can look up at the waterfall sailing off the rim of Laurel Gorge and making the naked dive to the rocky bottom of the cliff line below. Backtrack to the last intersection.

0.6 Keep right at the intersection, heading toward the Main Trail. Walk a short distance then reach the Main Trail and head left in woods.

0.8 The Creekside Trail comes in on your right. Keep straight on the Main Trail and soon complete the loop portion of the hike and begin to backtrack to the trailhead.

1.0 Arrive back at the trailhead, completing the waterfall hike.

20 Falls of Glade Branch

Seemingly appearing out of nowhere, the three waterfalls of Glade Branch will surprise. Leaving from a nondescript trailhead, the hike passes a solid spiller near the parking area and then a long, tall, faucet-like cataract. From there, head toward Glade Branch and come to a 25-foot chute cutting from uplands into a slot canyon. To fully appreciate this pour-over, work around the stream then approach the falls from the bottom and you will see the crevice through which this waterfall flows, creating a beautiful scene of which the fall is the centerpiece.

Waterfall height: In order, 12 feet, 35 feet, 25 feet
Waterfall beauty: 5
Distance: 1-mile out-and-back
Difficulty: Easy; does require some scrambling
Hiking time: About 0.7 hour
Trail surface: Gravel, natural
Other trail users: A few equestrians

Canine compatibility: Leashed pets allowed
Land status: Army Corps of Engineers property
Fees and permits: None
Maps: Paintsville Lake Wildlife Management Area; USGS Oil Springs
Trail contact: Kentucky Department of Fish & Wildlife Resources, #1 Sportsman's Ln., Frankfort 40601; (800) 858-1549; https://fw.ky.gov

Finding the trailhead: From US 23 at the intersection with US 460 near Staffordsville, take the exit east then immediately head north onto KY 40 west. Follow KY 40 west for 1.5 miles to KY 172 west. Turn right and follow KY 172 for 3.2 miles to Stonecoal Road. Turn left and follow Stonecoal Road for 0.6 mile, then take the left turn (and down) onto obscure Glade Branch Road. Follow Glade Branch Road to its dead end after 0.6 mile. The parking area is a large grassy turnaround and the trail starts on the west side of the field, following a partly gravel doubletrack past a gate. GPS: N37° 51.6436' / W82° 53.2902'

The Hike

Paintsville Lake in eastern Kentucky is an Army Corps of Engineers impoundment of Paint Creek, itself a tributary of the Levisa Fork. Glade Branch—where these waterfalls can be found—flows into Paintsville Lake. The lake encompasses 1,139 acres, but more importantly for us waterfall hikers, the Army Corps of Engineers owns 13,156 acres surrounding the lake. It is on this public land where the falls of Glade Branch can be found. The Army Corps of Engineers has conferred most land management around the lake to the Kentucky Department of Fish & Wildlife Resources.

The trail to the falls of Glade Branch is shown on the Paintsville Lake Wildlife Management Area map. The trail, really a gated doubletrack road, has no name but it leaves the parking area then circles around Glade Branch and up the Paint Creek arm of the lake to exit at Stonecoal Road. To find the waterfalls of Glade Branch, we follow only the first half-mile of the trail. In fact, the first two waterfalls are just a short

Glade Branch Falls charges through a mossy rock cleft.

stroll from the trailhead, before you can even get any momentum. They are located on a tributary of Glade Branch.

To view these tributary falls, you have to drop off the main track and follow a user-created trail. The uppermost tributary falls is easy to reach. It first dances down an angled slide then makes a 12-foot curtain drop into a classic, circular plunge pool. The second tributary fall is another matter. You follow this same waterway downstream, then the creek simply free-falls 35 feet from the cliff line above Glade Creek. This faucet-like falls is quite a spiller and you must scramble to reach its base. Be very careful near the top of this cataract.

Next, you rejoin the unnamed trail and curve away from the tributary falls, clearly audible from the official path, and pass under a power line. It isn't long before more falling water sounds hit your ears. As you creep toward the edge of the gorge below, you find it but a crevice, a slot canyon, where Glade Branch Falls leaves the rolling hills and disappears into a world of rock and moss below.

Seeing Glade Branch Falls from its base is not difficult and is a must to fully appreciate the magnificence of this cataract. Simply continue curving around the gorge, crossing Glade Branch by culvert then arriving at the other side. You will soon find a break in the cliff line. Leave the trail and take a faint path toward the falls. You will see the gorge walls narrow to a slot, and here is where Glade Creek makes its slender

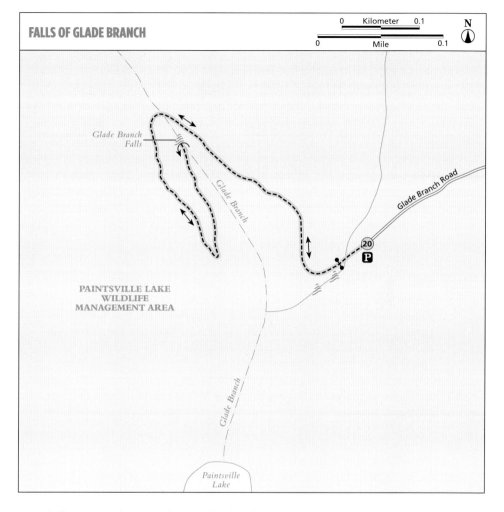

pinballing, stage-by-stage descent bordered by mossy stone walls to slow in a shallow sandy pool before moving on downstream, where the slot widens. The slot is easy to reach and rewarding, but beware slippery surfaces.

I for one am thankful Paintsville Lake came to be, preserving this waterfall and the trail to access it. The lake is also home to Paintsville Lake State Park, which offers up some excellent walk-in tent campsites as well as a more standard campground. The walk-in tent area fills only on summer holiday weekends, whereas the RV area fills most summer weekends. Campers come here because it is a quiet destination yet accessible to Paintsville Lake and the town of Paintsville.

While at Paintsville Lake, check out the Mountain HomePlace, open April through October. Like the trail, the Mountain HomePlace is located on nearby Army Corps of Engineers land. The plot is a working farm from the 1850s. Historic buildings include an old homestead, school, and church. You can also see a barn, working blacksmith shop, and gristmill. Explore on your own, take a guided tour, or visit the Mountain HomePlace on special event weekends.

Fishing at Paintsville Lake is reputed to be good; the lake is stocked with smallmouth and largemouth bass, channel catfish, walleye, and bream. Rainbow trout are also stocked annually. A full-service marina, located within sight of the state park, rents boats in case you want to head out and try your luck. The tailwaters below Paintsville Lake Dam are also stocked with trout and make for a different fishing experience.

Want to check out some other area trails? Take the 1.6-mile foot-traffic-only Kiwanis Trail, across from the Mountain HomePlace Welcome Center, where you can enjoy some views along the way. The star of the trail show in these parts is the 18-mile Dawkins Line Rail Trail, a converted former railroad line that is a blast to bicycle. Therefore, if you come to the falls of Glade Branch, consider all the other nearby offerings here at Paintsville Lake.

Miles and Directions

0.0 From the large grassy parking area, head southwest, crossing an unnamed small tributary of Glade Branch by culvert then passing around a metal gate, to join a doubletrack partly gravel road/trail. However, if you want to see the first two tributary falls, immediately split left from the trail near the metal gate and follow a faint path to the upper tributary fall. The lower tributary fall requires a scramble to reach its base. Resume the main official trail, curving away from the tributary to pass under a power line.

0.2 Come to the slot into which Glade Branch tumbles. The falls can't be accessed from here; therefore, continue curving around the stream, crossing it by culvert. Ignore old roads spurring away from the main trail into nearby fields and woods.

0.4 Diverge from the main trail at a wide break in the cliff line. Aim for Glade Branch Falls, passing a rock house on your left.

0.5 Arrive at 25-foot Glade Branch Falls and its slot canyon, a special and scenic parcel of the Bluegrass State. Backtrack to the trailhead.

1.0 Arrive back at the trailhead, completing the waterfall hike.

21 Broke Leg Falls

This exciting set of cataracts in Menifee County has been a draw for generations, despite the name. It is easy to see why, for this park offers four exciting waterfalls, culminating in the big-time spiller, 70-foot Broke Leg Falls. A set of nature trails takes you along Broke Leg Creek to see these aquatic wonders.

Waterfall height: In order, 12 feet, 10 feet, 14 feet, 70 feet
Waterfall beauty: 3
Distance: 0.4-mile out-and-back
Difficulty: Easy
Hiking time: About 0.5 hour
Trail surface: Natural
Other trail users: None

Canine compatibility: Leashed pets allowed
Land status: County park
Fees and permits: None
Map: USGS Ezel
Trail contact: Menifee County, 12 Main St., PO Box 105, Frenchburg 40322; (606) 768-3482; www.menifeecounty.ky.gov

Finding the trailhead: From the intersection of US 460 and KY 36 in Frenchburg, take US 460 east for 9.9 miles to reach the left turn into signed Broke Leg Falls Park. This left turn will be on a sharp right curve. GPS: N37° 54.3822' / W83° 29.3712'

The Hike

The natural beauty of Broke Leg Falls has existed from time immemorial. Here, Broke Leg Creek drops off the hills of Menifee County into a steep gorge, and it is where the stream spills into the gorge that the cataracts can be found. Seventy-foot Broke Leg Falls and its gorge drew attention in the 1940s. A fellow named Wells developed a regular tourist attraction off US 460, an important east–west Kentucky thoroughfare in the days before interstates laced our land. Wells charged a ten-cent admission to view the falls but also had nine cabins overlooking the gorge that he would rent overnight, as well as a restaurant for hungry travelers and waterfall visitors.

The state of Kentucky wanted in on the act. In 1958 they created a roadside park here, leasing the land from the owners. Walkways to the falls, restrooms, and picnic areas were built, making it an official wayside for travelers driving US 460.

However, times changed as they always do. The traffic on US 460 fell off as the nearby interstate-like Mountain Parkway opened for business in 1963, all but killing off all incidental visitors to Broke Leg Falls. I-64 siphoned still other visitors. Ten years after opening Broke Leg Falls as a wayside park, the state of Kentucky abandoned the preserve. The adjacent restaurant closed in the 1970s. In 1988 the state conferred the land back to the owners, leaving Broke Leg Falls an eyesore, with weeds sprouting up in the frequently vandalized destination.

By 2002 Menifee County had had enough and decided to purchase the land and develop Broke Leg Falls as its own county park. Progress took a while—over nine years actually—from purchasing to park opening. The county added a new gazebo, renovated the picnic shelter, added cooking grills, and generally cleaned up the 15-acre preserve. Broke Leg Falls once again shone. Hikers, passersby, and waterfall enthusiasts like us appreciated not only the waterfalls but also the deep gorge grown up with hemlock, tulip trees, birch, and white pine, nestled in thickets of rhododendron. Picnickers and visitors began filtering back here to see this highlight of Menifee County.

Then on March 2, 2012, a mere five months after the park renovations were completed, a venomous tornado tore through the area, not only wreaking havoc on the man-made structures and trails, but also tearing down nearly every tree at the park. A lot of money and time had been invested in Broke Leg Falls, and citizens were shocked at the carnage. Since then, the main part of the infrastructure has been restored, but some old trails have yet to be renovated. Nevertheless, Broke Leg Falls has once again risen from the ashes. The park is open; trees are regrowing. It will take a long time for the forces of nature to recover from the tornado—you can still see hundreds of cut stumps—yet natural recovery will occur on its own schedule.

Enough of the trails have been restored to allow you to view the four major falls here as well as observe the amazing power of what a tornado can do. From the parking area, take a little trail upstream to view three set of falls. The trail ends at a cataract with a plunge pool that is easy to access.

You return to the trailhead then work your way to an incredible, immense stone cathedral into the gorge of the stream. Here you can gain face-on views of the 70-foot plunge made by Broke Leg Falls. (Incidentally, legend has it that Broke Leg Falls and creek got their name when an ox broke its leg hereabouts.) An alluring but difficult-to-reach plunge pool lies below.

A trail leads you behind the falls into the overhanging amphitheater, where you can get more looks at the cataract. Unfortunately, beyond here the trail system has not been renovated. Perhaps it will be in the future, but given the park's history, you cannot blame the government of Menifee County of being wary of investing too much in this park that has seen both good days and bad. Nonetheless, the beauty of the waterfalls here has been constant. See for yourself.

Miles and Directions

0.0 From the parking area, take a narrow trail upstream along Broke Leg Creek, making your way past two waterfalls. The path ends at the uppermost fall, dropping in two stages into a wide and easily accessible plunge pool. Backtrack to the trailhead.

0.1 Arrive back at the trailhead. Stay with the path winding along the rim of the gorge above Broke Leg Falls. Descend past a picnic shelter, then drop to see the another waterfall, descending upstream of the trail bridge over Broke Leg Creek.

Broke Leg Falls makes a 70-foot swan dive from a rock rim.

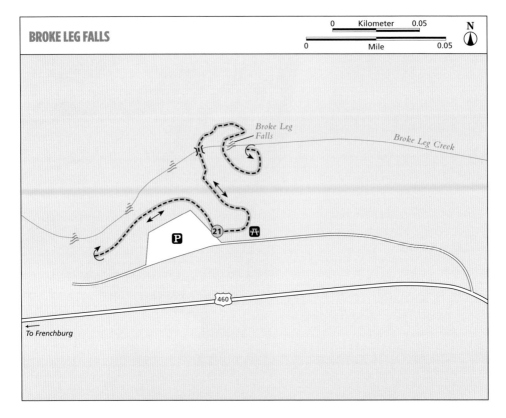

Broke Leg
Falls

Broke Leg Creek

21

P

460

To Frenchburg

0.2 Reach the base of 70-foot Broke Leg Falls after walking a slender path with rails next to the falls then enjoying a face-on view. After that you can circle behind Broke Leg Falls on a trail to gain a face-on view from the other side of the falls. Carefully explore, then back-track to the trailhead.

0.4 Arrive back at the trailhead, completing the waterfall hike.

22 Copperas Falls

An aquatic highlight of the Clifty Wilderness within the Red River Gorge, Copperas Falls is the centerpiece of a memorable scene of Kentucky beauty. Here you will find a crystalline stream dashing from an overhung rim, making a curtain dive onto a sand-bottomed plunge pool, encircled in junglesque vegetation. The hike to the falls is alluring as well, but it does entail at least a dozen crossings of Copperas Creek.

Waterfall height: 25 feet	**Land status:** National forest
Waterfall beauty: 5	**Fees and permits:** None
Distance: 3.4-mile out-and-back	**Maps:** Red River Geological Area, Daniel Boone
Difficulty: Moderate	National Forest; USGS Pomeroyton
Hiking time: About 2.2 hours	**Trail contact:** Daniel Boone National Forest,
Trail surface: Natural	Cumberland Ranger District, 2375 KY 801
Other trail users: None	South, Morehead, KY; (606) 784-6428; www.fs
Canine compatibility: Leashed pets allowed	.usda.gov/dbnf

Finding the trailhead: From exit 40 on the Bert Combs Mountain Parkway, take KY 15/KY 715 north for 0.7 mile, then turn right onto KY 715 north. Follow it for 4.9 miles then veer right, staying with KY 715 as a road goes straight to Sky Bridge. Continue on KY 715 north for 1.4 more miles to reach the trailhead on the right, just after crossing the bridge over the Red River. GPS: N37° 49.209' / W83° 34.480'

The Hike

Located in the heart of the Clifty Wilderness, Copperas Creek flows through an incredibly attractive valley with everywhere-you-look beauty—from the clear stream and its tributaries running through regal woods to big boulders, cliff lines, and other geological fascinations found within the Red River Gorge. The sight of Copperas Falls reminds me of a tropical scene from a book where castaways of a sunken ship make their stand. The cliff line over which the waterfall tumbles forms a backdrop—and the overhanging rock house a shelter of sorts—and the sand-lined pool below the waterfall would be where the castaways would bathe and get their water. Nearby, the flats populated by pines, hemlocks, and hardwoods would be the location of their hut.

You may not get as carried away by your imagination when coming to Copperas Falls, but you will agree it is a stimulating and stunning part of Kentucky. Plan to linger at the falls and enjoy the atmosphere, perhaps having a picnic here. However, realize you are within the boundaries of the Clifty Wilderness and want to preserve this untamed land, keeping it attractive for the next visitor.

The Clifty Wilderness, covering 12,646 acres, came to be in 1985. Within this wild area exists fifteen sensitive, rare, or endangered plants. Prior to becoming part of the Daniel Boone National Forest and being designated a wilderness, as well as part of the National Natural Landmark that is the Red River Gorge, many of the streams, valleys, and ridges were logged and farmed. However, with decades and decades for nature to do its work, the Clifty Wilderness is once again one of Kentucky's special wild places.

What is wilderness anyway? After 18,600 pages of testimony and the consolidation of 65 bills, the Wilderness Act of 1964 was passed by Congress. The legal definition of wilderness, spelled out in the bill, is as follows: "A wilderness, in contrast with those areas where man and his works dominate the landscape, is hereby recognized as an area where the earth and its community of life are untrammeled by man, where man . . . is a visitor and does not remain." Ranging from 6 to over 9 million acres in size, wilderness areas have multiple uses. Most visitors to the Clifty Wilderness hike, backpack, climb, and go waterfalling.

Even though the trail to Copperas Falls is unofficial, the path is well trampled and you should have no problem staying found. However, since the hike to the falls requires multiple crossings of Copperas Creek, you will often find trails on both sides of the waterway, since all the creek crossings are not uniform and hikers aplenty scramble up the valley in search of ways to reach Copperas Falls. Therefore, your only confusion may be when to cross the creek and what side of the creek to be on at any given moment. Nevertheless, you should not have any trouble reaching Copperas Falls. On busy days there will be plenty of other hikers making their way to the cataract.

Finding the proper time to visit can be tricky. The waterfall will be boldest from winter through spring. This is also when Copperas Creek will be at its highest and coldest. Lucky is the hiker who can make it to the waterfall without getting their feet wet. That is why many visitors come during the summer, when they can simply slosh through the creek if necessary. Rock-hopping is also easier then. Also, the warmth and humidity of summer makes dipping in the pool at the base of Copperas Falls a just reward.

So factor these considerations into your visit. In addition, the limited parking area can be troublesome. Get here early on nice weekends to secure a spot. Remember, the trail is not marked and maintained; therefore, expect to step over plenty of fallen trees.

You will first leave the trailhead and walk northwesterly away from the Red River on KY 715. A well-trammeled path will leave KY 715, turning up the Copperas Creek valley. At first you will be traveling up the right-hand side of the valley. It is not long before coming to the first creek crossing and the divergence of paths heading for the valley on both sides of the creek. Trekking poles or hiking sticks greatly aid your crossings. Copperas Creek is not big but does have plenty of sections that will go over the tops of your shoes. I do not recommend hiking sandals, as there are too many rough sections where you are working through rhododendron and other brushy areas. Consider using old hiking shoes that you do not mind getting wet.

Copperas Falls forms the centerpiece of the Clifty Wilderness.

Along the way you will enjoy wilderness-level beauty. Most hikers do not see the very unusual aquatic feature on the right-hand bank not too far from KY 715. Here a side stream flows toward Copperas Creek and then spills about 10 feet into its own sinkhole. Observant hikers will also find places where springs are pushing forth from the bases of bluffs. Deeper pools in the creek exude a gorgeous bluish cast. Other times, the mixture of tall trees, mosses, rocks, and rhododendron create memorable woodland scenes.

The falling noise of 25-foot Copperas Falls will give away its presence. Here, in a junglesque woodland glen, you will find this narrow curtain-type spiller diving into a sandy catch basin and pool. The beauty of the spot may stimulate your imagination, too. Please take extra-special care of this place. It deserves your attention, respect—and regard.

Miles and Directions

0.0 Walk away from the Red River along KY 715 west, passing the side road to the Copperas Creek paddler access. Quickly turn right, following a well-trod, user-created trail up the Copperas Creek valley. Trace an old roadbed up the vale, northbound, with Copperas Creek to your left.

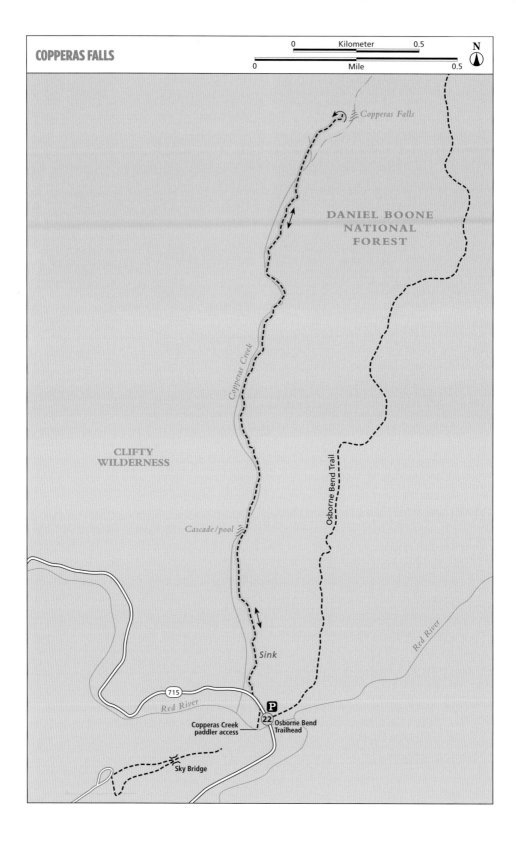

COPPERAS FALLS

0   Kilometer   0.5

0   Mile   0.5

N

Copperas Falls

DANIEL BOONE
NATIONAL
FOREST

Copperas Creek

CLIFTY
WILDERNESS

Osborne Bend Trail

Cascade/pool

Sink

715

Red River

Red River

P

22

Copperas Creek
paddler access

Osborne Bend
Trailhead

Sky Bridge

0.2 Come to the first split in the trail. From here forward expect to have multiple trail choices as to which side of the creek to hike on as well as exactly where to cross the creek, which you will be doing over and over again.

0.5 Copperas Creek squeezes through boulders well below the path, forming a small cascade and big plunge pool. Soon begin crisscrossing the stream with frequency. Small tributaries flow into Copperas Creek.

1.3 Copperas Creek runs under a rising cliff line on the right-hand side as you head upstream.

1.7 Come to 25-foot Copperas Falls and its magical scene. This is one waterfall you can circle around and behind and get multiple angles without difficulty. Backtrack to the trailhead.

3.4 Arrive back at the trailhead, completing the hike.

23 Creation Falls, Turtle Falls

Hike to two gorgeous yet contrasting waterfalls, plus see one of Kentucky's most picturesque arches. The first part of the hike is quite popular as you head to 12-foot Creation Falls and its big pool. Next stands Rock Bridge Arch, a stone span stretching across Swift Camp Creek. The hike then joins the Swift Camp Creek Trail, entering the Clifty Wilderness. Traverse this gorgeous vale to reach 20-foot Turtle Falls, a tapered cataract diving from a cliff line.

Waterfall height: In order, 12 feet, 20 feet
Waterfall beauty: 4
Distance: 4-mile loop with spur
Difficulty: Moderate
Hiking time: About 2 hours
Trail surface: Mostly natural, some asphalt
Other trail users: None
Canine compatibility: Leashed pets allowed

Land status: National forest
Fees and permits: None
Maps: Red River Geological Area, Daniel Boone National Forest; USGS Pomeroyton
Trail contact: Daniel Boone National Forest, Cumberland Ranger District, 2375 KY 801 South, Morehead 40351; (606) 784-6428; www.fs.usda.gov/dbnf

Finding the trailhead: From exit 40 on the Mountain Parkway near Pine Ridge, take KY 15 north for 1.3 miles to KY 715 north. Turn right and follow KY 715 for 0.4 mile to Rock Bridge Road. Turn right and follow Rock Bridge Road for 3.3 miles to its dead end at the Rock Bridge Picnic Area. GPS: N37° 46.206' / W83° 34.022'

The Hike

This waterfall hike takes you to two very different but both comely cataracts, with a bonus of viewing a super-cool arch along the way. Creation Falls is a wide, classic cataract with a big pool, while Turtle Falls is a narrow spiller diving over a cliff line. In between Creation Falls and Turtle Falls stands Rock Bridge Arch. The stone bridge stretches across Swift Camp Creek and is a sight to behold.

The Rock Bridge Trail, which this hike uses, is a very popular trail in Kentucky's fabled Red River Gorge, part of the Daniel Boone National Forest. The Rock Bridge Trail leaves the Rock Bridge Picnic Area then descends to Rockbridge Fork, passing a high, imposing rock house along the way to find Creation Falls. This pour-over makes its 12-foot drop after running over a long rock slab. The upper part of the falls makes a vertical curtain drop then spreads in angled white froth before gathering in a dark pool. To reach the beach below the falls, make a bridgeless crossing of Rockbridge Fork above the falls, then walk downstream along Rockbridge Fork. However, if you stay along the trail, a developed overlook will give you an alternate dry-footed view of Creation Falls, named for nearby Rock Bridge Arch being an arch formed by water erosion.

Turtle Falls splashes into its sandy base, framed by iron-stained rock walls.

Creation Falls makes its wide, classic drop during autumn.

Beyond Creation Falls, you will turn down the scenic Swift Camp Creek valley, where lush vegetation topped with regal trees grows amid rock outcrops. Of course, the stream itself presents aquatic splendor. And the spot where Rock Bridge crosses the creek will astound first-time arch viewers. The natural bridge extends 60 feet, completely across Swift Camp Creek, about 8 feet above the stream. Its bridge-like form completes the tableau.

The eye-pleasing hike leads onward to Turtle Falls. Here a tributary of Swift Camp Creek makes its vertical nosedive from a cliff line into a colorful grotto beside Swift Camp Creek. The trail takes you directly beside the waterfall, but getting to its base can be challenging. Turtle Falls is also known as Turtleback Falls and Pooch Turtle Falls. The derivatives of the turtle moniker come from nearby Turtle Back Arch, located on a user-created spur trail.

The tributary forming Turtle Falls flows across the trail, making the waterfall a cinch to find. However, accessing the base of the falls is anything but a cinch. Be careful. The view from the falls' base reveals this waterfall plummeting from a rock rim to splash into a sand floor. Iron-stained rock walls fashion an arresting framework for the pour-over.

After backtracking from Turtle Falls, rejoin the loop of the Rock Bridge Trail. The path climbs from Swift Camp Creek along a steep and narrow piney ridgeline.

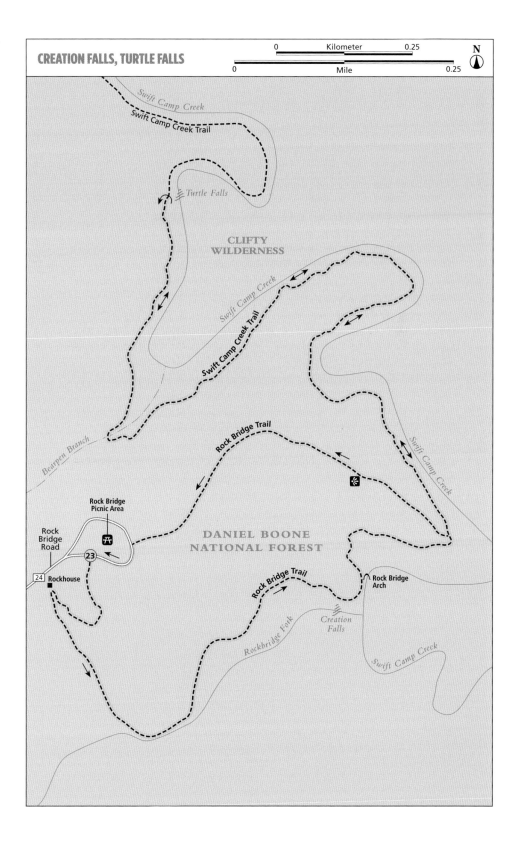

CREATION FALLS, TURTLE FALLS

0   Kilometer   0.25

0   Mile   0.25

N

Swift Camp Creek

Swift Camp Creek Trail

Turtle Falls

CLIFTY
WILDERNESS

Swift Camp Creek

Swift Camp Creek Trail

Swift Camp Creek

Bearpen Branch

Rock Bridge Trail

Rock Bridge
Picnic Area

Rock
Bridge
Road

23

DANIEL BOONE
NATIONAL FOREST

24 Rockhouse

Rock Bridge Trail

Rock Bridge
Arch

Rockbridge Fork

Creation
Falls

Swift Camp Creek

A developed overlook stands above Swift Camp Creek. Climb a bit more on neat-looking carved stone steps. The trail levels off before reaching hike's end on the north side of the picnic area.

Miles and Directions

0.0 Leave from the south side of Rock Bridge Picnic Area on the Rock Bridge Trail, a path asphalted long ago. Leave upland hardwoods for moister woods.

0.1 Reach a high, imposing rock house with a very low-flow, part-time waterfall dripping from its heights. Beyond here, turn down a tributary of Rockbridge Fork, shaded by white pines.

0.3 Come alongside Rockbridge Fork, and turn down this charming valley.

0.4 Come to 12-foot Creation Falls, found where Rockbridge Fork tumbles downstream of a long rock slab. Good views can be had from across the creek or just down-trail at a developed overlook. From here, turn along Swift Camp Creek.

0.5 Arrive at Rock Bridge Arch. The stone span completely crosses Swift Camp Creek. Keep downstream. The path delivers views of Rock Bridge Arch from both sides.

0.9 Intersect and join the natural surface the Swift Camp Creek Trail. You will return to this intersection later. For now, enter the Clifty Wilderness, undulating down the Swift Camp Creek gorge under pines aplenty, along with other evergreens. The trail runs the gorge rim, allowing looks into Swift Camp Creek.

1.3 Make a 180-degree northwest-to-southeast bend as the trail mimics the curves of the creek.

1.9 Turn up Bearpen Branch. The trail leads through a mini-gorge, leaving you to briefly walk directly up the small creek. Turn back out to Swift Camp Creek's rim.

2.2 Reach the top of Turtle Falls as it spills into a stone alcove below. The slender 25-foot spiller is difficult to access for a bottom-up view. Backtrack to the Rock Bridge Arch Trail.

3.5 Rejoin the Rock Bridge Arch Trail, to finish the loop. Climb away from Swift Camp Creek.

3.7 Come to a developed overlook above Swift Camp Creek.

4.0 Arrive back at the picnic area, completing the hike.

24 Upper Whittleton Falls

This waterfall—despite being on the Sheltowee Trace—sees few visitors, simply because it is located between popular Natural Bridge State Park and even more popular Red River Gorge. The walk is short, simple, and sweet. You take the Sheltowee Trace from KY 11 into the Whittleton Branch watershed along pretty little streamlets and over quaint hiker bridges to meet this classic ledge-spiller that makes its plunge into a rock jumble. Photographers can access the spiller from multiple angles without difficulty.

Waterfall height: 10 feet
Waterfall beauty: 3
Distance: 1-mile out-and-back
Difficulty: Easy
Hiking time: About 0.8 hour
Trail surface: Natural
Other trail users: None
Canine compatibility: Leashed pets allowed

Land status: National forest
Fees and permits: None
Maps: Red River Geological Area, Daniel Boone National Forest; USGS Slade
Trail contact: Daniel Boone National Forest, Cumberland Ranger District, 2375 KY 801 South, Morehead 40351; (606) 784-6428; www.fs.usda.gov/dbnf

Finding the trailhead: From exit 33 on the Mountain Parkway near Slade, take KY 15 south for 3.3 miles to Tunnel Ridge Road. The Sheltowee Trace starts on the south side of KY 15 here at the intersection with Tunnel Ridge Road. However, parking here can be problematic. You may therefore have to park your car at the Pinch Em Tight trailhead parking, on your left about a half-mile up Tunnel Ridge Road. GPS: N37° 47.833' / W83° 39.239'

The Hike

Natural Bridge State Park and the Red River Gorge are arguably two of Kentucky's most popular outdoor destinations. And the Sheltowee Trace, which links Natural Bridge State Park and the Red River Gorge, is Kentucky's most celebrated long-distance path. Judging by all this popularity, you would think that Upper Whittleton Falls would be a more popular destination, but it is not. Part of this problem is being in a "no man's land" parcel of the Daniel Boone National Forest between the two attractions. Also, the parking situation for this hike is not the greatest—at least if you want to park very close to the hike starting point.

However, do not let a lack of popularity or an imperfect parking situation deter you from coming here. The falls are pretty and easy to photograph. The walk is easy and short and delivers a lot, considering it is only a half-mile one way to the falls. First, you will leave KY 15, joining the Sheltowee Trace. Kentucky's master path immediately takes you downhill, first passing a rock house before making a series of switchbacks that take you to the head of the Whittleton Creek valley. Here several streams

Upper Whittleton Branch Falls is an unexpected highlight along the Sheltowee Trace.

converge to form the headwaters of this creek that ultimately feeds the Middle Fork Red River. These smallish streams unite to give enough aqua to push Whittleton Creek literally over the edge of a rock rim in a constricted part of the valley.

This is where Upper Whittleton Falls forms, making a uniform curtain drop over the slick rim into an irregular rock pile, forcing the stream to flow every which way before regrouping below. You cannot miss the falls, as the Sheltowee Trace takes you directly beside it. A little scrambling will allow you to view this cataract from multiple angles and perhaps visit the rock house on the far side of the falls. Enjoy the walk back uphill, reflecting on why other visitors do not seem to seek out this waterfall directly alongside Kentucky's most important trail.

Miles and Directions

0.0 Leave the signed trailhead on KY 15, joining the Sheltowee Trace under pines, oaks, maples, and mountain laurel. Work your way down along a cliff line.

0.1 Come to a switchback in the trail. A side path leads right to a nearby rock house. Continue downhill, into an increasing number of evergreens from rhododendron to hemlock.

0.4 Cross a tributary of Whittleton Branch on a footbridge. Soon cross another footbridge over a wet area. The valley narrows into a defile.

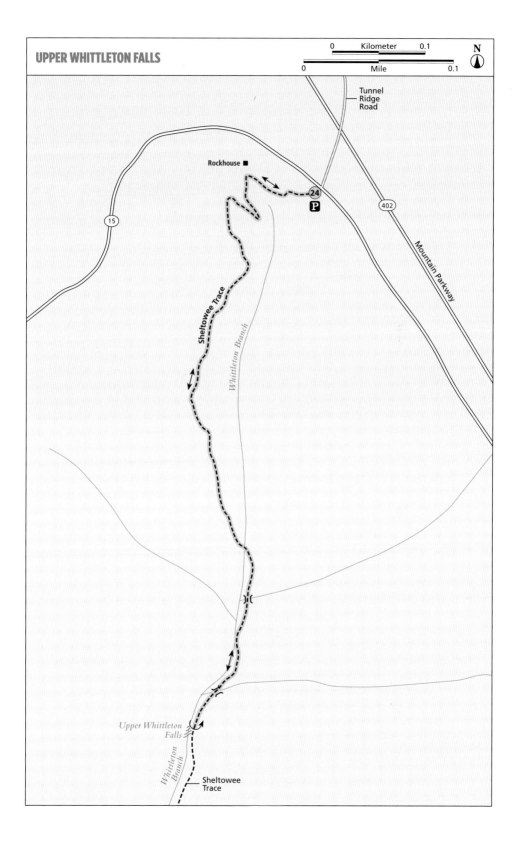

UPPER WHITTLETON FALLS

0 — Kilometer — 0.1

0 — Mile — 0.1

N

Tunnel
Ridge
Road

Rockhouse ■

24

P

402

15

Mountain Parkway

Sheltowee Trace

Whittleton Branch

Upper Whittleton
Falls

Whittleton Branch

Sheltowee
Trace

A face-on view of Upper Whittleton Falls

0.5 Come to Upper Whittleton Falls. The Sheltowee Trace takes you directly beside the classic ledge cataract, pouring 10 feet over a rock ledge. A short downhill scramble leads you to a face-on view of the falls. Backtrack to the trailhead.

1.0 Arrive back at the trailhead, completing the hike.

25 Sand Gap Trail Falls

This waterfall hike at Natural Bridge State Resort Park takes place on the seldom-trod Sand Gap Trail. It leads from the busy skylift parking area and visits a remote parcel of the park inside the protected confines of 1,188-acre Natural Bridge State Resort Park Nature Preserve, where flora and fauna are accorded an additional layer of protection. It is within this preserve that you will find Sand Gap Trail Falls. This 5-foot spiller takes a trailside tumble from a rock lip then goes on its way to feed its mother stream, Lower Hood Branch.

Waterfall height: 5 feet
Waterfall beauty: 3
Distance: 2.6-mile out-and-back
Difficulty: Easy
Hiking time: About 1.3 hours
Trail surface: Natural
Other trail users: None
Canine compatibility: Pets prohibited

Land status: State park
Fees and permits: None
Maps: Natural Bridge State Resort Park; USGS Slade
Trail contact: Natural Bridge State Resort Park, 2135 Natural Bridge Rd., Slade 40376; (606) 663-2214; www.parks.ky.gov/parks/resortparks/natural-bridge

Finding the trailhead: From exit 33 on the Mountain Parkway near Slade, head south on KY 11 for 2 miles, then turn right into the Natural Bridge State Park entrance indicating lodge, dining, and skylift. Cross the bridge over the Middle Fork Red River, then immediately turn right toward the skylift and mini-golf. Follow the park road to its dead end near the restrooms and mini-golf area. GPS: N37° 46.891' / W83° 41.465'

The Hike

Now just because this waterfall is a mere 5 feet high, do not immediately discount it. Not only is the spiller attractive and a worthy destination, but the scenery around it meets the high Kentucky standard of a state nature preserve, home to the endangered Virginia big-eared bat among other species. Furthermore, the Lower Hood Branch watershed is one of the healthiest, cleanest streams in Kentucky, as proven by its rich macroinvertebrate communities, and part of the reason for establishing the sanctuary is to sustain this vigorous watershed.

Solitude is another attraction of the Sand Gap Trail. When other paths in the Natural Bridge/Red River Gorge complex are crowded, solitude reigns on the Sand Gap Trail. Most people avoid the trail because to do the whole thing requires a 10-mile hike, with no bailout options for the first 7 miles—unless you backtrack. Of course, our waterfall hike is a 2.6-mile out-and-back adventure.

However, I do encourage hiking the entire Sand Gap Trail. It will take you to Natural Bridge—the long way—for which the park is named. From Natural Bridge,

Very few people view this cataract along the Sand Gap Trail.

you can return to the trailhead via the Hood Branch Trail, fashioning the 10-mile circuit, full of seclusion and first-rate Kentucky scenery.

The trailhead for the hike contrasts mightily with your impending entry into the Kentucky state nature preserve. It begins next to the state park's mini-golf course, which is in turn next to the large parking area serving the park's skylift, which takes visitors to within a quarter-mile of Natural Bridge.

The hike leaves the potentially busy trailhead and climbs on the Hood Branch Trail before quickly joining the Sand Gap Trail. Solitude is guaranteed on this path, as demonstrated by the relatively faint trail bed. The signed and blazed track works its way up the vale of Lower Hood Branch under a mantle of beech and pine. The path rises far above the stream on a steep hillside while bridging numerous feeder branches.

You then reach Sand Gap Trail Falls, on a larger tributary of Lower Hood Branch. Here, just below the path, this tributary pours from a cleft of stone then gathers itself and flows onward onto Lower Hood Branch. This spiller is easy to photograph and get around for different angles. Being a wet-weather waterfall, I recommend visiting it from winter through spring. Furthermore, spring is excellent for wildflowers along Lower Hood Branch. Contrastingly, I have seen this cataract completely dry in autumn.

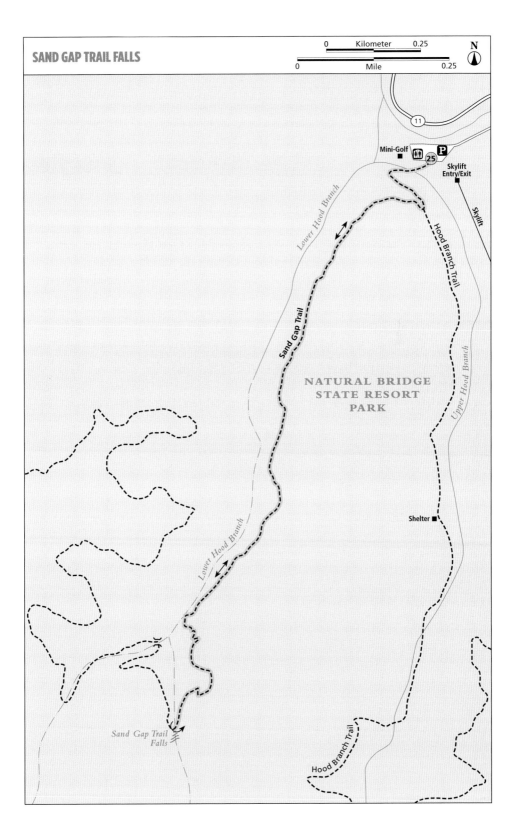

SAND GAP TRAIL FALLS

0   Kilometer   0.25
0   Mile   0.25

N

Mini-Golf
P
25
Skylift
Entry/Exit

Skylift

Lower Hood Branch

Sand Gap Trail

Hood Branch Trail

Upper Hood Branch

NATURAL BRIDGE
STATE RESORT
PARK

Shelter

Lower Hood Branch

Sand Gap Trail
Falls

Hood Branch Trail

In addition to visiting the falls, there is plenty more to do here at Natural Bridge State Resort Park. Accommodations not only include two campgrounds but also a lodge with an accompanying restaurant. However, the natural attributes of the land, namely Natural Bridge, are the reasons why this park is here in the first place. In addition to the Sand Gap Trail, Natural Bridge can be reached via several park pathways. The Original Trail reaches the arch after three-quarters of a mile and links to other paths, visiting geological wonders such as Balanced Rock, Battleship Rock, Devils Gulch, Needles Eye, and Lookout Point, among other features. If you want to see Natural Bridge the easy way, take the skylift. It can be picked up near this hike's trailhead.

In summer the activities and nature center offers daily programs for park visitors from 3 to 93. Consider paddling a rental boat around Hoedown Island Lake, or swim in the park pool, or fish Middle Fork and Mill Creek Lake. In addition, if hiking to Sand Gap Trail Falls in the summertime, you can cap off your trek with a round at the mini-golf course adjacent to the trailhead.

Miles and Directions

0.0   Leave the skylift/mini-golf parking area near the restrooms, then walk southwest across a lawn to find the signed Hood Branch Trail. Enter the 1,188-acre Natural Bridge State Park Nature Preserve. Ascend on an old roadbed.

0.1   Turn right onto the Sand Gap Trail. Posted signs apprise hikers of the distance and difficulty of the trail.

1.3   Turn into the unnamed tributary of Lower Hood Branch and reach Sand Gap Trail Falls. The pour-over tumbles just below the trail and cannot be missed. Backtrack to the trailhead.

2.6   Arrive back at the trailhead, completing the waterfall hike.

26 Waterfall of Whittleton Arch

Take a hike that delivers a double reward: massive Whittleton Arch—a natural bridge—and the waterfall that drops from its heights. The low-flow cataract forms just one part of this scene of water, stone, and forest. Start at Natural Bridge State Resort Park, then follow the Sheltowee Trace to meander up the attractive vale of Whittleton Branch. A spur trail leads up a tributary of Whittleton Branch to Whittleton Arch and the waterfall that discharges from its face.

Waterfall height: 25 feet
Waterfall beauty: 3
Distance: 3-mile out-and-back
Difficulty: Easy to moderate
Hiking time: About 1.4 hours
Trail surface: Natural
Other trail users: None
Canine compatibility: Leashed pets allowed
Land status: State park, national forest
Fees and permits: None

Maps: Red River Geological Area, Daniel Boone National Forest; USGS Slade
Trail contact: Natural Bridge State Resort Park, 2135 Natural Bridge Rd., Slade 40376; (606) 663-2214, www.parks.ky.gov/parks/resort parks/natural-bridge/. Daniel Boone National Forest, Cumberland Ranger District, 2375 KY 801 South, Morehead 40351; (606) 784-6428; www.fs.usda.gov/dbnf

Finding the trailhead: From exit 33 on the Mountain Parkway near Slade, head south on KY 11 for 2.2 miles, passing the entrance to the Whittleton Campground at Natural Bridge State Resort Park on your left. Just beyond the campground entrance road, turn right and cross the Middle Fork Red River on a low-water bridge to reach a parking area with restrooms. Do not park in Whittleton Campground then hike to the arch. GPS: N37° 46.788' / W83° 40.550'

The Hike

To most visitors, Whittleton Arch is the primary reason for doing this hike. However, for us waterfallers the eye-pleasing trek delivers an additional aquatic punch. I recommend coming here during the wetter times, winter through spring, to see the best of the waterfall. However, no matter the time of year, at least you will be able to enjoy Whittleton Arch and the attractive Kentucky woodlands hiked through along the way.

The beginning of the hike leaves a parking area on KY 11, near the entrance to Natural Bridge State Resort Park's Whittleton Campground, one of two campgrounds here under state park auspices. (Whittleton Campground offers water, campsites with or without electricity, and hot showers, set along Whittleton Branch.) The trek then leads through the main campground road (don't park here, or anywhere within the campground). Enjoy the tour of the campsites before picking up the Sheltowee Trace at the end of the campground road to enter a woodland of white pines as well as deciduous trees shading Whittleton Branch. This crystalline watercourse

This bridge over Whittleton Branch leads you to Whittleton Falls and Arch.

flows through state park and national forest land flanked with stone bulwarks. You are following an old logging railroad grade, though the trail jumps off it here and there. Back in the late 1800s, the Mountain Central Railway was part of a timber operation connecting the Natural Bridge area to Chimney Top.

Wood hiker bridges span Whittleton Branch, helping keep your feet dry. Back on land the path is bathed in golden needles from white pines. It is a pleasant hike. The trek leaves Whittleton Branch for an unnamed tributary flowing off Whittleton Ridge. Here the Whittleton Arch Trail squeezes up a rhododendron-filled hollow, crossing the small streamlet along the path. Wildflowers blossom here in spring, followed closely by ferns. The walls of this chasm narrow as you head deeper into it, ultimately closing at a semicircular wall of rock—except the rock wall is not entirely closed, as revealed by the light opening of Whittleton Arch. Here you will also see the spilling and nosedive of the 25-foot waterfall of Whittleton Arch.

Here, in this boulder-strewn dead end of a chasm, the sound of splattering water echoes off the walls. The bulk of Whittleton Arch towers overhead. By mass it is said to be one of Kentucky's biggest arches. Since you can easily circle the waterfall of Whittleton Arch, photographing the spiller can be turned to an art form—and a challenge since the cataract is often flowing faintly and the locale can have strong contrasts of light and shade. Try to capture the fall and the arch in one photograph.

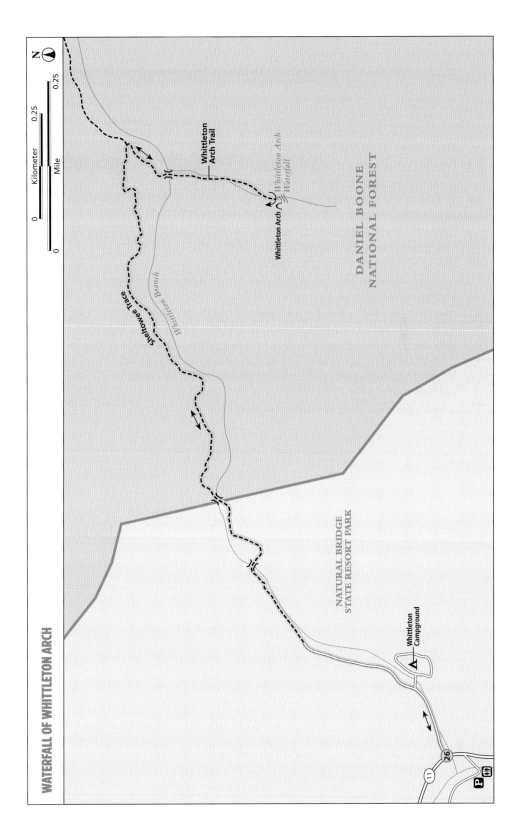

WATERFALL OF WHITTLETON ARCH

Whittleton Arch Trail

Whittleton Arch

Whittleton Arch Waterfall

Sheltowee Trace

Whittleton Branch

DANIEL BOONE NATIONAL FOREST

NATURAL BRIDGE STATE RESORT PARK

Whittleton Campground

N

Kilometer

Mile

0   0.25

0   0.25

11   26   P

Miles and Directions

0.0   From the parking area on the west side of Middle Fork Red River, walk the low-water bridge over the river then carefully cross KY 11 to enter seasonally open Whittleton Campground.

0.1   Hike past the campground entrance station and follow the asphalt campground road along Whittleton Creek. Campsites spur off the road leading deeper into the Whittleton Branch hollow.

0.3   Leave the campground at an auto turnaround. Join the singletrack Sheltowee Trace at a trailhead kiosk. Whittleton Branch is flowing to your right.

0.6   Enter national forest land and leave the state park after crossing Whittleton Branch twice on footbridges.

1.1   Leave left from the old railroad grade that once ran through a boulder jumble ahead. The trail climbs farther up the valley, avoiding the boulder jumble.

1.2   Intersect the Whittleton Arch Trail. Turn right here, descending to cross Whittleton Branch on a footbridge. At this point, Whittleton Branch can run underground, upstream of the aforementioned boulder jumble.

1.5   Reach Whittleton Arch and its waterfall, situated at the head of a stone chasm. The waterfall pours over the top of the arch deck then down its side and free-falls from the stone span onto a permanently wet rock pile. A sizable boulder stands directly next to the base of the falls, while other stone rubble lies beneath the arch. The low-flow cataract is often reduced to a trickle but will be a compelling sight when flowing boldly. Backtrack to the trailhead.

3.0   Arrive back at the trailhead, completing the waterfall hike.

27 Anglin Falls

Enjoy this walk up a rugged valley preserved by the state of Kentucky to visit a delicate spiller diving from a sheer cliff. Located within the John B. Stephenson State Nature Preserve, this steep tributary valley of Anglin Fork shows off not only this 75-foot cataract but also wildflowers in season as well as geologically intriguing scenes.

Waterfall height: 75 feet
Waterfall beauty: 4
Distance: 1.6-mile out-and-back
Difficulty: Easy
Hiking time: About 1 hour
Trail surface: Natural
Other trail users: None
Canine compatibility: Dogs not allowed

Land status: State nature preserve
Fees and permits: None
Maps: John B. Stephenson State Nature Preserve; USGS Johnetta
Trail contact: Kentucky State Nature Preserves Commission, 801 Teton Trail, Frankfort 40601; (502) 573-2886; www.naturepreserves.ky.gov

Finding the trailhead: From exit 76 on I-75 near Berea, join KY 21 east for 3.5 miles to the center of Berea. Turn right at the light (staying on KY 21), past the Boone Tavern, and drive another 5 miles. Turn right (south) onto US 421 and drive 2.6 miles to turn right on Burnt Ridge Road and drive 0.2 miles, then turn left on Hammonds Fork Road and drive 3.4 miles. Look for a red brick house on the right; approximately 0.1 mile beyond the house make an acute left turn down a steep hill, joining Anglin Falls Road. Drive 0.8 miles on Anglin Falls Road to a sign that says Anglin Falls next to a mailbox marked 842 (this looks like you are turning into someone's private driveway, especially with houses along this gravel drive, but it is the road to Anglin Falls trailhead). Turn left onto the driveway-like gravel road and follow it 0.2 mile to its dead end at the parking area. GPS: N37° 29.597' / W84° 13.577'

The Hike

Owned by Berea College but managed by the Commonwealth of Kentucky, 123-acre John B. Stephenson State Nature Preserve is best known to the public for Anglin Falls but it is also a place of study for Berea College students. And the namesake of the preserve would want it that way, since John B. Stephenson was president of Berea College from 1984 to 1994. Mr. Stephenson saw not only the educational value of this richly vegetated deep hollow ringed in majestic cliffs and littered with big boulders, but also the intrinsic beauty of this vale highlighted by Anglin Falls. He lobbied to have the falls preserved. Brought into the state nature preserve system on December 10, 1996, the land was initially owned by the Cobb-Venable family, who sold it to Friends of Anglin Falls, a nonprofit organization, for preservation purposes. The friends group then deeded the property to Berea College.

The 75-footer makes a graceful dive from an imposing beige stone rim, spreading its spray before bespattering a perpetually wet rock garden below. Anglin Falls is actually not on Anglin Fork, but on a tributary of that stream and has a historically low flow. Therefore, waterfall lovers will be wise to visit this cataract from early winter through spring, or after heavy rains. By autumn it will be a disappointment unless a hurricane has passed through, a rare event in Kentucky.

However, you will not be disappointed with the hike to Anglin Falls, as it offers fine scenery along the way. You will leave the trailhead and start heading up the valley nestled between Cruse Ridge to the northwest and an unnamed ridge to the south-east, rising over 400 feet above you. The tributary of Anglin Fork dances off to your right, while beech, pines, and oaks rise above. In spring you will find an abundance of wildflowers, from trout lily to columbine to rue anemone. Club moss and ferns aplenty find their place.

A hiker bridge soon takes you over the creek. The trail works its way up the right bank, rising in places well above the watercourse on a steep slope. When the leaves are off the trees, you will see bluffs rimming the valley. Expect the well-used trail to be a bit sloppy when Anglin Falls is running. Trailside boulders become common at

Anglin Falls dives 75 feet from a rugged cliff.

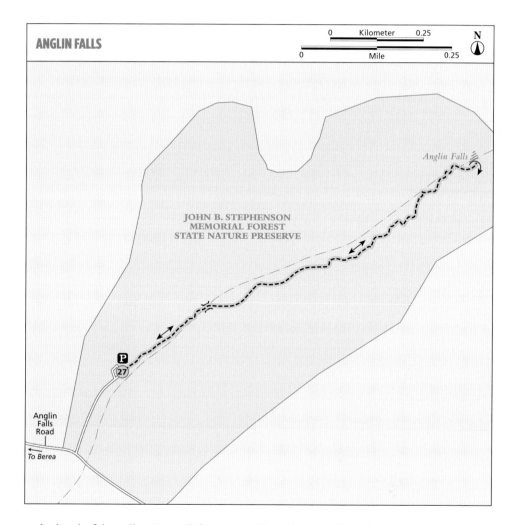

0   Kilometer   0.25

0   Mile   0.25

N

JOHN B. STEPHENSON
MEMORIAL FOREST
STATE NATURE PRESERVE

Anglin Falls

P
27

Anglin
Falls
Road

To Berea

the head of the valley. You will find yourself steeply scrambling through a rock garden before arriving at Anglin Falls, diving from the head of the canyon. Here you can view the falls from multiple angles, including from a midlevel ledge and deep rock house at which the trail dead-ends. Fallen boulders lie below the falls. You can walk to its splattering base, and go on to the far side of the boulders below the falls for an additional look.

Miles and Directions

0.0   Leave the parking area, passing through a fence and hiking the trail up the left bank of the tributary of Anglin Fork. Note the stone memorial to John B. Stephenson.

0.1   Cross over to the right-hand bank of the stream on a low-slung hiker bridge. Continue up the valley as a sharp bluff rises on the opposite stream bank.

0.7 The trail reaches a boulder field. Stay with the path as it gets much steeper and works its way up toward Anglin Falls.

0.8 Come to Anglin Falls. This 75-foot free-flowing cataract pours over a rim and free-falls into a stone cathedral, splattering on a rock jumble then gathering to flow downward. Examine the falls from all angles before backtracking to the trailhead.

1.6 Arrive back at the trailhead, completing the hike.

28 Alcorn Branch Falls

Take an easy hike to see Alcorn Branch Falls, a 31-foot spiller located on a seldom-visited tract of the Daniel Boone National Forest. The seasonal cataract dives from a rock rim into a semicircular rock house that you can access. The hike is easy as you use the Sheltowee Trace following an old roadbed to then descend into the vale of Alcorn Branch where Alcorn Branch Falls makes its desperate dive. Make sure to visit this cataract during winter and spring for the most beauty.

Waterfall height: 31 feet	**Land status:** National forest
Waterfall beauty: 4	**Fees and permits:** None
Distance: 1.6-mile out-and-back	**Maps:** Daniel Boone National Forest, Central
Difficulty: Easy	Section; USGS Leighton
Hiking time: About 1 hour	**Trail contact:** Daniel Boone National Forest,
Trail surface: Natural	London Ranger District, 761 S. Laurel Rd.,
Other trail users: None	London 40744; (606) 864-4163; www.fs.usda
Canine compatibility: Leashed pets allowed	.gov/dbnf

Finding the trailhead: From the town square in Irvine, take KY 89 south/KY 52 west for a short distance before KY 89 splits. Stay with KY 89 south for 7.2 miles to meet KY 1209. Turn left and follow KY 1209 for 13 miles to the Sheltowee Trace, leaving south from KY 1209 just bit east of the old Arvel post office. Park at the eastern intersection of KY 1209 and Old Arvel Post Office Road. There is room for one car. If you reach KY 587 beyond Old Arvel Post Office Road, you have gone 0.1 mile too far. GPS: N37° 31.058' / W83° 53.121'

The Hike

Alcorn Falls is one of Kentucky's forgotten trail-accessible cataracts. The trailhead is located next to a lesser-known parcel of the Daniel Boone National Forest, but the waterfall is along its most famous trail—the Sheltowee Trace. It is but a short distance to the falls.

The hike leaves from the small community of Arvel. The Sheltowee Trace leaves south from KY 1209 on an old doubletrack right-of-way, the former Polly Sparks Road, which has reverted to an eroded-in-places dirt track. The route of the Sheltowee Trace then crosses a forest road and becomes a standard singletrack hiking trail.

Uppermost Alcorn Branch and its tributaries flow through the hollow to the left of the trail, cutting the beginnings of a gorge. Listen for the sounds of moving water. Hopefully, noisy water sounds will waft upward to your ears. If so, Alcorn Branch Falls will be running well.

Alcorn Branch Falls is an underappreciated Kentucky cataract.

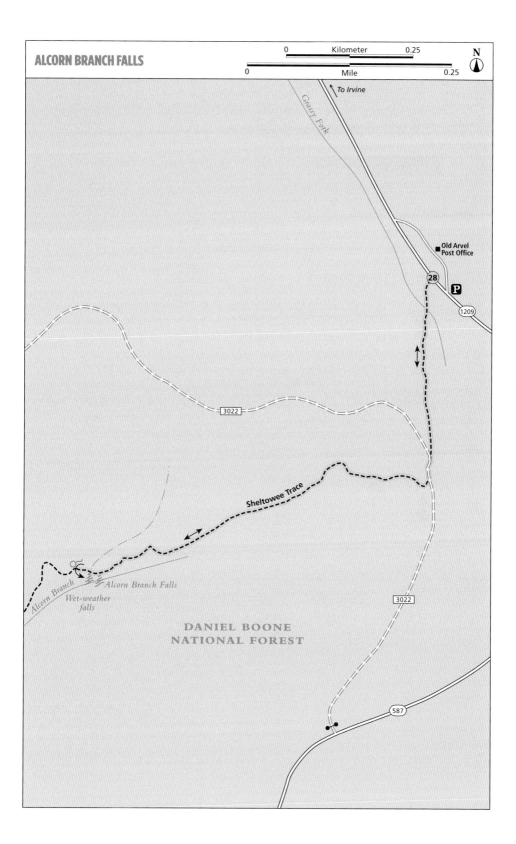

0   Kilometer   0.25

0   Mile   0.25

N

To Irvine

Grassy Fork

Old Arvel
Post Office

28

P

1209

3022

Sheltowee Trace

3022

Alcorn Branch

Alcorn Branch Falls

Wet-weather
falls

DANIEL BOONE
NATIONAL FOREST

587

The hike takes you to the precipice of the falls then curves around the rim over which the cataract tumbles. Watch out for a side stream diving off the same rim. However, both of these streams can run dry by autumn.

Be careful reaching the bottom of Alcorn Branch Falls. Your best bet in reaching the falls is to continue downstream on the Sheltowee Trace until the slope of the land below you becomes tenable, then work your way up Alcorn Branch. As you continue on, look for an overhanging bluff to the right of the trail with a spring below it, in which lie some old barrels and a sign placed by the Forest Service not to drink the water.

Once at Alcorn Branch Falls, you can walk in front of and behind the ribbon of white water. Multiple photography angles are available. These views give you a true idea of the rock rim from which Alcorn Branch Falls makes its gambit.

Miles and Directions

0.0 Leave KY 1209 south on a doubletrack trail, veering left and passing a memorial to an equestrian by the name of Embry Curry. The doubletrack trail is bordered by fence on both sides, where woods and fields roll in the distance.

0.2 Come to FR 3022. Turn left on the doubletrack then quickly veer right onto a signed single-track path. The Sheltowee Trace turns west in rich forest, aiming toward Alcorn Branch.

0.7 Saddle alongside the rim of Alcorn Branch Falls. Here the Sheltowee Trace curves right along the rim, where you can look into the curved undercut cliff line over which Alcorn Branch plunges before dashing onto a perpetually wet rock pile. The trail then goes by a side stream of Alcorn Branch that also makes a waterfall when the water is up.

0.8 Reach Alcorn Branch Falls. Here Alcorn Branch spills from a cut in the curved rock rim, dropping 31 feet onto a sloped, rocky bottom, then gathers in a shallow pool before flowing onward. Backtrack to the trailhead.

1.6 Arrive back at the trailhead, completing the hike.

29 Turkey Foot Cascade

This relatively short waterfall hike starts at the fine destination known as Turkey Foot. The Daniel Boone National Forest recreation area features a picnic area and swimming hole on War Fork as well as a nice little tent campground. The hike to Turkey Foot Cascade starts at the picnic area then rises to the campground, where you pick up a foot trail running above War Fork on an old logging railroad grade. The path then drops off the grade to find a tributary of War Fork diving from a stone lip, creating a 12-foot spiller dashing onward to meet its mother stream.

Waterfall height: 12 feet
Waterfall beauty: 3
Distance: 1.2-mile out-and-back
Difficulty: Easy
Hiking time: About 0.5 hour
Trail surface: Natural
Other trail users: None
Canine compatibility: Leashed pets allowed

Land status: National forest
Fees and permits: None
Maps: Daniel Boone National Forest, Central Section; USGS McKee
Trail contact: Daniel Boone National Forest, London Ranger District, 761 S. Laurel Rd., London 40744; (606) 864-4163; www.fs.usda .gov/dbnf

Finding the trailhead: From exit 76 on I-75 near Berea, head east on US 421 18 miles to McKee. Once in McKee, turn left on KY 89, passing through the town square. Follow KY 89 north 3 miles to a sharp, signed right turn onto paved FR 17/Macedonia Road. Follow Macedonia Road for 0.5 mile, turning left onto a paved road that becomes FR 4/Turkey Foot Road after 1 mile. Continue on gravel FR 4 for 2 more miles to FR 345. Turn left onto FR 345 and follow it 0.2 mile to the right turn into Turkey Foot Campground, crossing a low-water bridge. Stay left on the recreation area road when it makes a loop and park at the picnic area, near the restrooms. GPS: N37° 28.0821' / W83° 55.0324'

The Hike

When coming here to view Turkey Foot Cascade, consider expanding your adventure beyond the short just-over-a-mile waterfall hike. This can be done by continuing on the Turkey Foot Loop and making the entire 4.1-mile circuit through the hills above the recreation area (a shortcut trail allows for a circuit hike of a little over 2 miles), or picnicking here, or overnighting at the free campground. Or you could walk a section of the Sheltowee Trace to Resurgence Cave, or fish or swim in War Fork, which flows through the recreation area. Nevertheless, the waterfall will stand out on its own if you want to make a quick trip of it.

Turkey Foot is situated on a swath of the Daniel Boone National Forest near the town of McKee. Finding the start of the trail can be tricky when visiting here for the first time. You will actually walk to the campground loop road then pick up the Turkey Foot Loop near campsite #1. Do not park at the campsite when day-hiking.

Come during the springtime to see 12-foot Turkey Foot Falls.

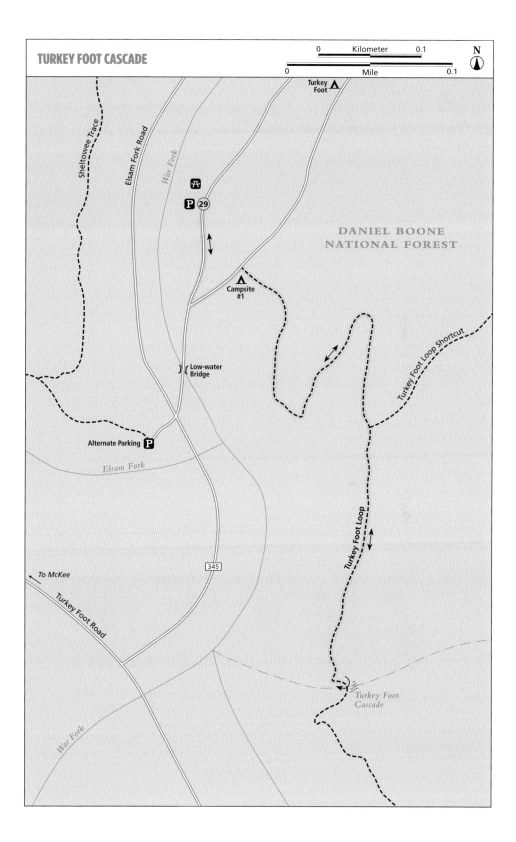

TURKEY FOOT CASCADE

0 Kilometer 0.1
0 Mile 0.1

N

Turkey Foot

Sheltowee Trace

Elsam Fork Road

War Fork

29

DANIEL BOONE
NATIONAL FOREST

Campsite #1

Turkey Foot Loop Shortcut

Low-water Bridge

Alternate Parking

Elsam Fork

Turkey Foot Loop

345

To McKee

Turkey Foot Road

Turkey Foot Cascade

War Fork

Turkey Foot Campground is open from mid-April through mid-November. Each site offers a tent pad, picnic table, fire ring, and lantern post in a shady forest. As mentioned, camping is free.

By the way, if the recreation area is gated, you can simply park your vehicle at the Sheltowee Trace parking area near the low-water bridge over War Fork at the entrance to Turkey Foot. Either way, make your way to campsite #1, then follow the blazed Turkey Foot Loop through a mix of hardwoods and evergreens. The path winds uphill using switchbacks before intersecting the marked and maintained trail shortcutting the Turkey Foot Loop. You are now picking up an old railroad grade, probably used for logging the locale way back. You will see the forest has since recovered nicely. The shortcut trail uses the railroad grade as it heads the other way.

Ahead, the trail splits right away from the railroad grade, leaving the level wider track for a more primitive but maintained path. You then come to 12-foot Turkey Foot Cascade. This seasonal stream drops a dozen feet in two stages over a rock rim. You cannot miss the falls, as the Turkey Foot Loop runs just above the lip of the cataract as it makes a two-stage curtain drop from a rock rim. To view the falls you will have to scramble downhill. *Note:* This tributary of War Fork can run dry by late summer and autumn. Therefore, make sure to visit this cataract from winter through spring and you will be well rewarded.

If continuing the Turkey Foot Loop, the hike will lead you back along the railroad grade then for very short road walk along FR 4 and Hughes Fork. Next, you will climb the hills above Turkey Foot to rejoin the railroad grade. Ahead, the loop nears private land then dips down a hollow to curve along the sinkhole-pocked valley of War Fork before returning to the recreation area on the far side of the campground. Interestingly, the valley of War Fork is riddled with springs, seeps, and underground streams—and Turkey Foot Cascade.

Miles and Directions

0.0 Leave the Turkey Foot picnic parking area and walk back toward the bridge over War Fork to then turn left onto the campground loop road.

0.1 Pick up the Turkey Foot Loop, a standard hiking trail, near campsite #1. Climb away from the campground and switchback uphill.

0.4 Reach a trail intersection and a railroad grade. Turn right here, staying with the Turkey Foot Loop on the railroad grade, as a shortcut to the Turkey Foot Loop heads left along the railroad grade.

0.5 The Turkey Foot Loop leaves right from the railroad grade, irregularly descending through woods.

0.6 Arrive at the top of 12-foot Turkey Foot Cascade. Here a nameless tributary of War Fork pours over the trail then makes a two-stage dive from a stone lip. A little scrambling is required for a face-on view of the spiller. If you want to make the whole loop, it is 3.5 miles back to the recreation area from Turkey Foot Cascade. Otherwise, backtrack to the trailhead.

1.2 Arrive back at the trailhead, completing the waterfall hike.

30 McCammon Branch Falls

Upon arriving at Gray Hawk Community Park, you will wonder, "Where is McCammon Branch Falls?" Despite having the look of a traditional park with ball fields, playgrounds, and other such facilities, the craggy gorge of McCammon Branch lies just beyond, in nearby woods. Immediately take a short but steep trail to enter the canyon. Here you walk along a cliff line to find a tall, multifaceted cataract plunging, splashing, and pirouetting in stages onto a boulder-and-rock-laden bottom. A second short spur trail leads to an overlook of the uppermost part of the wild whitewater.

Waterfall height: 55 feet
Waterfall beauty: 5
Distance: 0.4-mile out-and-back
Difficulty: Easy
Hiking time: About 0.2 hour
Trail surface: Natural
Other trail users: None

Canine compatibility: Leashed pets allowed
Land status: County park
Fees and permits: None
Map: USGS McKee
Trail contact: Jackson County Parks and Recreation, PO Box 175, McKee 40447; (606) 348-8534; www.jacksoncounty.ky.gov

Finding the trailhead: From downtown McKee, take US 421 south and follow it for 5.3 miles to JCHS Road (Jackson County High School) Road. Turn right and follow JCHS Road for 0.1 mile, then turn left on Gray Hawk Community Park Road. Follow it for 0.6 mile to end at the park picnic shelter. GPS: N37° 23.5351' / W83° 56.8032'

The Hike

Talk about contrasts! Upon arriving at Gray Hawk Community Park, it seems the last place to find an untamed, multitiered waterfall crashing into a rock-strewn, boulder-laden gorge. However, it is. Yet you are still doubting when looking around at parents watching their tots on the playground and people exercising on the walking track, and still others dining under the shade of the picnic shelter.

And then you disembark from your vehicle and walk across a mown area, leaving the picnic shelter for the woods. Then the sound of McCammon Branch Falls rushes into your ears. Your heart beats a little faster, for there *is* a waterfall here! You find yourself perhaps going too fast down the steep trail in anticipation of seeing this tall cataract, dropping in different stages and forms. You mentally go over your photography equipment or make sure your phone is at least handy for a snapshot.

Then comes a split in the trail. You keep down toward the gorge, descending a low cliff line that even has a stout knotted rope to aid your progress. Once in the gorge you walk along a cliff line toward the now-pitching cataract.

McCammon Branch Falls shows many faces during its 55-foot descent.

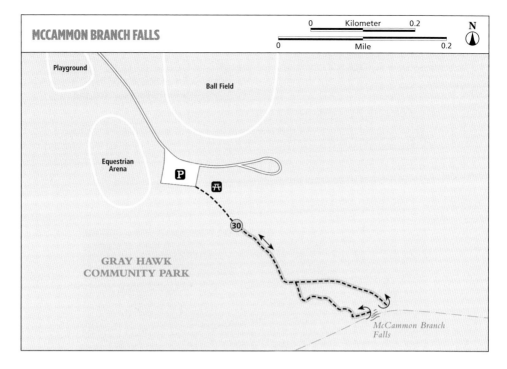

0   Kilometer   0.2

0   Mile   0.2

N

Playground

Ball Field

Equestrian
Arena

P

30

GRAY HAWK
COMMUNITY PARK

McCammon Branch
Falls

And there it appears, making an initial curtain drop onto a slightly sloped, very overhung ledge, then flowing a bit before leaping from the stone rim and scattering onto piled rocks and layered stone strata. A large, quite deep, and partly wet rock shelter envelops the falls in a semicircle. The very handsomeness of the waterfall and ruggedness of this gorge is truly hard to fathom after seeing the trailhead.

Before long you have clambered all about the depths of the gorge, gaining the best vantages of McCammon Branch Falls. But there is still an additional vista point. You climb back out, once again using the short rope to make your way to the upper rim of the gorge, then walk along the rim among mountain laurel. Here a view opens of the uppermost drop of the falls, and a repose bench . . . and one final surprise. This view is on the very edge of park property and to your left up the hill stands a private house!

Despite the very close proximity of community and nature, McCammon Branch Falls is worth a visit. And when you share your photos of the cataract, no one will believe that this waterfall is but a small swath of natural Kentucky surrounded by civilization.

Miles and Directions

0.0 With your back to the park picnic shelter, walk downhill and pick up a hiking trail entering forest under hemlock and hardwoods. The trail quickly splits. Save the trail going left for later. For now, keep descending, reaching a low cliff line with a knotted rope to aid your descent. This isn't too difficult or dangerous for your average waterfall hiker. Along the way you will pass a trail going left along the cliffline above McCammon Branch.

0.2 Reach McCammon Branch Falls after cruising at the base of the cliff line. Here you will view the waterfall making its tiered plunge. Backtrack to the trail going along the gorge rim.

0.4 Arrive back at the trailhead, completing the waterfall hike, after hiking out to the contemplation bench and viewpoint of the upper descent of McCammon Branch Falls.

The upper descent of McCammon Branch Falls

31 Flat Lick Falls

A visit to this Jackson County park will yield a short, fun hike to a gorgeous cataract that you can view from different vantages. A short paved path leads to a developed and cleared overlook of 30-foot Flat Lick Falls, hurtling from a stone ledge into a deep boulder-bordered plunge pool. From this easy overlook, join a natural surface path leading into the gorge of Flat Lick, where you turn up the creek, passing a deep but relatively low rock house. The path then leads to the base of Flat Lick Falls, where you can admire the cataract face on.

Waterfall height: 30 feet
Waterfall beauty: 4
Distance: 1-mile out-and-back
Difficulty: Easy
Hiking time: About 0.6 hour
Trail surface: Asphalt and natural
Other trail users: None

Canine compatibility: Leashed pets allowed
Land status: County park
Fees and permits: None
Map: USGS Tyner
Trail contact: Jackson County Parks and Recreation, PO Box 175, McKee 40447; (606) 348-8534; www.jacksoncounty.ky.gov

Finding the trailhead: From downtown McKee, take US 421 south and follow it for 6.7 miles to Begley Road. Turn right and follow Begley Road for 100 feet, then quickly veer left onto Hays Road. Follow Hays Road for 1 mile, then veer right at the sign for Flat Lick Falls Recreational Area. Follow this paved road for 0.6 mile to end at the park trailhead. GPS: N37° 22.3312' / W83° 56.3148'

The Hike

Flat Lick Falls is a pretty spiller that is the centerpiece of a Jackson County park. Of course, people have been coming to Flat Lick Falls long before the land became a park. However, one way to preserve a resource is to build a park around it, allowing visitors from near and far to give it a gander. Jackson County has since added a picnic shelter and log cabin building (with restrooms open during the warm season), along with a paved trail leading to a developed overlook with rails, allowing waterfall lovers of all ages to make their way 0.2 mile to the viewpoint of Flat Lick Falls. They also made a short asphalt loop for park exercise.

Better still, park personnel added a natural surface trail leading to the base of Flat Lick Falls. It leads along the rim of the Flat Lick Creek gorge before dropping to the confluence of Flat Lick Creek and its mother stream, Laurel Fork. Here you pass the foundation of an old building before crossing Flat Lick Creek on a hiker bridge. In the gorge, rock bluffs rise overhead and a low, long rock house stands to the right of the trail, while Flat Lick Creek dances under stone walls. The hike ends at the base of the pool of Flat Lick Falls. Here we find the stream plummeting faucet-like from a layered stone precipice, filling a gently waving pool bordered by imposing pillars.

Flat Lick Falls charges 30 feet from a stone precipice.

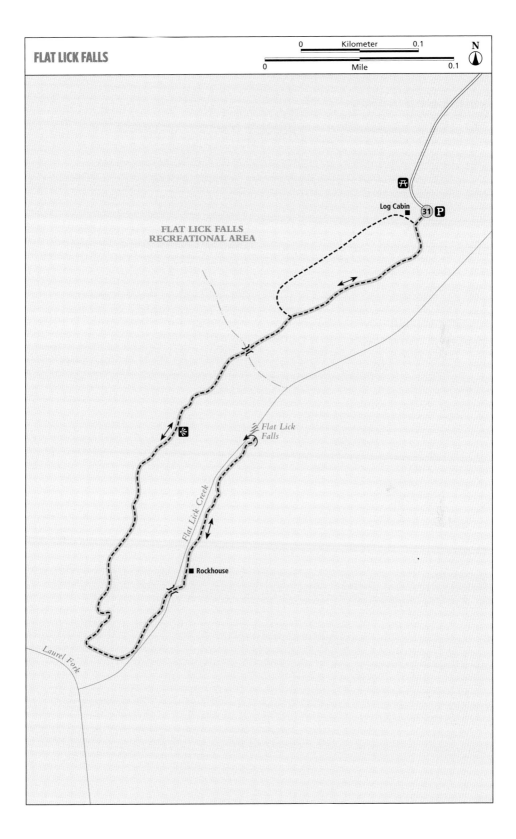

FLAT LICK FALLS

FLAT LICK FALLS
RECREATIONAL AREA

Log Cabin
31
P

Flat Lick
Falls

Flat Lick Creek

Rockhouse

Laurel Fork

N

Kilometer
0   0.1
0   0.1
Mile

This face-on viewpoint complements the top-down panorama from the developed overlook.

Miles and Directions

0.0 Leave the trailhead log cabin on the paved path closest to Flat Lick Creek. Cruise the perimeter between a field to your right and woods to your left.

0.1 Reach a trail split. Here a paved trail loops back to the trailhead. However, we keep straight on another paved track entering woods. Soon bridge a tributary of Flat Lick Creek.

0.2 Reach the developed overlook of Flat Lick Falls. Here a cleared view opens down to the cataract, spilling into a deep plunge pool. After enjoying the overlook, join the natural surface path continuing down the rim of the Flat Lick Creek gorge.

0.3 The trail squeezes between a boulder and a cliff line, then descends along the cliff line to reach the confluence of Laurel Fork and Flat Lick Creek. From here, turn up the left-hand bank of Flat Lick Creek, passing the foundations of an old concrete block structure.

0.4 A rising rock wall forces you to cross Flat Lick Creek. Fortunately, a hiker bridge has been built here, allowing a dry-footed crossing. Continue up the creek, passing a low and deep rock house.

0.5 Reach trail's end and the base of Flat Lick Falls. Here you can look across the plunge pool, framed by big boulders, at Flat Lick Falls somersaulting 30 feet from a ragged ledge. Backtrack to the trailhead.

1.0 Arrive back at the trailhead, completing the waterfall hike.

32 Bad Branch Falls

The centerpiece of a Kentucky state nature preserve, Bad Branch Falls tumbles 60 feet into a wild vale where you can see not only this falls but other cascades, all set in a pristine highland gorge cut into Pine Mountain. The preserve hosts over thirty species of rare flora and fauna, and the stream itself is noted for its high water quality, too. Additional trails allow you to expand your hike beyond Bad Branch Falls.

Waterfall height: In order 15, 100, 60 feet
Waterfall beauty: 4
Distance: 2-mile out-and-back
Difficulty: Easy
Hiking time: About 1.2 hours
Trail surface: Natural
Other trail users: None
Canine compatibility: Dogs not allowed

Land status: State nature preserve
Fees and permits: None
Maps: Bad Branch State Nature Preserve; USGS Whitesburg
Trail contact: Kentucky State Nature Preserves Commission, PO Box 102, Whitesburg 41858; (606) 633-0362; www.naturepreserves.ky.gov/naturepreserves

Finding the trailhead: From Whitesburg, take KY 15 south for 1.4 miles to US 119 south. Turn right and follow US 119 south for 7 miles to KY 932 east. Turn left and follow KY 932 east for 1.7 miles to reach the Bad Branch State Nature Preserve parking area on your left. GPS: N37° 4.049' / W82° 46.316'

The Hike

Bad Branch is deserving of its status as a Kentucky state nature preserve. Upon entering the scenic stream valley at the southern foot of Pine Mountain, natural splendor is instantaneous and evident. A clear, sparkling stream dashes over multicolor stones bordered by sandy banks over which rises a regal forest of hemlock, yellow birch, and Fraser magnolia. Bad Branch State Nature Preserve stands close to the border of Virginia in easternmost Kentucky. This part of the state harbors Kentucky's highest elevations and also more closely recalls the Southern Appalachians rather than the Cumberland Plateau to the west. However, Bad Branch certainly has its share of geological wonders, and you will surely admire the stone palace from which Bad Branch makes its dive, as well as the incredible boulder field lying below the waterfall.

Established in 1985, Bad Branch Preserve was originally 485 acres, protecting the core of the stream gorge, including Bad Branch Falls. Later the preserve was expanded to over 2,700 acres, including the south side and crest of Pine Mountain. Additionally, the 5-mile Bad Branch trail system links to the famed Pine Mountain Trail, which runs along the crest of Pine Mountain past overlooks, arches, and other phenomena.

The hike to Bad Branch Falls will reveal this attractiveness. You will immediately enter the gorge and be enveloped in a high-canopied forest with hemlocks reigning.

The opportunity to see Bad Branch—a tributary of the Poor Fork of the Cumberland River—up close comes quickly as the trail leads to two bridge crossings of the mountain stream. The exceptional-quality water harbors blackside dace, among other fish. Now blackside dace may not be high on your list of important fish, but the finned wonder is rare in American waters and worth preserving. The Cumberland arrow darter, a rare state species, also swims the waters of Bad Branch.

Beyond these two crossings, you continue up the trail. The deep canyon and elevation conspire to create a climatic situation resembling lands much farther north. The vegetation reflects this cooler environment. Wildflowers are also abundant in the preserve. A spring hike to Bad Branch Falls will yield not only a strongly flowing cataract, but also abundant flowering plants such as painted trillium. However, there is a threat in Bad Branch. The hemlock woolly adelgid, a nonnative insect, is killing hemlocks throughout the eastern mountains, and the 20,000-plus hemlocks at Bad Branch State Nature Preserve are being treated for the insect through soil injection. Let us hope it works.

Continuing up the trail, you will pass hemlocks aplenty. The rapids and shoals of Bad Branch sing you along, then you take the spur to the falls. If the water is high, you can hear the roar of the 60-foot cascade. Wind your way up to a sandstone wall, the same wall from which Bad Branch plunges 60 feet, dashing to rocks then working its way down a boulder jumble of the first order.

Your first view of Bad Branch Falls will be sidelong, but then you can maneuver to a front-on view of the cataract as well as getting to its base. Don't climb to the top of the falls. Many visitors have fallen from the top and gotten severely hurt and worse.

Miles and Directions

0.0 From the Bad Branch parking area, walk past a trail sign and fence on a singletrack path. Bad Branch is off to your right. Pass an informational kiosk.

0.1 Cross Bad Branch on a trail bridge, and enter a big flat roofed with hemlocks. Quickly bridge the stream a second time. You are now ascending the left bank of the stream under yellow birch aplenty.

0.3 The trail is well above the stream.

0.4 Look down to admire a two-tiered slide cascade, dropping perhaps 15 feet over 100 feet of creek. Look for other lesser shoals. Bluffs form in the valley.

0.6 Step over a tributary of Bad Branch flowing across the trail. Just ahead, you can look across the creek at a multitiered 100-foot waterfall across the creek. When the leaves are on, this spiller will be hard to see and at lower flows will be nothing but a trickle. However, in winter, when the water is up, it is a sight to behold. A huge bluff also develops on the far side of the vale.

0.8 Reach a signed trail intersection. Here the main trail goes straight for High Rock, atop the crest of Pine Mountain along the Pine Mountain Trail, while we turn right toward Bad Branch Falls. Descend to rock-hop a tributary of Bad Branch, then climb among huge mossy rocks toward a sandstone cliff ahead.

This tributary falls complements Bad Branch Falls.

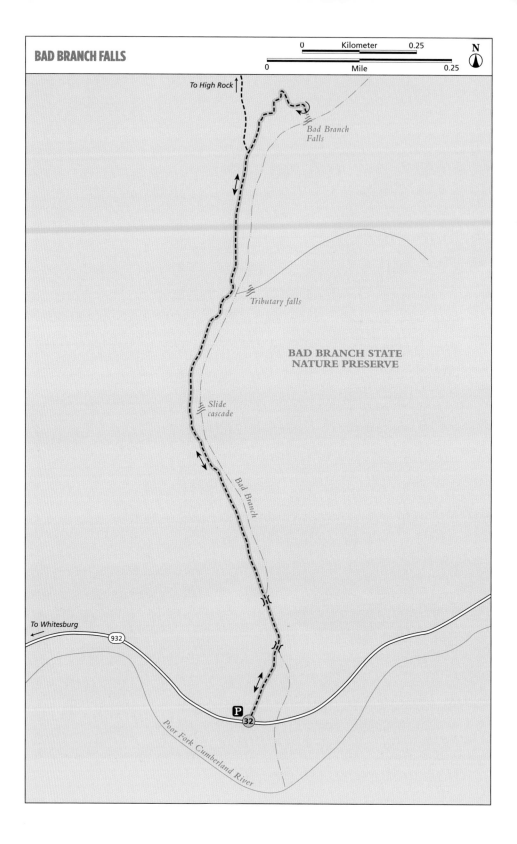

To High Rock

Bad Branch
Falls

Tributary falls

BAD BRANCH STATE
NATURE PRESERVE

Slide
cascade

Bad Branch

To Whitesburg

932

P 32

Poor Fork Cumberland River

N

0   Kilometer   0.25

0   Mile   0.25

1.0 Come to Bad Branch Falls after ascending wooden steps and walking along the base of a cliff. Here you come to a sidelong view of the 60-foot cataract somersaulting off a ledge then bashing its way down among a long and implausible boulder jumble. Be very careful when exploring here, and do not climb to the top of the falls under any circumstances. Backtrack to the trailhead.

2.0 Arrive back at the trailhead, completing the waterfall hike.

A sidelong view of Bad Branch Falls at a high flow

33 Gabes Branch Falls

It is a short walk but a long drive to visit Gabes Branch Falls. However, the waterfall is worth the journey. Located in the coal country of Harlan County, this cataract charges from a stone diving board into a big plunge pool, tailor-made for a backwoods dip. A nearby companion fall adds to the already impressive scenery. The walk to the falls isn't bad either, and even includes wooden steps to aid your passage to the spiller and the enticing swimming pool.

Waterfall height: In order, 18 feet, 25 feet
Waterfall beauty: 3
Distance: 0.2-mile out-and-back
Difficulty: Easy
Hiking time: About 0.4 hour
Trail surface: Natural
Other trail users: None
Canine compatibility: Pets on leash

Land status: County attraction
Fees and permits: None
Map: USGS Bledsoe
Trail contact: Harlan County Recreation Board Authority, Convention and Tourist Information Center, 201 S. Main St., Harlan 40831; (606) 837-3205; www.harlancountytrails.com

Finding the trailhead: From downtown Harlan, take US 421 north for 9 miles to turn right on KY 221 east and follow it for 2.5 miles to turn left on KY 2009 north. Follow KY 2009 for 6.2 miles to turn right onto KY 2008. Follow KY 2008 for 6.8 miles to an unsigned right turn. This is Gabes Branch Road, and the right turn is a short distance after passing through a coal processing area. Turn right on Gabes Branch Road, immediately bridging Greasy Creek, and continue for 0.8 mile to a pullover on your right. There is no official parking area. GPS: N36° 57' 58.95" / W83° 15' 2.24"

The Hike

Advertised on the Harlan County website as an area scenic natural attraction, Gabes Branch Falls more than holds up to its publicized billing. Although it may be advertised on their website, the scenic cataract is not signed en route to it. A little signage would help, because you don't know you are really there until you really are there. In fact, you have to drive to the back of beyond and out the other side before getting there—or at least it seems that way when taking remote roads through folded mountain lands and along twisting streams.

Gabes Branch has its origins in small springs and creeks flowing down the north side of imposing Pine Mountain. It is a tributary of Greasy Creek, which is in turn a tributary of the Middle Fork Kentucky River. The deep pool of Gabes Branch Falls is arguably as much of an attraction as the spiller itself, since this spot has attracted visitors to it as long as locals have been swimming in the creeks during those steamy summer days in southeastern Kentucky.

Gravel bar view of 18-foot Gabes Branch Falls.

The walk is easy. You can hear the noise of falling water from the roadside where you park. From there it is a simple matter of winding down the steep hillside on a wide track to a gas line access, then turning away from the access on the trail leading to the already audible falls. You are soon atop a bluff overlooking the 18-foot waterfall and its outsize pool. The trail turns downstream, winding amid big boulders and along carved steps downstream of the cataract. Finally, a wooden walkway leads to a gravel bar and Gabes Branch.

Ahead, the waterway makes its plunge. Below the waterfall, waves radiate in the rock-lined swimming hole. To your right, at higher flows, a companion waterfall flows down a stair-step stone ledge about 25 feet, giving its quota to Gabes Branch. Continuing up the gravel bar you reach the down side of the expansive circular pool, inviting a dip, as it has for generations. Come in the summer and see why Harlan County advertises Gabes Branch Falls—and its famed swimming hole.

Miles and Directions

0.0 From Gabes Branch Road, descend on a gas line access. Turn right on a foot trail and quickly reach a bluff overlooking Gabes Branch Falls. Continue downstream, winding through big boulders, then reach wooden steps leading to a gravel bar below the falls. From here, walk upstream on the gravel bar.

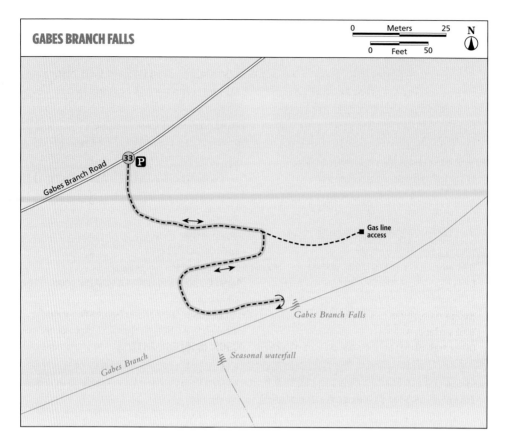

Gabes Branch Road

33 P

Gas line access

Gabes Branch Falls

Gabes Branch

Seasonal waterfall

0   Meters   25   N

0   Feet   50

0.1 Reach Gabes Branch Falls and its companion cataract on the right-hand side of the creek. Backtrack to the pullover.

0.2 Arrive back at the pullover, completing the hike.

34 Sand Cave Falls

This Kentucky waterfall hike actually starts in Virginia at Cumberland Gap National Historical Park, shared by Kentucky, Virginia, and Tennessee. The trek first scales Cumberland Mountain, forming the border between Kentucky and Virginia, then wanders the highlands, making its way to phenomenal Sand Cave, a huge rock house enclosing a sea of grains that will impress. Nearby, Sand Cave Branch plummets 25 feet off the red rock rampart adjacent to Sand Cave, not surprisingly onto a bed of sand. Hikers can add a side trip to White Rocks, a fantastic overlook at this fantastic national park. Be apprised this hike entails a 1,700-foot ascent from the trailhead.

Waterfall height: 25 feet
Waterfall beauty: 4
Distance: 7.4-mile out-and-back
Difficulty: Moderate to difficult; does have 1,700-foot gain
Hiking time: About 3.8 hours
Trail surface: Natural
Other trail users: Equestrians on part of hike

Canine compatibility: Leashed pets allowed
Land status: National park
Fees and permits: None
Maps: Cumberland Gap National Historical Park; USGS Ewing
Trail contact: Cumberland Gap National Historical Park, 91 Bartlett Park Rd., Middlesboro 40965; (606) 248-2817; www.nps.gov/cuga

Finding the trailhead: From Middlesboro, Kentucky, take US 25E south for 2.3 miles to the US 58 east ramp, passing through the Cumberland Gap Tunnel. Join US 58E and follow it for 14 miles to VA 724/Sand Cave Road in Ewing, Virginia. Turn left and follow VA 724 for 1 mile to its dead end at Ewing Civic Park. GPS: N36° 39.167' / W83° 26.160'

The Hike

Sand Cave Falls is quite a sight, but it is arguably contested by its namesake Sand Cave. More of a rock house than an actual cave, Sand Cave stretches 1.25 acres in size, according to the Park Service, and has an opening 250 feet wide. The floor of the rock house is covered deep in more sand than you can imagine occurs naturally, a result of cave erosion. A commonly repeated legend (also repeated here) is that Sand Cave has twenty-one different colors of sand.

In pre–national park days, Sand Cave was accessible by auto. It became a popular gathering spot, especially in the heat of summer. Not only would the air temperature be cooler here at 3,000 feet, but the rear of the rock shelter would be cooler still. Sand Cave was also known for its audibility; therefore, group sing-alongs would be held in the colossal rock house. Today the only way to get here is by trail, and after you come to see Sand Cave and its falls, you will be singing its praises both inside and outside the rock shelter, often argued to be the single largest rock shelter in the Bluegrass State, which is saying a lot.

Sand Cave Falls drops 25 feet over a reddish-hued ledge.

Looking out from Sand Cave. Note Sand Cave Falls to the right.

The hike leaves Ewing Civic Park on a hiker-only path bordered by scads of mountain laurel. Cruise up a tributary of Roaring Branch, crossing it twice to meet the equestrian trail leading up from lower Ewing Park. The path now angles its way up the slope of Cumberland Mountain, easing the ascent as it crosses tributaries of Indian Creek. The Ewing Trail ascends below White Rocks but then joins the Ewing Trail Connector, making still more upward switchbacks to make a total climb of 1,700 feet to reach the Kentucky-Virginia state line.

At this point the waterfall trek picks up the also wide Ridge Trail, as it heads west on the Kentucky side of the state line. The trail travels through thick woods, rife with rhododendron. You will cross the uppermost reaches of Sand Cave Branch—the stream forming Sand Cave Falls—before picking up the side trail to Sand Cave and Sand Cave Falls. This path is hiker only, and descends by switchbacks through rhododendron thickets. Wood and concrete steps aid your passage toward Sand Cave.

Step over a gravelly streambed, then come to Sand Cave. You will be impressed with the size and beauty of this geological wonder that redefines rock house. Sand Cave Falls spills from the east side of the cave edge, making a noisy drop as it pours forth over a slightly overhung ledge then splashing 25 feet later onto a shallow grainy pool. In late summer and autumn, Sand Cave Branch can shrink to a trickle up here at 3,000 feet.

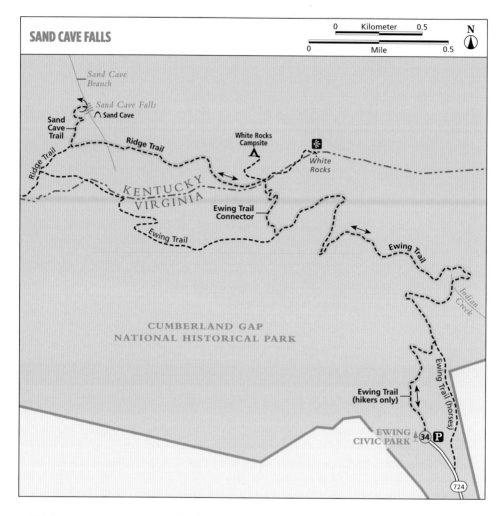

While up in these majestic highlands, take the opportunity to gain the 360-degree views that can be had from this landmark once looked upon by those taking the Wilderness Road into Kentuck'. It's a mile backtrack to the spur trail leading up to White Rocks, then a 0.3-mile climb to this naked rock knob proffering first-rate panoramas into Kentucky, Virginia, and Tennessee. From the intersection with the trail to White Rocks, it is 2.7 miles back to the trailhead at Ewing Civic Park.

Miles and Directions

0.0 Join the Ewing Trail, leaving from near the pavilion at the uppermost part of Ewing Civic Park. This trail is hiker only. Ascend along an unnamed tributary of Roaring Creek and cross it twice.

0.6 Intersect the equestrian trail coming up from the lower end of Ewing Civic Park. Continue working up the slope of Cumberland Mountain. The path is wider.

0.9 Cross the upper reaches of Indian Creek. Ahead, make a big switchback to the left, recrossing additional intermittent tributaries of Indian Creek.

1.8 Make a big switchback to the right. Keep ascending.

2.3 Meet a trail intersection on the south slope of Cumberland Mountain. Here the Ewing Trail goes left, but we stay with the Ewing Trail Connector, aiming for the top of the state-line ridge. Ascend by switchbacks.

2.7 Come to the top of Cumberland Mountain and the intersection with the Ridge Trail, the spur trail to White Rocks campsite, and the spur trail to White Rocks. Head left on the Ridge Trail, briefly cruising the state line before turning fully into Kentucky.

3.3 Cross the upper reach of Sand Cave Branch, the stream of Sand Cave Falls.

3.5 Turn right onto the hiker-only Sand Cave Trail. Descend through evergreens.

3.7 Reach Sand Cave and Sand Cave Falls. Explore both the 25-foot cataract and the immense shelter. Backtrack to the trail intersection.

4.7 Return to the four-way intersection with the Ridge Trail, spur trail to White Rocks campsite, and spur trail to White Rocks. Here is your chance to make the 0.3-mile climb to White Rocks for 360-degree views. Otherwise, continue backtracking.

7.4 Arrive back at the trailhead, completing the hike.

35 Falls of Shillalah Creek

Come explore one of the cleanest, purest streams in Kentucky. Here you follow a well-maintained doubletrack trail through an easement to enter Shillalah Creek Wildlife Management Area, where the watercourse drains untamed land atop Cumberland Mountain. The seasoned waterfaller will find three exciting cataracts, creating highlights in this valley of everywhere-you-look beauty.

Waterfall height: In order, 18 feet, 8 feet, 15 feet
Waterfall beauty: 4
Distance: 2-mile out-and-back
Difficulty: Easy; does have 350-foot climb
Hiking time: About 1.2 hours
Trail surface: Gravel
Other trail users: None
Canine compatibility: Leashed pets allowed

Land status: State wildlife management area
Fees and permits: None
Maps: Shillalah Creek Wildlife Management Area; USGS Varilla
Trail contact: Shillalah Creek Wildlife Management Area, Kentucky Department of Fish and Wildlife Resources, #1 Sportsman Ln., Frankfort 40601; (502) 564-7109; www.fw.ky.gov

Finding the trailhead: From Pineville, take US 25E south for 1 mile to US 119 north. Turn left and follow US 119 for 5.1 miles the intersection with KY 1344. Turn right on KY 1344, bridging the Cumberland River. Turn left, still on KY 1344, and stay with it for 5.5 miles to intersect KY 217. Immediately turn left onto KY 217 and follow it for 0.3 mile to the access road to Shillalah Creek Wildlife Management Area on your right. The parking area is on the left-hand side of KY 217. GPS: N36° 40' 4.12" / W83° 34' 56.77"

The Hike

Draining the 3,000-plus-foot peaks of Cumberland Mountain and Brush Mountain, fast against the Virginia border, Shillalah Creek is one of Kentucky's purest, clearest waterways and one of only two naturally reproducing trout streams in the commonwealth, a place native brook trout call home. The waterway also has a few waterfalls, naturally. Protected within the confines first of Cumberland Gap National Historical Park, then downstream on state-owned Shillalah Creek Wildlife Management Area (WMA), Shillalah Creek lies within sheltered highlands, a special addition to Kentucky's aquatic reserve. Upon seeing the creek, you will instantaneously note these special characteristics—clear-as-air water, cool to the touch on the hottest summer day, frothing white as it dances steeply downward among giant boulders into marine-blue pools then speeding over gravel bars, a moving ribbon rich in aquatic life.

Simply put, Shillalah Creek is a Southern Appalachian mountain stream extraordinaire. The stream access, as well as the access to the wildlife management area and the famed Hensley Settlement (see sidebar), is a gated doubletrack road, open only to national park and WMA personnel. Therefore, your waterfall venue is this wide track.

Lowermost Shillalah Falls is scenic but difficult to reach.

It leaves Kentucky 217, passing behind a cabin cluster on a right-of-way. A rich forest already rises along the gravel track as it wastes no time in rising forth in hardwoods, complemented by scads of rhododendron. In winter, views extend through the trees of the valley of the Clear Fork, the stream into which Shillalah Creek flows.

You gain elevation and turn toward Shillalah Creek, crashing well below. The air cools and the mountainside rises in earnest. Before long the trail enters the wildlife management area—Kentucky public lands for you and me to enjoy. The stream then comes into view below, hurtling forth betwixt boulder and rock in continuous collisions of solid and liquid, echoing up to your ears, raising your pulse beyond which the climb has already brought it up.

However, the slope is such that only hardened waterfallers—and agile ones at that—are able to explore these lower pour-overs. Down there tumbles one special fall, Lowermost Shillalah Falls, an 18-foot wonder of white, slowing and swirling in a trouty pool before continuing on. Other cataracts noisily clamor for attention.

Ahead are two waterfalls easily visited from the doubletrack, and they are the falls most associated with Shillalah Creek. Here, at the exact bend where the doubletrack comes closest to the creek before turning away, you will find a short trail leading to what is commonly called Shillalah Falls. At this point, deeply nestled in vegetation, the stream is forced between a pair of boulders, surging 8 feet through the opening

ABOUT THE HENSLEY SETTLEMENT

In the headwaters of Shillalah Creek, where springs emerge from atop Cumberland Mountain, lies the famed Hensley Settlement. The Hensley Settlement protects and preserves lifeways long abandoned in the Southern Appalachian Mountains. This former community is set 3,300 feet high in a perched mountaintop flat, where uppermost Shillalah Creek flows between Brushy Mountain to the north and Cumberland Mountain to the south. The locale remains a remote and scenic spot, the place where Sherman Hensley, back in 1904, decided to retreat from the lower reaches of Harlan County and make his home along the Kentucky-Virginia state line. Sherman brought his wife and built on the former pasturage and woodland, set apart from the rest of the world.

Relatives of Hensley and his wife joined the settlement and a bona fide community was established. Despite inroads of such things as indoor plumbing, electric lighting, and the like had made in the Southern Appalachians, the Hensley Settlement remained cast in the nineteenth century, inadvertently preserving a self-sufficient, simple subsistence life that—despite its primitive conditions—seems romantic and unpretentious compared to today's rush-rush digital world.

By 1908 enough children were in the settlement to establish a simple school. The place of learning went through several incarnations, yet you can see the final wooden clapboard schoolhouse, with its wooden desks and cast-iron stove for heat. The settlement continued to expand, ultimately reaching over one hundred residents in the mid-1920s. Residents grew their own food, raised their own animals, and used horses, wagons, or foot power for transportation. The residents did leave regularly to trade their products, such as corn—and corn juice (read: moonshine)—down in Caylor, Virginia, using the Chadwell Gap Trail to make their runs.

Ultimately, the lure of civilization and money that could be made down there drew its residents from the settlement. By 1949 only its founder, Sherman Hensley, remained. Two years later, at age 71, Hensley left the mountain himself. The buildings fell into disrepair, and the forest began reclaiming once-productive fields. The Hensley Settlement was no more. Sherman Hensley, the settlement's founder, lived to be 98 years old, spending the last 28 years of his life off the mountain and away from the community that bore his name.

After the establishment of Cumberland Gap National Historical Park in 1959, plans were made to restore the Hensley Settlement as a historical window to the past. In the 1960s the Job Corps restored many structures, and they continue to be maintained to this day. Come see this isolated mountaintop community, a fine complement to viewing the waterfalls of Shillalah Creek.

Lower Shillalah Falls runs clear as air while dashing between immobile boulders.

and spreading in a pool of its own. This is the most visited and photographed cataract on the stream simply because it is the easiest to view.

Nevertheless, just downstream is an unusual waterfall—Lower Shillalah Falls. Here, gravity forces the creek behind massive boulders, falling as a sheet of white. The boulders give way, exposing the lower half of the falls. The spiller creates a fine pool as well.

Beyond here the doubletrack turns away from Shillalah Creek up the WMA and into Cumberland Gap National Historical Park to reach the celebrated Hensley Settlement. The Park Service uses this route when guiding visitors through the Hensley Settlement, otherwise the preserved agglomeration of historic buildings is visited only by a vigorous walk. The most common route to the Hensley Settlement is via the Chadwell Gap Trail, a 4-mile one-way trip from the Virginia side of the park, even though the settlement lies in Kentuck'.

Alternatively, you can continue up this access road, simply staying with the doubletrack for a total of 5 miles from the trailhead to reach the Hensley Settlement. The mountaintop village frozen in time is a must-visit in Kentucky. If you (or your loved ones) aren't up for the climb, Cumberland Gap National Historical Park also includes a guided tour of the Hensley Settlement, eliminating all but 1 mile of walking (no stops at the waterfalls, though). The four-or-so-hour tour—including the ride to the

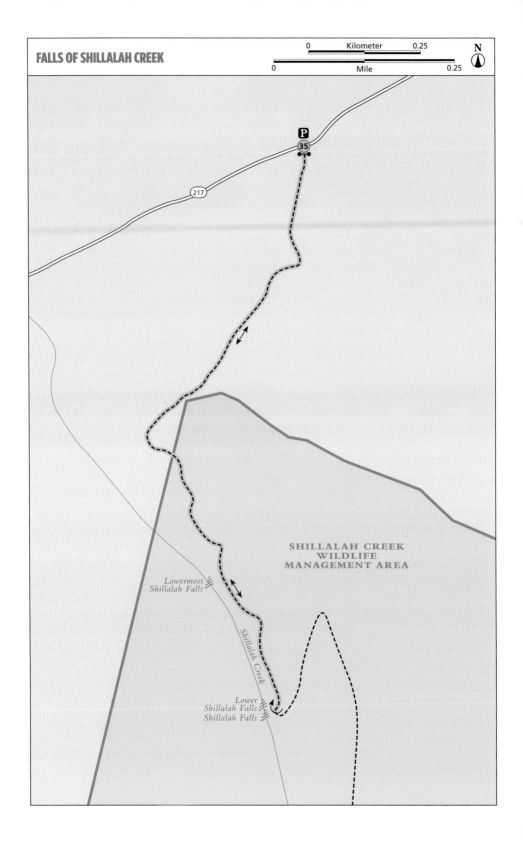

FALLS OF SHILLALAH CREEK

N

Kilometer
0   0.25

Mile
0   0.25

P
35

217

SHILLALAH CREEK
WILDLIFE
MANAGEMENT AREA

Lowermost
Shillalah Falls

Shillalah Creek

Lower
Shillalah Falls
Shillalah Falls

Hensley Settlement then the 1-mile walk through the settlement—is held daily from Memorial Day weekend through October. There is a fee. To reserve your spot on the tour, call the park visitor center at (606) 248-2817.

Undoubtedly other waterfalls, cataracts, and rapids can be found on Shillalah Creek, but before you explore, realize that the terrain along the watercourse is rugged to the extreme. Be prudent. Also don't explore downstream of the WMA boundaries. Respect private property.

Miles and Directions

0.0 From the parking area on KY 217, cross the road and walk around the pole gate, accessing the road to Shillalah Creek WMA and the Hensley Settlement. Hike among mountain laurel and oaks, morphing into birch and rhododendron in cooler, moister areas. The doubletrack is working a side slope on an easement, aiming for the Shillalah Creek watershed.

0.5 Turn left (south), entering the steep-sloped gorge of Shillalah Creek.

0.6 Enter Shillalah Creek WMA, marked with a sign. Not far beyond this point you can hear—and in winter see—Lowermost Shillalah Falls. The cataract is difficult to reach, requiring a steep downhill scramble. Be careful if you try this. Going down to Lowermost Shillalah Falls is probably more difficult than coming back up. Those who do will be rewarded with an 18-foot curtain of white making a slightly angled drop into a chilly mountain pool.

1.0 The doubletrack comes very near Shillalah Creek before making a sharp left turn away from the water. At the exact point of the left curve, you will find a short foot trail leading right to Shillalah Falls, an 8-foot spiller squeezing between a pair of boulders. Just downstream tumbles 15-foot Lower Shillalah Falls, pouring from behind huge boulders, exposing its lower half in a sheet flow. Backtrack to the trailhead.

2.0 Arrive back at the trailhead, completing the hike.

36 Honeymoon Falls, Divorce Falls

Visit the signature cataract of Pine Mountain State Park, one of Kentucky's most heralded preserves. Rising high in southeastern Kentucky, Honeymoon Falls drops as a slender spiller tucked away in a rock alcove. While the waterfall makes a well-ordered faucet plummet, across the narrow valley so-called Divorce Falls sprays chaotic from an irregular rock wall on a different stream. When at Pine Mountain State Park, integrate other activities into your waterfall hike.

Waterfall height: In order, 18 feet, 26 feet
Waterfall beauty: 4
Distance: 0.6-mile out-and-back
Difficulty: Easy
Hiking time: About 0.6 hour
Trail surface: Natural
Other trail users: None
Canine compatibility: Leashed pets allowed

Land status: State park
Fees and permits: None
Maps: Pine Mountain State Park trails; USGS Middlesboro North
Trail contact: Pine Mountain State Resort Park, 1050 State Park Rd., Pineville 40977; (606) 337-3066; www.parks.ky.gov

Finding the trailhead: From Pineville, take US 25E south for 1.9 miles and turn right onto KY 190. At 1.6 miles keep right on KY 1491. Drive 1.7 miles, then veer right to enter Pine Mountain State Park. Drive 0.6 mile farther, passing the left turn to the park lodge. Continue for 0.4 mile beyond the turn to the lodge to reach the Honeymoon Falls Trail on your right. *Note:* There is limited parking on both sides of the road. Be considerate and also do not block the gate at the trail's beginning. GPS: N36° 44' 16.42" / W83° 44' 26.06"

The Hike

It is hard not to chuckle a bit upon hearing the names of these two waterfalls at Pine Mountain State Park, a Kentucky signature preserve. I suspect that upon being established as a state park, the powers that be decided to name the park waterfall that happened to be within walking distance of the park lodge Honeymoon Falls in order to attract newlyweds. After all, a short stroll to a picturesque cataract can only enhance a honeymoon, right? However, Kentucky state park personnel did not anticipate the other nearby waterfall—a decidedly less-attractive seasonal spiller—would acquire the moniker "Divorce Falls" from humor-minded visitors checking out Pine Mountain State Park's aquatic features. And the state park does have features aplenty, both aquatic and land-based. Officially a state resort park, attracting honeymooners comes naturally.

The trek to the falls is short and sweet, just 0.3 mile each way. However, if you want to extend the walk, it is an easy matter. The Honeymoon Falls Trail makes a 1.5-mile circuit, returning you back to where you started. The hike to the falls leaves

Honeymoon Falls spills 18 feet in aquatic splendor.

the parking area then comes to an unnamed tributary of Clear Creek. You will note a small dam, now abandoned, likely built by the Civilian Conservation Corps as a water supply for the park. The path briefly joins a concrete track along the old pond dam. Rich vegetation of rhododendron, black and yellow birch, and hemlock rises above the slender trail and small creek. Hop over the clear, smallish stream, flowing over a sand and rock bed. You will cross the creek a total of five times on the way up, experiencing the catch-22 of waterfall hiking: When a stream is up, the waterfalls will be bold, but that also means the creek crossings will be more difficult. This particular stream is small, so it should not present much difficulty.

Continue up the tight valley, perched a little below 2,000 feet. The land opens a bit at the confluence of two streams, and this is where you find the two waterfalls each on its own waterway. Honeymoon Falls is tucked away in a little rock grotto, uniformly pouring from a stone cleft straight down from an overhung rock house, fauceting 18 feet to a pebble-and-rock-strewn base below. You can admire the discharging water from multiple angles.

Nearby, a trail bridge leads onward to Divorce Falls. The two cataracts are close enough to be visible from one another. This more-disjointed water feature rolls and flows along an irregular rock ledge before free-falling the final stage, landing on an angled slope of stone, sheeting to regroup and join the stream of Honeymoon Falls.

No doubt you will notice the zipline canopy tour facilities overhead, since the line takes participants directly above Honeymoon Falls and Divorce Falls. In fact, a highlight of the tour is the bird's-eye view of these pour-overs from the trees above. The two-and-a-half-hour tour requires strict weight limits of participants.

In addition to this waterfall hike, Pine Mountain State Park offers 12 miles of pathways, including a trek to Chained Rock, the park's most publicized feature. Here a precipitously situated huge boulder on the edge of the mountain above the city of Pineville is linked to terra firma by a chain. Originally installed in 1933 ostensibly to protect Pineville below, the placement of the chain was meant as a folly, but then became a tourist attraction. The 100-foot-long, 2,500-pound chain was hauled up the mountain by mules and pegged to the lone stone, then anchored to the main rock outcrop atop the ridge. This unusual phenomenon drew loads of attention, which continues to this day. A stellar panorama enhances the site at Chained Rock.

Less outdoorsy pursuits at Pine Mountain State Park include golf, miniature golf, and swimming in the park pool. Overnighters can pitch their tent or RV in the campground. As you might suspect, honeymooners prefer the lodge, where each of the thirty rooms has a patio or balcony from which they can lovingly gaze over the waves of mountains in the yon. For an even more private setting, cottages are available in either one- or two-bedroom styles. Honeymooners prefer the one-bedroom log cabins, since they have stone fireplaces before which to curl up.

Pine Mountain was Kentucky's first state park, established in 1924. It took a while to get going, until the Civilian Conservation Corps helped construct facilities in the 1930s—including the log cabins as well as the roads, bridges, and hiking trails.

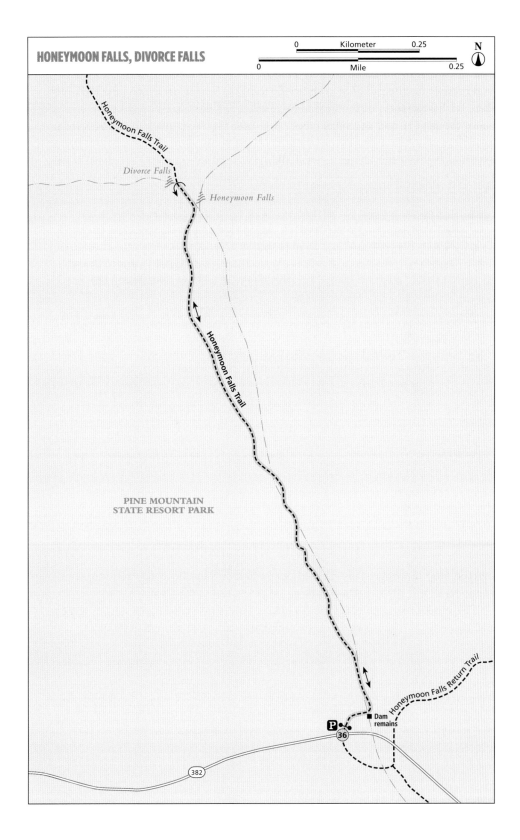

0   Kilometer   0.25

0   Mile   0.25

N

Honeymoon Falls Trail

Divorce Falls

Honeymoon Falls

Honeymoon Falls Trail

PINE MOUNTAIN
STATE RESORT PARK

Honeymoon Falls Return Trail

P

Dam
remains

36

382

This rustic touch is reflected throughout the park. Today the preserve is one of Kentucky's most popular. Park naturalists lead programs throughout the warm season to keep visitors occupied, with woodsy walks, paddling trips on the nearby Cumberland River, camping skills classes, and specific seasonal events.

So whether you are a honeymooner or a divorcee—or none of the above—marry yourself to the idea of a visit up here to Honeymoon Falls and its accompanying cataract, Divorce Falls.

Miles and Directions

0.0 From the parking area, join the Honeymoon Falls Trail (not the Honeymoon Falls Return Trail). Pass around a gate then head left, passing a small former dam and pond. Quickly make the first crossing of the creek of Honeymoon Falls.

0.3 Come to Honeymoon Falls, situated in a grotto to the right of the trail. There is no chance of missing it, since the sound of the spiller will alert you. After exploring this fall, walk the forthcoming trail bridge and come to Divorce Falls. You can enjoy the erratic spiller from the trail but have to work around some fallen boulders to reach its stone-slab base. Backtrack to the trailhead, although you can continue the Honeymoon Falls Trail to make a 1.5-mile loop.

0.6 Arrive back at the trailhead, completing the waterfall hike.

Waterfall Hikes of the Lower Cumberland Plateau

37 Hawk Creek Suspension Bridge Falls

The Hawk Creek valley in the Daniel Boone National Forest is the setting for this waterfall hike where you bag two spillers on one adventure. The main attraction, Hawk Creek Suspension Bridge Falls, plummets 36 feet from a rock lip into a bouldery abyss, while a secondary fall drops 12 feet. The hike to these spillers is attractive throughout, including a segment that travels rich woods—and a cool hiker suspension bridge on Hawk Creek.

Waterfall height: In order, 12 feet, 36 feet
Waterfall beauty: 4
Distance: 3.4-mile out-and-back
Difficulty: Moderate
Hiking time: About 1.8 hours
Trail surface: Natural
Other trail users: None
Canine compatibility: Leashed pets allowed

Land status: National forest
Fees and permits: None
Maps: Daniel Boone National Forest, South Section; USGS Bernstadt
Trail contact: Daniel Boone National Forest, London Ranger District, 761 S. Laurel Rd., London 40744; (606) 864-4163; www.fs.usda .gov/dbnf

Finding the trailhead: From exit 41 on I-75 near London, take KY 80 west for 0.7 mile to KY 1956. Turn right onto KY 1956 west and follow it for 7 miles to the signed Sheltowee Trace trailhead on the right. GPS: N37° 9.766' / W84° 14.421'

The Hike

This waterfall hike uses the Sheltowee Trace to enter the deep and picturesque valley of Hawk Creek to then find a tributary of Hawk Creek creating a 36-foot waterfall echoing off a stone chamber. Not only is this waterfall—known as Hawk Creek Suspension Bridge Falls—alluring, but so is Hawk Creek and its other tributaries, one of which features yet another waterfall with a height of 12 feet. In addition to these cascades, you will also enjoy bluffs, boulders, and deep woods magnificence located within the Daniel Boone National Forest. The Hawk Creek suspension bridge, for which the falls is named, is a man-made highlight and allows views of Hawk Creek. The flats adjacent to Hawk Creek make for ideal picnicking or backpacking sites.

The hike leaves KY 1956, located in uplands dividing feeder streams of the Rockcastle River. The singletrack path, marked with plastic white diamonds, parallels the road for a minute then turns north toward Hawk Creek under hickories, maples, and oaks. It then picks up a faint old doubletrack, descending into hemlock and rhododendron to cross a stream.

The old roadbed is left behind and keeps winding north to eventually come along the base of a cliff line. The trail enters the valley of Hawk Creek proper among rock palisades, turning east after downward switchbacks, entering a sea of rhododendron.

The scramble is worth this view of Hawk Creek Suspension Bridge Falls.

The suspension bridge over Hawk Creek.

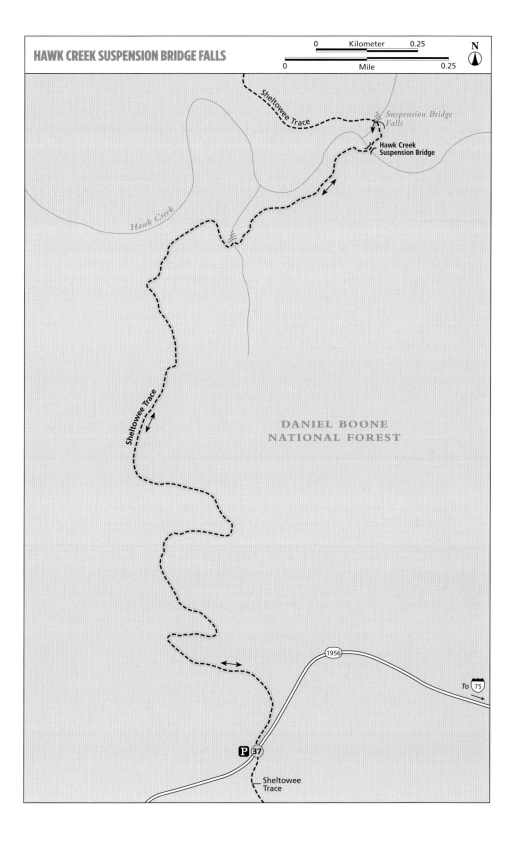

0 Kilometer 0.25

0 Mile 0.25

N

Sheltowee Trace

Suspension Bridge Falls

Hawk Creek Suspension Bridge

Hawk Creek

Sheltowee Trace

DANIEL BOONE NATIONAL FOREST

1956

To 75

P 37

Sheltowee Trace

You then come upon an unnamed 12-foot tributary waterfall. The stream first pours down an angled rock slab then free-falls off a ledge to make a ground splash before flowing along a cliff line, aiming for Hawk Creek. This wet-weather cataract can be a mere trickle during the warm season.

Rock houses and cliff lines rise above the deep forest of moisture-loving trees such as black, birch, beech, and hemlock, including one old-growth hemlock located directly alongside the trail. Enjoy looking down on Hawk Creek alternating in pools and rapids, with gravel bars bordering the stream in spots. The hike wanders across flats then comes to the long wooden suspension bridge over Hawk Creek. Enjoy the watery view from atop the span of this stream flowing west for the Rockcastle River.

After crossing the trail bridge, Hawk Creek Suspension Bridge Falls becomes audible. To reach the falls, keep on the Sheltowee Trace, coming to the waterfall tributary. At this point you can squeeze right among a boulder jumble to reach the falls, or climb the hill on the far side of the waterfall tributary. Here you will see the slender spiller launching from a stone rim to splash from a lower ledge before splattering to the ground below. Neither waterfall lookout is easy to reach, but it is worth your effort. From here it is a simple backtrack to the trailhead via the Sheltowee Trace. However, I recommend you spend some time down here in this cool, wild valley that is Hawk Creek.

Miles and Directions

0.0 Pick up the Sheltowee Trace, leaving north from the KY 1956 trailhead. The Trace edges the national forest boundary next to a residence.

0.6 The Sheltowee Trace turns past a small streamlet.

1.1 Come along a tall rock bluff, then walk the margin between the rock rim above and Hawk Creek below.

1.4 Come to the 12-foot waterfall located along a curve of the trail. Here an unnamed tributary makes an angled descent followed by a vertical dive, then flows along an adjacent cliff line.

1.6 The Sheltowee Trace takes you past an old-growth hemlock imperiled by an exotic pest known as the hemlock woolly adelgid that is killing hemlocks in Kentucky and beyond. Drop into a flat with a campsite.

1.7 Come to and cross the wooden suspension bridge over Hawk Creek. Reach another flat. From here you can hear Hawk Creek Suspension Bridge Falls. Follow the Trace just a short distance more to reach the cataract. Backtrack to the trailhead.

3.4 Arrive back at the trailhead, completing the waterfall hike.

38 Big Dog Falls

What a beautiful waterfall! This wide cataract forms where Big Dog Branch and Little Dog Branch merge, creating a stretched-out slide of stone that pours two creeks over a single ledge into a very outsize plunge pool. It is yet another demonstration of the variety of waterfalls found the Bluegrass State. The hike to the waterfall—using the Sheltowee Trace—isn't too bad either. You start in a remote area of the Daniel Boone National Forest, working your way along Pond Ridge to pass the McFadden Cemetery. From there you descend to Big Dog Branch, fording it once before reaching its confluence with Little Dog Branch at Big Dog Falls.

Waterfall height: 10 feet
Waterfall beauty: 5
Distance: 3-mile out-and-back
Difficulty: Easy
Hiking time: About 1.6 hours
Trail surface: Natural
Other trail users: Mountain bikers, equestrians, illegal ATVs
Canine compatibility: Leashed pets allowed

Land status: National forest
Fees and permits: None
Maps: Daniel Boone National Forest, South Section; USGS Ano, London SW
Trail contact: Daniel Boone National Forest, London Ranger District, 761 S. Laurel Rd., London 40744; (606) 864-4163; www.fs.usda .gov/dbnf

Finding the trailhead: From exit 38 on I-75 near London, head west on KY 192 for 5.7 miles and turn right onto paved Line Creek Road. Follow Line Creek Road for 2.7 miles, then veer left onto gravel FR 56. After 1.8 miles, veer left onto FR 119 (away from New Hope Baptist Church). After 3.2 miles, split right and uphill with FR 457 as FR 119 goes left. Follow FR 457 for 2.8 miles to end at a wide turnaround. (**Note:** A primitive track splits up and to the right from the turnaround, and a lesser-maintained segment of FR 457 continues beyond here. However, do not continue on FR 457 beyond this point unless you have four-wheel drive, and even then it could be iffy after rains.) GPS: N37° 5.603' / W84° 15.909'

The Hike

Big Dog Falls is nestled deep in the valley of Big Dog Branch, where Little Dog Branch flows into its mother stream. Looking up at the falls, you can admire Big Dog Branch surging over the wide ledge with Little Dog Branch coming in from the left and then dropping off the same ledge. Above the falls, both waterways feature flat rock slabs over which the water flows. Below the falls, small rock houses can be found. You will be surprised at the length and depth of the plunge pool here.

However, Big Dog Falls is not quite as busy of a swimming and admiring destination as you might think. For starters, the sides and base and plunge pool of the waterfall are not easy to reach. Your approach to the cataract is from the top. Thickets of rhododendron and low cliff lines add to the difficulty of reaching the falls. However,

Big Dog Falls drops wide, low, and white.

intrepid waterfall enthusiasts like us can carefully reach and admire this spiller. In summer and autumn, when the water is warm, it is a simple and much easier matter of traipsing through the aqua to access Big Dog Falls and its alluring plunge pool.

Big Dog Falls is a year-round waterfall attraction. At lower flows the two streams will spill separately over the same ledge, with Little Dog Branch making a lesser plunge.

To reach Big Dog Falls, you use the Sheltowee Trace. The parking area on FR 457 is where the Sheltowee Trace comes in and follows FR 457. However, beyond the parking area FR 457 is primitive and often riddled with potholes and muddy sections. I certainly would not drive this last portion unless I had a four-wheel-drive vehicle, and during the winter and spring the road is liable to be very muddy. Additionally, since you are following the Sheltowee Trace, it is better to walk.

From the turnaround, the Sheltowee Trace runs along Pond Ridge for a little over a half-mile then makes a sharp right turn, descending to the McFadden Cemetery and a gate. The internment is to the right of the trail with headstones shaded by rising forest, although the graves are easy to spot. Beyond the cemetery the Sheltowee Trace is open only to equestrians, bicyclers, and hikers, although illegal ATVs follow the trail also. Begin an extended descent into the plush forest of Big Dog Branch, where the humidity is thick in summer and evergreens are found in copious quantities.

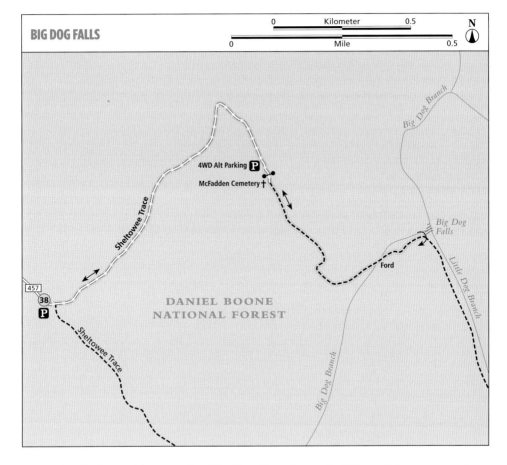

The Sheltowee Trace reaches Big Dog Branch at a ford. You might get across by rock-hopping in summer and autumn, but if the water is up, expect to ford. Beyond the creek crossing, the trail takes you along Big Dog Branch a short distance to the confluence with Little Dog Branch. Look for a spur trail leading left to the top of the falls. From here you can cross Big Dog Branch and circle below the falls, bordered by bountiful rhododendron. The two-creek 10-foot-high and 35-foot-wide spiller takes on many forms depending upon water volume and is a good cataract to visit in different seasons, including when other waterfalls may be running dry.

Miles and Directions

0.0 From the parking area, head left, easterly, on the primitive continuation of FR 457 (a primitive track goes up and right here). After a few feet, the Sheltowee Trace comes in on your right. Continue on FR 457, rolling over a couple of hills in mixed pines and hardwoods, now heading northeasterly. Look for Sheltowee Trace markers along the ragged roadbed.

0.6 Veer sharply right, southeasterly, as a faint track keeps straight. Descend away from Pond Ridge.

0.8 Come to a gate and the McFadden Cemetery, in the woods to your right. This is as far as a passenger vehicle should go. Here the Sheltowee Trace is closed to motor vehicles, but unfortunately that regulation is ignored by some. Continue a downgrade on a narrower track, and enter a dense forest rife with evergreens.

1.3 Come to the Big Dog Branch crossing just after passing a pretty little campsite on your right. Cross the stream, then stay left along Big Dog Branch as an illegal ATV track leaves up and to your right.

1.5 Come to a spur trail leading left to the top of Big Dog Falls. You can access the falls this way, either crossing Big Dog Branch or walking down along Little Dog Branch. Beyond here the Sheltowee Trace curves right and begins running up Little Dog Branch. Backtrack to the trailhead.

3.0 Arrive back at the trailhead, completing the waterfall hike.

39 Vanhook Cascade, Vanhook Falls

This loop hike takes you not only by two named waterfalls but also by four other unnamed lesser cascades. Your circuit traverses the Rockcastle River valley within a remote, lesser-visited section of the Daniel Boone National Forest. The Rockcastle Narrows East Trail and the Sheltowee Trace lead you past two unnamed falls before reaching Vanhook Cascade, a 10-foot angled slide spiller. Next comes one of the national forest's signature spillers—35-foot Vanhook Falls. The hike turns down Cane Creek then up the Rockcastle River, passing the legendary rapid known as The Narrows. View one last low-flow cataract before completing the loop.

Waterfall height: In order, 5 feet, 7 feet, 10 feet, 35 feet, 22 feet, 30 feet
Waterfall beauty: 5
Distance: 6.6-mile lollipop loop
Difficulty: Moderate
Hiking time: About 3.6 hours
Trail surface: Natural
Other trail users: None
Canine compatibility: Leashed pets allowed

Land status: National forest
Fees and permits: None
Maps: Daniel Boone National Forest, South Section; USGS Ano
Trail contact: Daniel Boone National Forest, London Ranger District, 761 S. Laurel Rd., London 40744; (606) 864-4163; www.fs.usda .gov/dbnf

Finding the trailhead: From exit 38 on I-75 near London, head west on KY 192 for 5.7 miles and turn right onto paved Line Creek Road. Follow Line Creek Road for 2.7 miles, then veer left onto gravel FR 56. After 1.8 miles, veer left onto FR 119 (away from New Hope Baptist Church). After 3.2 miles, stay left with FR 119 as FR 457 goes right and uphill. Continue for 2.1 miles more miles on FR 119, parking at the intersection of FR 119 and FR 1198. Park in the gravel to the right of the road, just after FR 1198 goes right. GPS: N37° 2.977' / W84° 17.506'

The Hike

The fact that this hike visits two named falls along with four other cataracts makes it an outstanding adventure, but the trek is further enhanced by trailside beauty along feeder streams of the Rockcastle River, as well as its remote setting in the Daniel Boone National Forest. Therefore, expect to see six waterfalls amid some of Kentucky's most scenic locales. Furthermore, on the drive to the trailhead you will pass two roadside natural arches, an added perk of the hike.

As far as waterfalls are concerned, Vanhook Falls (often misspelled as Van Hook) is the star of the show. It makes a 35-foot dive from a rock rim into a stone-bordered cathedral of overhanging rock lording over scads of rhododendron. Vanhook Cascade slides into a dark grotto and is often quickly passed by since it is found a quarter-mile before Vanhook Falls. Don't make this mistake.

Vanhook Falls makes its signature curtain drop from an overhung ledge.

Also, appreciate the other less-heralded spillers on the way. The first unnamed fall you will encounter is a 5-foot ledge drop on Yuel Branch, just before this stream merges with Vanhook Branch. The next one is on Vanhook Branch. It makes a distinctive horseshoe-shaped 7-foot drop into a stone-walled mini-gorge. The two named falls then come next. Beyond them, the trail goes directly by a low-flow fall making a 6-foot slide then dropping an additional 16 feet from a rim into a maw of darkness-enveloped in rhododendron. The path cuts back across the creek at a small ledge. The final cataract is near hike's end, where a low-flow seasonal creek drops 30-plus feet from a cliff line, but it can run dry by autumn.

Therefore, you will get plenty of waterfall action on this hike, especially in spring. Photographers need to allow ample shooting time—the cataracts are not all easy to shoot. The hike starts out easy enough, following gated FR 119 for a quarter-mile then joining the Rockcastle Narrows East Trail, a singletrack path heading into the valley of Yuel Branch. The forest is lush here as you slowly drift deeper toward the water, crossing Yuel Branch twice before Yuel gives up its waters to Vanhook Branch. This is also where you join the Sheltowee Trace and encounter your first bonus ledge drop.

The Sheltowee Trace and Vanhook Branch separate for a while, but when they come back together, you will find the 7-foot horseshoe-shaped fall. Just a little down-trail come to 10-foot Vanhook Cascade, located where the Sheltowee Trace crosses Vanhook Branch. Here the stream flows over layered strata then makes a final slide into a dark pool bordered by low but sheer rock walls. This whole area is slippery, so exercise caution.

Vanhook Falls is just a short piece down the Sheltowee Trace. Here you'll discover a wooden observation deck with a bench and an excellent view of Vanhook Falls. However, you can walk closer to the falls and even behind the cascade as it collapses from the overhanging brow of stone. The whole scene is enrapturing and worth a lengthy stop.

Next, the loop leaves the Sheltowee Trace and heads down the Cane Creek valley, curving into hemlock hollows and onto ridges of pine, well above Cane Creek. Ahead is a tributary fall that is difficult to access. However, intrepid Kentucky waterfallers know that a little extra effort is required to reach these special places. This spiller slides to a straight drop, seemingly into a black hole.

The Rockcastle Narrows after an autumn thunderstorm.

You then open onto the perceptibly wider valley of the Rockcastle River, though these lowermost regions are often stilled as part of Lake Cumberland. When lake levels are down in winter, however, the Rockcastle will flow free. The trail winds among big boulders and thick woods in the almost junglesque valley, shortly reaching "The Nars," a tapered part of the Rockcastle River caroming through a boulder garden. While hiking this area you will understand why this part of the Rockcastle is a designated Kentucky Wild River.

The Rockcastle Narrows East Trail steeply climbs away from the river to pass the final waterfall of the loop—a low-flow dropper falling from a cliff line. Your 400-foot ascent ends upon picking up a grassy roadbed to soon reach closed FR 119. From there it is an easy, simple backtrack to the parking area.

Miles and Directions

0.0   Pass around the pole gate on FR 119, heading southbound on the doubletrack.

0.2   Come to a trail intersection. Head left onto the singletrack Rockcastle Narrows East Trail, leaving the forest road behind. Dip into thick woods.

0.9   Rock-hop evergreen-shaded Yuel Branch. You are now on the left-hand bank heading downstream.

1.1   Intersect the Sheltowee Trace. Head right here, southbound on Kentucky's master path. Quickly cross Yuel Branch a second time. Note the 5-foot ledge waterfall just below this second crossing.

1.9   Listen for a 7-foot horseshoe-shaped waterfall on Vanhook Branch spilling into a rhododendron-cloaked, eroded-stone fissure. The trail and creek are near one another at this point.

2.2   Reach a trail junction. Head left toward Vanhook Falls on the Sheltowee Trace, and descend to reach Vanhook Branch. Carefully cross the stream just above Vanhook Cascade, a 10-foot angled slide fall. It takes effort and balance to shoot this spiller. Continue toward Vanhook Falls.

2.4   Circle above the rim of Vanhook Falls, then turn onto a stairway and wooden deck at the falls. The 35-foot pour-over makes its curtain free-fall into an echo chamber of a rock hollow, reverberating the spill. Backtrack to the last trail intersection.

2.6   Reach the trail intersection just after again crossing above Vanhook Cascade. Here, head west on the continuation of the Rockcastle Narrows East Trail. Watch for a spur leading right, uphill, to the terminus of FR 119.

3.3   Walk near a low-flow falls sliding 6 feet then diving 16 additional feet off a rock rim. Listen for this falls, then work your way toward it.

4.2   Intersect the faint Winding Stair Gap Trail after coming along Cane Creek amid pines. The Rockcastle Connector Trail—with no bridge crossing Cane Creek—is across Cane Creek and leads you to Bee Rock Campground. Stay straight here, curving north along the Rockcastle River.

4.8   Reach the Rockcastle River Narrows. Continue upriver.

5.4   Work around a muddy hollow as the Rockcastle River curves west. Beware user-created trails working around this messy area. After crossing the stream of the hollow, stay west along the Rockcastle River.

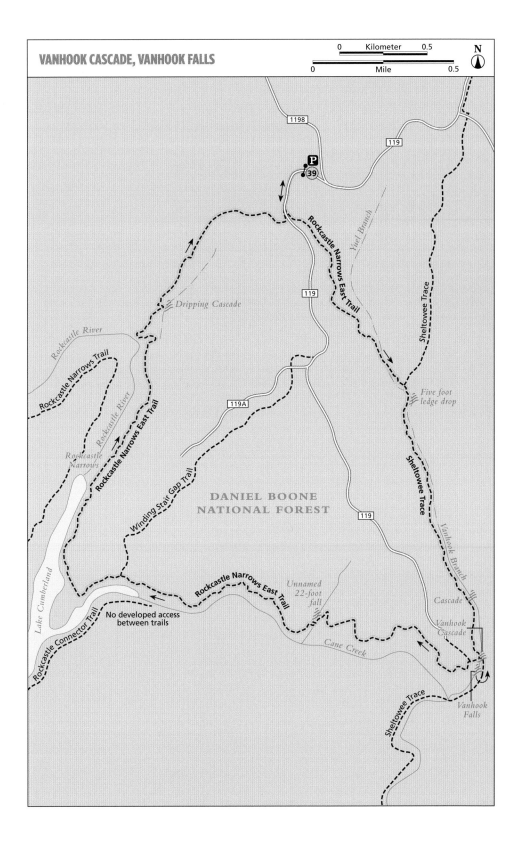

0   Kilometer   0.5

0   Mile   0.5

N

1198

119

P
39

Rockcastle Narrows East Trail

Yuel Branch

Sheltowee Trace

119

Dripping Cascade

Rockcastle River

Rockcastle Narrows Trail

Rockcastle River

119A

Five foot
ledge drop

Rockcastle Narrows East Trail

Rockcastle
Narrows

Winding Stair Gap Trail

Sheltowee Trace

DANIEL BOONE
NATIONAL FOREST

119

Vanhook Branch

Lake Cumberland

Rockcastle Connector Trail

No developed access
between trails

Rockcastle Narrows East Trail

Unnamed
22-foot
fall

Cascade

Vanhook
Cascade

Cane Creek

Sheltowee Trace

Vanhook
Falls

5.5 Turn right along the easily missed blazed path rising right, away from the water. Don't be deceived by a user-created trail continuing along the Rockcastle River bottom. Climb.

5.7 Come alongside a low-flow waterfall dripping from a cliff line. Keep climbing by switchbacks.

6.1 Level off at a closed forest road accessing a wildlife clearing. The walking is easy from here on out.

6.4 Turn left onto FR 119, northbound.

6.6 Arrive back at the trailhead, completing the hike.

40 Falls of Pounder Branch, Vanhook Falls

This is one of the best waterfall hikes in Kentucky, not only for the sheer number of waterfalls but also for the variety of spillers. The final highlight is Vanhook Falls, which puts an exclamation point on the adventure. The hike takes you from the ridgetops into the Pounder Branch valley to find a wealth of waterfalls while hopping over these streams and their tributaries. Reach your elevation low point at Cane Creek; however, the highlights continue here as you find rapids and sunning rocks. From Cane Creek make a short ascent to reach beautiful 35-foot Vanhook Falls making its curtain drop in an attractive alcove.

Waterfall height: In order, 6 feet, 6 feet, 10 feet, 25 feet, 50 feet, 30 feet, 35 feet
Waterfall beauty: 5
Distance: 5.2-mile out-and-back
Difficulty: Moderate
Hiking time: About 2.5 hours
Trail surface: Natural
Other trail users: None
Canine compatibility: Leashed pets allowed

Land status: National forest
Fees and permits: None
Maps: Daniel Boone National Forest, South Section; USGS Sawyer, Ano
Trail contact: Daniel Boone National Forest, London Ranger District, 761 S. Laurel Rd., London 40744; (606) 864-4163; www.fs.usda .gov/dbnf

Finding the trailhead: From exit 38 on I-75 near London, head west on KY 192 for 12.2 miles to the intersection with KY 1193 and a trailhead parking area. Follow the Sheltowee Trace leaving north from KY 192. GPS: N36° 59.865' / W84° 17.093'

The Hike

Make sure the water is flowing before you tackle this signature Kentucky waterfall hike. I recommend December through May. You will enjoy at least seven waterfalls of differing volumes, shapes, and heights and might find a few more if you are willing to explore along Pounder Branch. Rabid waterfall enthusiasts and photographers should give this adventure a full day.

Kentucky's master path, the Sheltowee Trace, is your trail conduit leading to this abundance of waterfalls along Pounder Branch, Cane Creek, and Vanhook Branch— all the streams by which this waterfall hike leads. Located in part of the Rockcastle River watershed inside the Daniel Boone National Forest, this hike takes you not only by waterfalls but also rock houses, cliffs, and streamside rock slabs perfect for relaxing or picnicking.

The hike starts up high then aims for Pounder Branch, where you will find many a waterfall on Pounder and its tributaries spilling over its gorge. When the water is up, the roar of moving water echoes throughout the valley while walking the

Sheltowee Trace. Around the stream, rhododendron, hemlock, and ferns keep things green. More scenic beauty awaits at Cane Creek, where you will see a slide cascade where Pounder Branch meets Cane Creek and rapids coursing past open rock slabs. Hiker bridges take you over both lower Pounder Branch and Cane Creek. The final part of the trek leads to renowned Vanhook Falls.

Your first waterfall is a 6-footer that spouts from an overhanging lip into a little pool. It seems an appropriate-size warm-up fall. The deeper you go in the valley, the more beautiful it becomes, and this remains the case with all the waterfalls. The second falls is very different. The 6-foot drop fills a pool far outsizing the size of the stream. As you face this cataract, a long, low ledge extends to your right.

The tributary you have been following soon joins Pounder Branch. Here a gorge begins forming as Pounder Branch cuts deeper toward Cane Creek. Soon enough Pounder Branch makes its own waterfall, a 10-foot-high stair-step spiller that is a little wider than high, dropping white over layered stone.

Lava Falls comes next, a tributary cataract spilling from the rim of the Pounder Branch gorge. It is hard to get a top-down look, but you can—with difficulty—get a face-on look by continuing down-trail just a bit to find a route down into the gorge. Lava Falls makes its descent in short stages, pinballing down stone layers. To add to the scenery, Pounder Branch makes its own short fall at the point where Lava Falls ends.

And there's more. Ahead, a short spur trail leads to the rim of the gorge where you can look at another tributary waterfall, making its crazy plunge across the gorge, stopping to bounce off one layer of rock to then free-fall to feed Pounder Branch. Ahead, you will walk just upstream of another tributary waterfall spilling from view on this side of the gorge. Alas, the gorge rim is too steep to descend. Therefore, you have to walk directly up or down along Pounder Branch to reach the bottom of this waterfall.

Relish views of sheer bluffs along Cane Creek before descending to a bridge over Pounder Branch near the confluence of the two streams. You cannot help but notice the long slide cascade sheeting beneath the Pounder Branch hiker bridge, still another scenic yet difficult-to-reach waterfall.

Cane Creek propounds still more beauty. Here the translucent waterway pushes beside streamside rock slabs begging for a stop. Sonorant rapids on Cane Creek make their play for attention. However, we have more falling water to see, thus take the elevated hiker bridge across Cane Creek. This perch allows still more eye-pleasing looks at Cane Creek.

Continuing beyond Cane Creek, the Sheltowee Trace climbs along a cliff line pocked with rock shelters. Vanhook Branch flows through thickets of rhododendron to your left. Then abruptly you are at Vanhook Falls, where an observation deck with a resting bench contrasts the untamed scene where Vanhook Branch makes a curtain crash of 35 feet, landing on an ever-wet stone jumble. An overhung rock rim frames the cataract. It is a simple matter to descend to the rock house below and even walk behind the falls, capturing it from many perspectives.

Lava Falls dances down layers of stone to meet Pounder Branch.

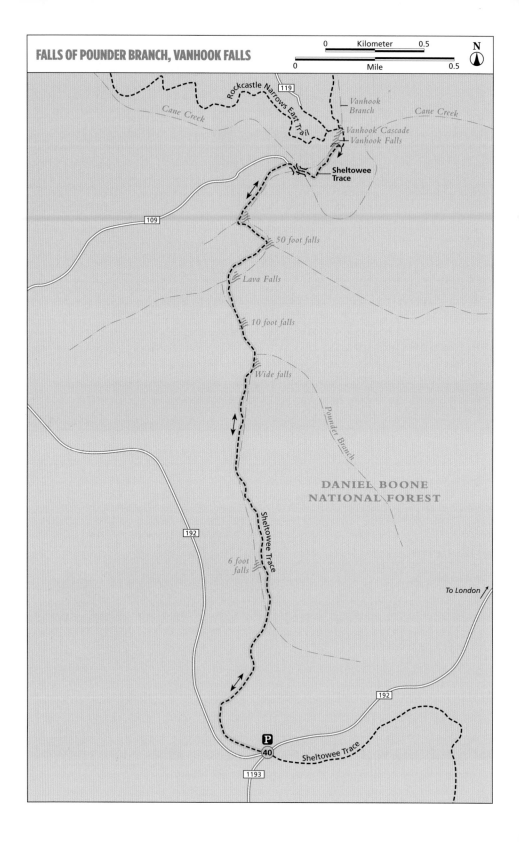

FALLS OF POUNDER BRANCH, VANHOOK FALLS

0   Kilometer   0.5

0   Mile   0.5

N

Rockcastle Narrows East Trail

119

Cane Creek

Vanhook Branch

Cane Creek

Vanhook Cascade

Vanhook Falls

Sheltowee Trace

109

50 foot falls

Lava Falls

10 foot falls

Wide falls

Pounder Branch

DANIEL BOONE NATIONAL FOREST

Sheltowee Trace

192

6 foot falls

To London

192

P

40

Sheltowee Trace

1193

If you haven't had enough waterfalls, continue on the Sheltowee Trace for 0.2 mile to see modest 10-foot Vanhook Cascade, an angled slide a little upstream of Vanhook Falls. Otherwise, backtrack to see again all the falls along Pounder Branch.

Miles and Directions

0.0 Leave north from KY 192 on the Sheltowee Trace. Join a singletrack footpath under pines and oaks.

0.1 Veer right to pick up a beech-bordered faded doubletrack. Descend toward a feeder stream of Pounder Branch.

0.4 Step over a tributary flowing across the path.

0.7 Raised stone steps help in crossing the tributary of Pounder Branch you have been following. You are now on the right-hand bank of the main tributary, gaining volume from still other feeder streams.

0.8 Reach the first waterfall. This 6-footer fashions a short drop over a narrow undercut lip, then makes an angled slide over rock into a linear pool.

1.0 Use steps to cross the creek again. Begin walking through attractive streamside flats.

1.2 Make two more creek crossings using the placed stone steps.

1.4 A spur path leads right to a wide and short waterfall, with an outsize pool. The tributary of Pounder Branch has clearly gained volume.

1.5 It's a short walk right from the trail to another waterfall. Here, Pounder Branch overspills white atop stratified stone, making a measured descent of 10 feet.

1.7 A tributary of Pounder Branch crosses the trail and then cartwheels 25 feet into the gorge of Pounder Branch. This is known as Lava Falls.

1.9 Watch for a short spur trail leading right as the Sheltowee Trace curves left. Here you can look across Pounder Branch as a tributary forms a 50-foot waterfall, leaping from the rim of the gorge.

2.2 While walking the gorge rim, step over a 30 foot tributary waterfall that plunges from the rim and out of sight.

2.3 A side trail leads left up toward gated FR 109. The Sheltowee Trace angles right, traversing open rock slabs where you can look across Cane Creek. Descend by switchbacks toward Cane Creek.

2.4 Come to Cane Creek after bridging Pounder Branch above a slide cascade. Soon bridge Cane Creek as well, then saddle alongside a cliff line, aiming for Vanhook Falls.

2.6 Come to the observation deck and bench at Vanhook Falls. Enjoy the 35-foot cataract from here and closer if you please. Backtrack to the trailhead.

5.2 Arrive back at the trailhead, completing the hike.

41 Falls of Bee Rock

This fine waterfall hike starts at an equally fine national forest recreation area known as Bee Rock. Here you can not only see waterfalls and enjoy views, but also camp, fish, paddle, and motorboat. The waterfall hike takes you up tributaries in the Rockcastle River valley. First, climb to see a two-tiered spiller, then quickly find a second, longer cataract. From there, cruise oak uplands before coming out to a grand view. Make a final descent, passing an unusual faucet spiller that pours into a dark rock shelter.

Waterfall height: In order, 18 feet, 35 feet, 20 feet
Waterfall beauty: 4
Distance: 2.5-mile lollipop loop
Difficulty: Moderate
Hiking time: About 1.2 hours
Trail surface: Natural
Other trail users: None
Canine compatibility: Leashed pets allowed

Land status: National forest
Fees and permits: None
Maps: Daniel Boone National Forest, South Section; USGS Ano
Trail contact: Daniel Boone National Forest, London Ranger District, 761 S. Laurel Rd., London 40744; (606) 864-4163; www.fs.usda .gov/dbnf

Finding the trailhead: From exit 38 on I-75 near London, head west on KY 192 for 18 miles to the bridge over the Rockcastle River. Turn right into Bee Rock Campground on FR 624, the south side of the Rockcastle River, before crossing the river bridge. Follow FR 624 for 0.4 mile to the Sublimity Bridge on the left. Parking is available at the bridge. GPS: N37° 1.677' / W84° 19.293'

The Hike

You might not know that tourists have been visiting Bee Rock, along the Rockcastle River (now dammed and part of Lake Cumberland at Bee Rock), for over 200 years. It all started when a War of 1812 hero by the name of Columbus Graham established a resort known as Sublimity Springs, where the Bee Rock Campground now lies. The resort got much of its business from summertime visitors residing in the lower South who stayed for long periods, fleeing from yellow fever, malaria, and suffocating heat. A plaque at the trailhead quotes a brochure from that time describing Sublimity Springs as "an Eden for children, a sanitarium for invalids, a paradise for lovers, and a haven of rest for the tired." The hotel was later crushed by ice when a February thaw followed a hard freeze of the Rockcastle River.

In the early 1900s a lady by the name of Martha Bolton opened a boardinghouse on the same spot, which was used by local fisherman and timbermen floating logs downriver. By the 1920s the logging era around Bee Rock ended. Then in the 1930s the Civilian Conservation Corps (CCC) came to the Rockcastle River and built the

Early spring finds this 35-footer tumbling boldly.

Sublimity Bridge, the first span across the Rockcastle and now open for foot travel only. In fact, you start this hike by crossing this historic span. The CCC also worked on other projects throughout the adjacent Daniel Boone National Forest. Later, this part of the Rockcastle River was dammed as Lake Cumberland and now is silenced for most of the year, except when the lake is drawn down in winter and again flows free and sonorant past Bee Rock.

Today the site of the old Sublimity Hotel and later boardinghouse is now part of the Bee Rock Campground. The campground offers both drive-up and walk-in tent sites. I have stayed here at least twenty nights and give it a ringing endorsement.

I also endorse the Bee Rock Loop waterfall hike—even when the falls are running less than bold. Leave the south section of Bee Rock Campground, divided by the dammed part of the Rockcastle River. (The north part of Bee Rock Campground is generally open from April through October, while the south portion—where this hike starts—is open year-round.) Look up from the bridge at Bee Rock and the Bee Rock overlook. After reaching the west side of the bridge, the hike traces FR 623 a short distance and then you turn right, climbing an old roadbed along an unnamed tributary of the Rockcastle River. The walking is easy despite a steady ascent.

You soon reach the first two waterfalls of the hike. These are seasonal spillers, running best from winter through spring. The first one pours over a two-tiered ledge, splattering to the ground before flowing across the trail. Leave the 18-foot cataract behind and walk uphill just a bit, passing an unusual mushroom-shaped trailside rock, then come to the second waterfall. This 35-footer first rushes over an angled stone slide then makes a short drop before dashing over layered rock to pinball down the base of a cliff line, all in a zigzag fashion. The path leads you directly by the upper part of this pour-over.

From there the hike leaves the old roadbed and wanders level uplands. The hiking is easy and glorious. You are rewarded at a developed overlook from Bee Rock. Gain extensive views of the dammed Rockcastle River below, the KY 192 bridge, and the historic Sublimity Bridge as well as bluffs along the Rockcastle Valley.

The final part of the hike leads past more impressive bluffs then to a dark shelter. Here a stream of water funnels from a narrow cleft above the shelter, creating yet another singular Kentucky waterfall. The trail takes you through the rock shelter, forcing hikers to dodge the natural shower. From here the path works downhill, passing small tributaries to reach FR 623. At this point, walk past the site of the old Sublimity Resort before crossing the Sublimity Bridge a second time, completing the hike.

Before coming to Bee Rock, load up your favorite outdoor toys and expand your adventure. You can camp, fish, paddle, go motorboating, have a picnic—and see waterfalls.

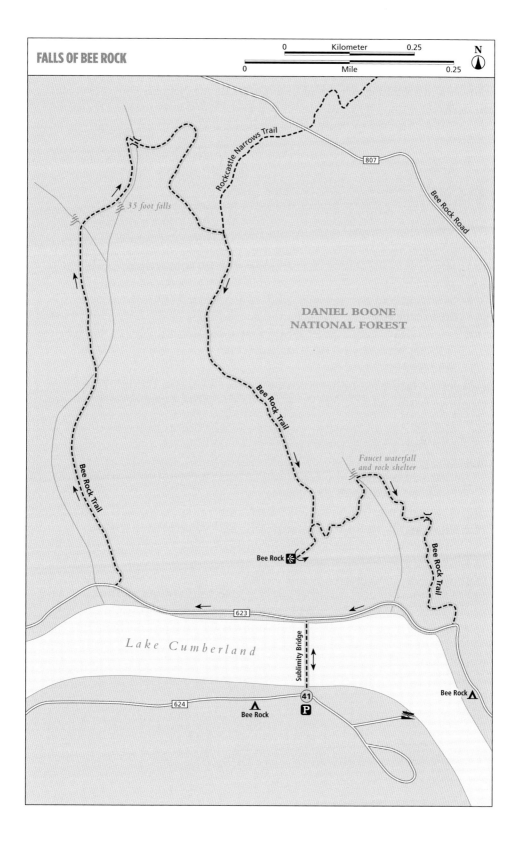

FALLS OF BEE ROCK

0 — Kilometer — 0.25
0 — Mile — 0.25

N

35 foot falls

Rockcastle Narrows Trail

807

Bee Rock Road

DANIEL BOONE
NATIONAL FOREST

Bee Rock Trail

*Faucet waterfall
and rock shelter*

Bee Rock Trail

Bee Rock

623

Bee Rock Trail

Lake Cumberland

Sublimity Bridge

41

Bee Rock

624

Bee Rock

P

Miles and Directions

0.0 Leave the trailhead on the south side of the Sublimity Bridge. Cross the historic span. Make sure to look up at Bee Rock, finding the developed overlook.

0.1 Head left on gravel FR 623.

0.3 Leave FR 623 and join the Bee Rock Trail, a singletrack path overlain on a rising roadbed. Ascend the valley of an unnamed tributary of the Rockcastle River under verdant woodland.

0.5 Cross the stream you have been following by culvert.

0.7 Come to the first waterfall. This vertical cataract is to the left of the trail, at the end of a rock house. It bounces down irregular rock before diving from a stone ledge and flowing on through rhododendron. Walk just a short distance and you will see the next waterfall, a twisting 35-footer with numerous forms and flows, starting as a slender shot of white then widening as it caroms down a low point between a cliff line to the right and a rock field to the left.

0.9 Leave the roadbed you have been following and head right on a hiker footbridge. Soon cruise upland woods.

1.2 Intersect the Rockcastle Narrows Trail as it makes its own worthy loop along the Rockcastle River then back to the upper end of Bee Rock Campground. Stay right here, still on the Bee Rock Trail.

1.6 Come to another trail intersection in low pines and mountain laurel. Here, keep straight to find the official Bee Rock Overlook and gain excellent vistas of the Rockcastle Valley below, including the Sublimity Bridge. Hopefully, you can still see your vehicle parked down there. Backtrack to the last intersection and begin a downgrade, finding a break in the cliff line below. Begin cruising the base of the cliff line.

1.8 Come to the faucet waterfall and rock shelter. Here a slender cataract makes a hose-like dive 20 feet into the rock shelter. During wet times hikers will be dripped on working through this shelter fronted by a big boulder.

2.0 A hiker bridge takes you over a shoaling stream.

2.1 Return to FR 623. Turn right here, passing campsites on the site of the old Sublimity Springs Hotel.

2.4 Cross the Sublimity Bridge a second time.

2.5 Arrive back at the trailhead, completing the hike.

42 Arch Falls, Bear Creek Falls

This rewarding waterfall trek in the Daniel Boone National Forest also features geological wonders such as an arch and magnificent cliff lines. The hike uses the Nathan McClure Trail, descending into the valley of the Rockcastle River. The first aquatic highlight is 18-foot Chimney Cascade. Next comes Arch Falls, a truly unique cataract that starts its 50-foot dive by passing through an arch. Ahead, lesser ephemeral waterfalls spill off ledges. Your end destination is perennial 20-foot Bear Creek Falls, a big, wide cataract that plunges from a ledge into Lake Cumberland. During the wet season photographers could take all day snapping shots of the wealth of cascades found along the route.

Waterfall height: In order, major falls only, 18 feet, 50 feet, 20 feet
Waterfall beauty: 5+
Distance: 7.4-mile out-and-back
Difficulty: Moderate
Hiking time: About 4.1 hours
Trail surface: Natural
Other trail users: Some equestrians
Canine compatibility: Leashed pets allowed

Land status: National forest
Fees and permits: None
Maps: Daniel Boone National Forest, South Section; USGS Sawyer
Trail contact: Daniel Boone National Forest, London Ranger District, 761 S. Laurel Rd., London 40744; (606) 864-4163; www.fs.usda.gov/dbnf

Finding the trailhead: From exit 38 on I-75 near London, head west on KY 192 for 18 miles to the bridge over the Rockcastle River. Continue on KY 192 for 3.5 more miles to turn left on Old Whitney Road. Follow it for 1.1 miles, then the road becomes gravel FR 122. Continue on FR 122 for 2.7 miles, then veer left onto FR 122A. Follow FR 122A for 2.6 miles to reach the Nathan McClure Trail, where it leaves acutely left and uphill from FR 122A. There is no official parking area; therefore, park on the road shoulder. GPS: N36° 58.504' / W84° 21.705'

The Hike

This is a spectacular hike, full of continuous beauty as well as high-level highlights. If you come when the water is up, you will be rewarded with waterfalls in addition to the "big three" cataracts on this hike: Chimney Cascade, Arch Falls, and Bear Creek Falls. For here in the valley of the Rockcastle River, many a seasonal tributary tumbles from rock rims, creating waterfalls that delight the hiker in winter and spring. Chimney Cascade and Bear Creek Falls are perennial waterfalls, while Arch Falls can reduce to a trickle. However, Arch Falls does have an unceasing highlight and that is the arch itself through which the waterfall flows. The hike takes place in the Rockcastle River arm of Lake Cumberland. The impoundment is a highlight unto itself. Additionally, majestic bluffs, spring wildflowers, and rock formations will also catch your eye.

Bear Creek Falls is located at hike's end, and is accessible not only by foot but also by boaters motoring up Lake Cumberland. The scenery around Bear Creek Falls is alluring—a point where mountain stream meets mountain lake, where a semicircular rock bluff provides an elevated perch to view Bear Creek Falls, and where thick eastern Kentucky woods add floral variety to the landscape. Bear Creek Falls even has a companion cataract from an adjacent branch.

The hike uses the Nathan McClure Trail, named for an eighteenth-century Indian fighter buried nearby. He was escorting some Kentucky settlers in 1788, heading west from the Cumberland Gap, when Indians stole the settlers' livestock and horses. McClure and his patrol went after them, but McClure was killed and then buried here. The path is primarily used by equestrians but is also open to hikers and mountain bikers. You should find it in decent to good shape.

The beginning of the hike belies its forthcoming beauty as the trail surmounts a nondescript brushy hill before descending into the gorgeous Pole Bridge Branch valley, luxuriantly vegetated. You will bridge the creek then squeeze through a narrow swath of the valley to soon find a lone chimney located beside the trail. From this point you can gaze down on Chimney Cascade. Though difficult to reach, the cataract pours through a narrow boulder jumble then widens and slides down a convex angled rock slab, dropping a total of 16 feet.

The Nathan McClure Trail leads out to the Rockcastle River arm of Lake Cumberland, not far from Rockcastle Campground, located across the water. The trail turns north up the lake arm, undulating along a rugged tree-covered hillside, ultimately rising to Arch Falls. Here a slender stream pours through an 8-foot-long arch then bounces down a few short ledges before free-falling to splatter at the base of a long rock house. It is a rare sight indeed to have a waterfall flowing through an arch. You can circle behind the waterfall and also climb up to viewpoints where you can see the water flowing through the arch.

It is important to pay attention to the trail along the way because the path goes on and off an old roadbed. Beyond Arch Falls the trail leads you past several cascades, including Morning Falls, so named because the morning light shines upon its flowing waters, and Lake Falls, which makes a drop just above Lake Cumberland.

Eventually you turn into the Bear Creek embayment of Lake Cumberland. Here you will find waterfalls on tributaries of Bear Creek if the water is up. However, the side falls can be problematic to access and photograph, although they are near the trail. And then comes the star of the show—Bear Creek Falls. This brawny wall of white is well known, since it can be accessed not only by trail but more commonly by boat. During the spring and summer, when the lake is at full pool, boaters regularly work their way to the base of this wide, curtain-like cataract. For hikers, the waterfall can be viewed from a cleared cliff.

At higher flows Bear Creek Falls will be accompanied by a tributary falls spilling into the water across the embayment from the overlook. You can safely walk to the top of Bear Creek Falls; however, viewing the falls from the lake level—unless you

Arch Falls literally flows through an natural arch before finishing its dive.

Morning Falls catches the early light.

are in a boat—is a challenge. Nonetheless, the cataract makes for a fine exclamation on a rewarding waterfall hike.

Miles and Directions

0.0   From where it leaves acutely left from FR 122A, join the doubletrack Nathan McClure Trail (Trail #530) and climb into pines, soon topping out in piney, brushy woods.

0.2   Curve left, westerly, then descend toward Pole Bridge Branch, curving right and keeping down into evergreens.

0.6   Cross Pole Bridge Branch on a trail bridge. Continue down the left bank of the creek, squeezing through a defile. The creek then falls away sharply.

0.9   Come along a lone chimney beside the trail on the right. From here, walk toward the cliff line and peer down on Chimney Cascade, making its convex slide. The steep terrain makes the spiller challenging to reach up close. However, you will see it has a companion tributary fall as well, when the rains have been falling.

1.3   Leave the embayment of Pole Bridge Branch and turn north up the Rockcastle River arm of Lake Cumberland. Soon cross the first of several tributaries flowing from cliff-laden Gulf Ridge above.

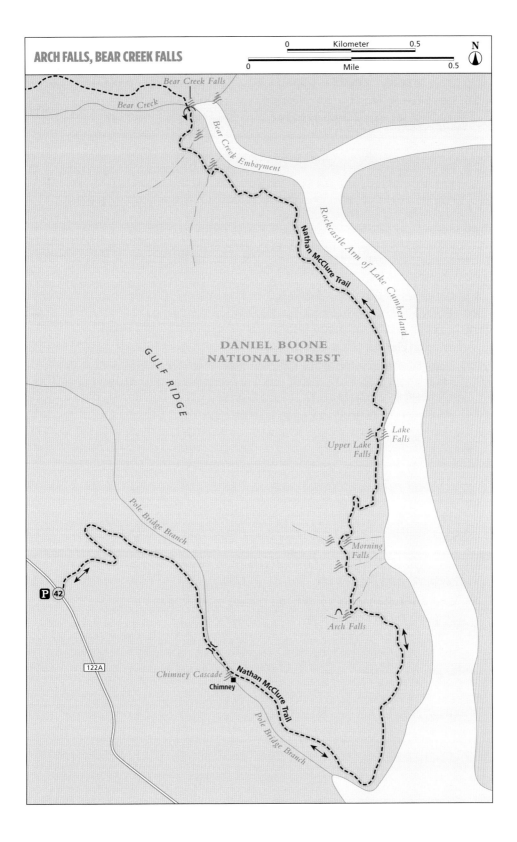

Kilometer
0   0.5

Mile
0   0.5

N

Bear Creek Falls

Bear Creek

Bear Creek Embayment

Rockcastle Arm of Lake Cumberland

Nathan McClure Trail

DANIEL BOONE
NATIONAL FOREST

GULF RIDGE

Lake Falls

Upper Lake Falls

Pole Bridge Branch

Morning Falls

P 42

Arch Falls

122A

Chimney Cascade   Nathan McClure Trail

Chimney

Pole Bridge Branch

1.9 Come to Arch Falls after climbing. Here a low-flow stream pours through a cliff-top arch then dances over layers of rock before diving past a vertical rock face. A big rock house stands to the right of the falls.

2.0 Pass a low-flow waterfall well upstream of the trail, dropping from a cliff line. This will be one of the first ephemeral falls to dry up.

2.1 Come to Morning Falls. This spiller lies just below the trail, diving 12 feet from a stone lip. An upper falls can be viewed on this same stream, plunging from a high cliff.

2.2 Pay close attention here. At this point an old roadbed, used as a social trail, keeps straight then curves left to climb to Gulf Ridge. This is the wrong way. Instead, look for the acute right turn descending toward Lake Cumberland. This correct route is blazed and gets closer to the water then turns back north.

2.5 Come to Lake Falls. Here a stream makes a narrow 12-foot drop below the trail, while Upper Lake Falls executes a wider 10-foot drop from an undercut rock lip. Neither is easy to reach. In winter you will see imposing cliff lines across the Rockcastle. Dip into other drainages ahead.

3.1 Turn left into the Bear Creek embayment.

3.4 Rock-hop a tributary of Bear Creek. Look for a falls here below the trail.

3.6 Pass one more tributary waterfall of Bear Creek. This cataract is especially difficult to see as it drops below the trail almost into the lake.

3.7 Reach the cliff-top overlook of Bear Creek Falls, a wide rumbler crashing 20 feet from a rock lip directly into Lake Cumberland. Look for the companion waterfall dropping into the lake very near Bear Creek Falls. Backtrack to the trailhead.

7.4 Arrive back at the trailhead, completing the waterfall hike.

43 Peter Branch Cascade

This waterfall hike features not only some fun little spillers, but also views of Lake Cumberland and a natural arch. The western section of the Nathan McClure Trail is your trail venue. Here, hike along the valley of the Cumberland River, backed up as Lake Cumberland. Wander along the lakeshore, turning into coves where you will find three falls, one of them spilling directly into Lake Cumberland. The next two are a bit unusual as they descend through a massive boulder jumble.

Waterfall height: In order, 8 feet, 5 feet, 10 feet, 10 feet
Waterfall beauty: 3
Distance: 6.8-mile out-and-back
Difficulty: Moderate
Hiking time: About 3.2 hours
Trail surface: Natural
Other trail users: Some equestrians
Canine compatibility: Leashed pets allowed

Land status: National forest
Fees and permits: None
Maps: Daniel Boone National Forest, South Section; USGS Sawyer, Hail
Trail contact: Daniel Boone National Forest, London Ranger District, 761 S. Laurel Rd., London 40744; (606) 864-4163; www.fs.usda .gov/dbnf

Finding the trailhead: From exit 38 on I-75 near London, head west on KY 192 for 18 miles to the bridge over the Rockcastle River. Continue on KY 192 for 3.5 more miles and turn left on Old Whitney Road. Follow it for 1.1 miles, then the road becomes gravel FR 122. Continue on FR 122 for 2.7 miles, then veer left onto FR 122A. Follow FR 122A for 3.5 miles to its dead end and a road circle. The trail starts on the southwest end of the road circle. GPS: N36° 57.926' / W84° 21.225'

The Hike

Highlights are interspersed all over this hike, keeping you satisfied throughout the trek. Set in the dammed Cumberland River valley where it flows through the Daniel Boone National Forest, the trail offers an attractive wooded setting in wild country. However, take note that even though you are in a remote area of the national forest, the close proximity of the lake—generally a plus for the lake views—also has its share of motorboat traffic, cutting into the "remoteness quotient" of this hike. This hike is also long on natural beauty, whether it is the arch at hike's beginning, the luxuriant forests rising along the lakeshore and in the stream valleys, the hills rising from the stilled waters of the Cumberland River, and, of course, cascading tributaries that we can enjoy, admire, and photograph.

However, these three pour-overs are not going to make any top 10 waterfalls in Kentucky nominations. Peter Branch Cascade makes a classic ledge drop where the stream meets Lake Cumberland. Speaking of that, I have seen Lake Cumberland so high that it nearly drowned Peter Branch Falls. I have also seen the lake 10 feet lower where Peter Branch spilled off its ledge then kept on going a ways before being stilled in Lake Cumberland.

Such is the nature of an impoundment. Water levels can change, though the changes are normally seasonal and cyclical. In a normal given year, lakes are drawn down in the fall, after the summer recreation season, in anticipation of winter rains. Reservoirs rise in winter and spring because of increased rain and often get well above normal summer pool when waters in dammed lakes are held back to prevent downstream flooding. (One negative: These floods also bring waterborne trash from roads into streams, then from streams into this lake. Expect to see some shoreline litter.) Lakes are then left at full pool through late spring and summer before being drawn down again, continuing the cycle. Therefore, these waterfalls might be affected by not only how much rain they have received lately, but also the level of the lake. It will not take long for you to ascertain the water and lake levels on this hike.

The hike begins atop a ridge near the now-stilled confluence of the Rockcastle River and the Cumberland River. As you descend, views of the two river valleys extend in the distance, a perhaps unexpected highlight. Another highlight comes in short order—an arch, sometimes known as Nathan McClure Arch. Though modest in size, a tad under 6 feet high and about 10 to 12 feet wide, the flattish span would make a good shelter except for one thing: The arch itself has a hole in its roof, technically an arch within an arch, adding character to the geological phenomenon.

From the arch, make your way down the first of many streamlets to reach the shore of Lake Cumberland and soon curve along the shoreline, soaking in bounteous lake views before turning into Peter Branch embayment. Here you will spot Peter Branch Cascade, an admittedly modest ledge fall, yet keeping the beauty going. From there the path leads back out to the lake and into the larger Big Lick Branch embayment, where a small cascade near the lake makes noise enough to grab your attention. You then come to the azure blue waters of Big Lick Branch and FR 272. Here the Nathan McClure Trail joins the gravel forest road along the Big Lick Branch embayment, then reverts to primitive trail as it pushes back out to Lake Cumberland. This is a scenic section of trail, cruising the riverside with hills rising on both sides of the slender impoundment.

The trail finally turns into an unnamed stream embayment. Here you find the last two falls, both resulting from water wending its way through a long, mossy, large clutter of boulders. These stones are house-size and create a complex of water, stone, and vegetation that is fun yet challenging and downright hazardous to explore. Be careful! The lowermost fall here is easier to see—a two-tiered tapered spiller jumping from rock to rock before giving its water to the lake.

The upper fall, Boulder Cascade, is upstream from the trail creek crossing. You can hear it but there is no good approach. Upon closer inspection, the unnamed stream makes a chute drop into the middle of the boulder cluster, landing a good 10 feet below. Listen for it to find it. Die-hard waterfallers can get a good look at the lower end of this cataract, while the upper part is perpetually in the shadows of the jumble.

This pour-over squeezes through massive boulders.

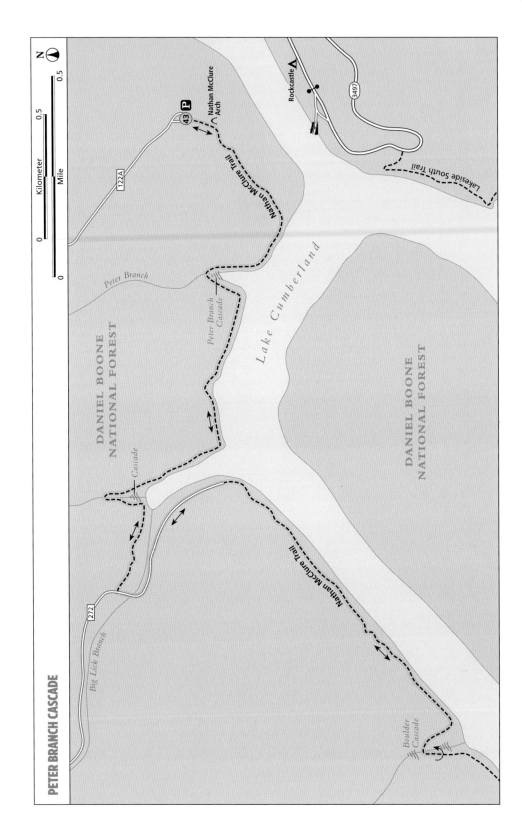

PETER BRANCH CASCADE

N

Kilometer
0   0.5

Mile
0   0.5

DANIEL BOONE NATIONAL FOREST

DANIEL BOONE NATIONAL FOREST

Lake Cumberland

Peter Branch

Peter Branch Cascade

Big Lick Branch

Cascade

Boulder Cascade

Nathan McClure Trail

Nathan McClure Trail

Nathan McClure Arch

Rockcastle

Lakeside South Trail

122A

272

43

P

3497

This watershed is a good place to backtrack, creating a 6.8-mile Kentucky waterfall hike that will satisfy your waterfall wants yet deliver added attractions you have come to expect here in the Bluegrass State.

Miles and Directions

0.0 Leave from the southwest end of the road circle at the end of FR 122A on the singletrack Nathan McClure Trail, walking among low pines, cedars, oaks, and brush. Partial views open of the valleys below.

0.1 Come to Nathan McClure Arch, just to the left of the trail. Note the small arch within the greater arch. Continue descending.

0.3 Step over a small creek. Soon begin cruising along the lake.

0.7 Circle around the embayment of Peter Branch, coming to Peter Branch Cascade as it makes its modest ledge drop. The trail then climbs away from the lake and circles back out to again parallel the shoreline.

1.2 Turn into the Big Lick Branch embayment.

1.5 Pass a small tributary cascade and turn toward Big Lick Branch.

1.9 Reach FR 272. Turn left, bridging Big Lick Branch on the forest road.

2.4 Leave the forest road and continue along the shore among cane. Small, ephemeral streams cross the Nathan McClure Trail. Pay close attention, as the path is faint in places.

3.4 Reach the stream of the last two falls after turning into the embayment of a valley pocked with big boulders and evergreens. Hop the stream then circle around to reach the lower falls of this creek. Here you will see stage-by-stage falls of water among boulders before pouring into the lake. The upper cataract, Boulder Cascade, is also 10 feet and is upstream of the trail in a heap of boulders. Use caution when seeking out this upper fall. Backtrack to the trailhead.

6.8 Arrive back at the trailhead, completing the waterfall hike.

44 Lakeside South Cascade

Do you want to combine a waterfall hike with a trek along a beautiful Kentucky mountain lake? If so, this is the hike for you. Set along the shoreline of Lake Cumberland ensconced in the Daniel Boone National Forest, we take the Lakeside South Trail along the impoundment where the Cumberland River has been dammed. Work in and out of hollows, passing a lonely chimney before turning into a watershed where you will find a nifty little waterfall spilling over a rock ledge. Although not spectacular, the waterfall makes a worthy destination on a worthy hike.

Waterfall height: 12 feet
Waterfall beauty: 3
Distance: 4.4-mile out-and-back
Difficulty: Easy to moderate
Hiking time: About 2 hours
Trail surface: Natural
Other trail users: None
Canine compatibility: Leashed pets allowed

Land status: National forest
Fees and permits: None
Maps: Daniel Boone National Forest, South Section; USGS Sawyer
Trail contact: Daniel Boone National Forest, London Ranger District, 761 S. Laurel Rd., London 40744; (606) 864-4163; www.fs.usda .gov/dbnf

Finding the trailhead: From exit 38 on I-75 near London, head west on KY 192 for 14 miles to KY 1193. Turn left on KY 1193, and follow it 1 mile to KY 3497. Turn right on KY 3497, and follow it 6 miles to reach the large boat ramp parking area just before entering Rockcastle Campground. GPS: N36° 57.643' / W84° 21.164'

The Hike

The Rockcastle area of the Daniel Boone National Forest is a hotbed of outdoor recreation, including fishing, boating, camping, and, of course, waterfall hiking. This particular adventure takes you to a somewhat modest cataract that provides you the excuse to enjoy this parcel of the Bluegrass State. And a pretty parcel it is. You are nestled deep in the valley of the Cumberland River where it has been dammed as ribbonlike Lake Cumberland. Near the trailhead, the Rockcastle River and the Cumberland River meet. This confluence is now stilled by a downstream dam but the river chasms are deep and steep; therefore, this section of Lake Cumberland exhibits a more riverine than lake aspect.

The hike starts at the large parking area near Rockcastle Campground. Do not be alarmed if the parking lot is filled with cars and trailers—most people use the area as a boat launch. In fact, even on the nicest days you will likely have few people for company on this hike. I recommend coming during the winter or spring when the waterfall is falling and the lake is at full pool. During summer the lake can get busy

Lakeside South Cascade drops over two ledges.

with boaters, adding motor noise. During autumn the lake will be drawn down and Lakeside South Cascade reduced to a mere dribble.

After leaving the large parking area, you have to backtrack up KY 3497 for a little more than a quarter-mile before joining the actual Lakeside South Trail near Goodin Branch. Work around the hollow and out toward the shoreline of Lake Cumberland. From here you will be cruising parallel to the water in a lush hillside wetland of evergreens and deciduous trees. This part of the trail faces northwest and has a wetter, lusher aspect, with ferns and mosses growing on anything that doesn't move.

You will soon turn into the hollow of Ike Branch, easily the biggest watershed along this hike and a perennial stream. Scan the woods for impressive beech trees. The hike continues mimicking the shoreline of Lake Cumberland, dipping in and out of lesser hollows, rife with wildflowers in spring. Picturesque rock bridges cross some of these seasonal streams flowing toward Lake Cumberland. After passing the rock chimney of an old hunting cabin, the Lakeside South Trail follows a major bend in the Cumberland and goes from traveling southwest to southeast. The forest takes on a drier aspect, with oaks dominating the woodland. The lake is quite narrow here.

Pass one more significant hollow before entering the stream branch of Lakeside South Cascade. Here the trail cuts below the 12-foot waterfall escaping in a stream over a rock lip, with lesser ribbons of water pouring alongside the primary flow. The

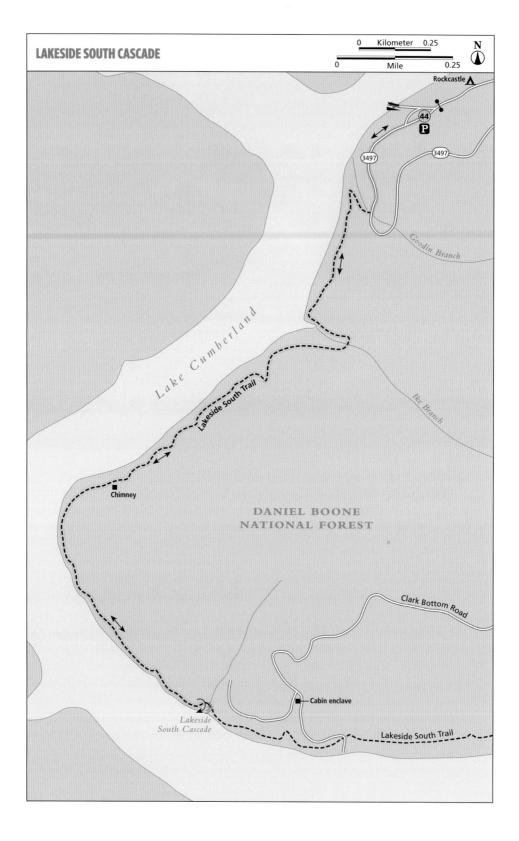

LAKESIDE SOUTH CASCADE

0   Kilometer   0.25

0   Mile   0.25

N

Rockcastle

44

P

3497

3497

Goodin Branch

Ike Branch

Lakeside South Trail

Lake Cumberland

Chimney

DANIEL BOONE
NATIONAL FOREST

Clark Bottom Road

Cabin enclave

Lakeside
South Cascade

Lakeside South Trail

stream then slides to make a smaller drop. From there the unnamed watercourse sla-loms toward Lake Cumberland, flowing over the trail and continuing to splash and dash until its waters join the impoundment.

You may notice cabins in the area of the waterfall. This is a private enclave of secondary dwellings accessed from Clark Bottom Road. From this point the Lakeside South Trail continues along the shoreline, crossing the cabin enclave access road about a half-mile from the waterfall before continuing on to meet the Twin Branch Trail and the Ned Branch Trail. Using these three trails, you can cobble together a reward-ing 8.5-mile loop hike that returns you to the boater parking area where you started.

Miles and Directions

0.0 Leave the Rockcastle boater parking area on Lake Cumberland. Backtrack on KY 3497, ascending away from Rockcastle Campground

0.3 Leave KY 3497 and join the Lakeside South Trail. Circle out of the hollow of Goodin Branch and run parallel to Lake Cumberland southwesterly.

0.7 Turn into the hollow of Ike Branch. Note the sizable beech trees here.

1.4 Pass a trailside rock chimney. Soon curve with a big bend and continue at a southeasterly orientation.

2.0 Work around a small hollow.

2.2 Reach 12-foot Lakeside South Cascade dropping above the trail. Backtrack to the trailhead.

4.4 Arrive back at the trailhead, completing the waterfall hike.

45 Ned Branch Falls

This hike starts at a popular recreation area in the Daniel Boone National Forest. The adventure first meanders up the Rockcastle River arm of Lake Cumberland before turning into Ned Branch, a deep backwoods valley with everywhere-you-look beauty. Here you will find a tributary of Ned Branch spilling over the stone rim of a layered cliff line. Consider combining your waterfall hike with other activities such as swimming, fishing, or camping—and visiting other nearby waterfalls.

Waterfall height: 14 feet
Waterfall beauty: 3
Distance: 3-mile out-and-back
Difficulty: Easy
Hiking time: About 1.4 hours
Trail surface: Asphalt then natural
Other trail users: None
Canine compatibility: Leashed pets allowed

Land status: National forest
Fees and permits: None
Maps: Daniel Boone National Forest, South Section; USGS Sawyer
Trail contact: Daniel Boone National Forest, London Ranger District, 761 S. Laurel Rd., London 40744; (606) 864-4163; www.fs.usda .gov/dbnf

Finding the trailhead: From exit 38 on I-75 near London, head west on KY 192 for 14 miles to KY 1193. Turn left on KY 1193, and follow it 1 mile to KY 3497. Turn right on KY 3497, and follow it 6 miles to reach the large boat ramp parking area just before entering Rockcastle Campground. Do not park in the campground. GPS: N36° 57.643' / W84° 21.164'

The Hike

The valley of Ned Branch is one of those places that make you glad much of Kentucky's portion of the Cumberland Plateau was preserved in its natural state as part of the Daniel Boone National Forest. This tributary of the Rockcastle River boasts not only a waterfall but also incredibly luxurious flora of rhododendron, mosses, and hemlock overlain upon geological features of steep cliffs, massive boulders, and sheer bluffs. The waters of Ned Branch, where they still in pools, exude an emerald color that adds an additional touch of green that would make an Irishman proud.

Ned Branch is also where I saw the biggest black bear I have ever seen in Kentucky, and thus became emblazoned in my memory. I was walking up the trail near the embayment of Ned Branch and spotted a black bear sniffing around some leaves. I was downwind and watched the 250-plus-pound bruin snorkeling around undetected for a couple of minutes. The animal's sixth sense must have finally noted my presence, for it stood up and looked at me for a few seconds—maybe a few too many seconds—before turning the other way and disappearing behind an enormous boulder. Unfortunately, the light was such that I could not get a good picture. C'est la vie.

This delicate spiller faucets down directly beside the trail.

The hike first passes through Rockcastle Campground, stretched along the shore of Lake Cumberland. The campsites are cut into the hillsides and accessed from the campground road via stairs and steps, making it a tent camper's paradise. Along the way you will pass by the Scuttle Hole trail system, home to 60-foot Dutch Branch Falls and detailed in this guide. As you walk through the campground, look for your favorite site.

Begin the Ned Branch Trail at the end of the campground turnaround road. You quickly curve into the still-water embayment of Ned Branch. The hollow tightens as you cut deeper into the valley, where tall trees rise among big boulders. You then hear Ned Branch gurgling over rocks and stilling in emerald pools. After bridging the stream, you will turn up the creek. In places the path rises well above the watercourse, navigating its way above steep cliff lines. Mountain laurel, rhododendron, and other vegetation flanks the pathway. It isn't long before you turn a corner and hear the splashing sounds of Ned Branch Falls. Here the unnamed tributary of Ned Branch makes its play, splashing from a rock rim directly beside the trail into a shallow pool.

You cannot miss the waterfall—unless the water isn't falling, or is merely trickling. If you want to extend the hike, continue up Ned Branch or hike along the Lakeside North Trail. It travels along the east bank of the Rockcastle River arm of Lake

NED BRANCH FALLS

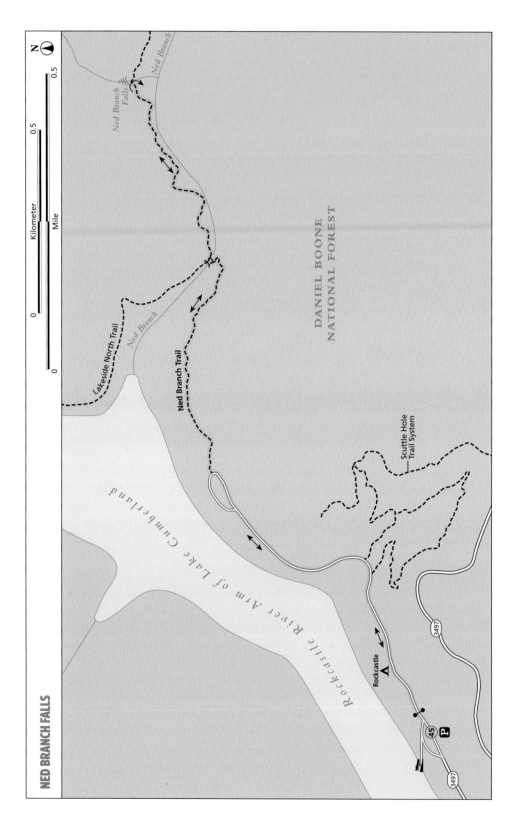

Ned Branch Falls

Ned Branch

Lakeside North Trail

Ned Branch

Ned Branch Trail

Rockcastle River Arm of Lake Cumberland

DANIEL BOONE
NATIONAL FOREST

Scuttle Hole
Trail System

Rockcastle

3497

45
P

3497

N

Kilometer
0   0.5   0.5

Mile
0   0.5

Cumberland. While here you can walk to the waterfalls of the Scuttle Hole and also visit Lakeside South Cascade.

Miles and Directions

0.0 Leave north from the boat ramp parking area. Hike along the asphalt Rockcastle Campground road, shaded by tall trees. Look for favored walk-in tent campsites beside the road.

0.3 Pass two paths connecting to the campground road, part of the Scuttle Hole nature trails. These trails have waterfalls of their own.

0.6 Reach the campground turnaround road. At this point join the singletrack Ned Branch Trail, entering woods. Quickly come to bridge a small stream, gradually curving into the Ned Branch valley.

1.1 Come to Ned Branch and a trail bridge nestled among massive boulders. Cross the bridge and reach a trail intersection. Here the Lakeside North Trail heads left, dead-ending after 3/4 mile. Turn right into the Ned Branch valley, where the mountain stream bordered by big boulders in repose lies below regal cliff lines, shaded by lush forest. Ahead, cross a couple of small tributaries rising well above Ned Branch.

1.5 Turn a corner and come to Ned Branch Falls, a tributary stream decanting 14 feet from a stone lip and landing in a small pool directly beside the trail. Backtrack to the trailhead.

3.0 Arrive back at the trailhead, completing the waterfall hike.

46 Falls of the Scuttle Hole

This highlight-filled short hike not only features 60-foot Dutch Branch Falls, but also offers a few lesser cascades plus three eye-opening overlooks of the river gorge of Lake Cumberland. Geological wonderments, from majestic cliff lines to a stone channel through which Dutch Branch flows before diving off a ledge, form the centerpiece cataract of this engaging Daniel Boone National Forest hike.

Waterfall height: In order, 12 feet, 5 feet, 60 feet, 6 feet
Waterfall beauty: 5
Distance: 2.7-mile lollipop loop
Difficulty: Moderate
Hiking time: About 1.5 hours
Trail surface: Natural
Other trail users: None
Canine compatibility: Leashed pets allowed

Land status: National forest
Fees and permits: None
Maps: Daniel Boone National Forest, South Section; USGS Sawyer
Trail contact: Daniel Boone National Forest, London Ranger District, 761 S. Laurel Rd., London 40744; (606) 864-4163; www.fs.usda .gov/dbnf

Finding the trailhead: From exit 38 on I-75 near London, head west on KY 192 for 14 miles to KY 1193. Turn left on KY 1193, and follow it 1 mile to KY 3497. Turn right on KY 3497, and follow it 5.1 miles to the Scuttle Hole trailhead on your right. GPS: N36° 57.632' / W84° 20.897'

The Hike

The waterfalls on this hike—especially Dutch Branch Falls—give reason enough and more to visit this neck of the woods. However, other highlights await, namely the views of Lake Cumberland, where the stilled waters of the Cumberland River and the Rockcastle River merge. The Daniel Boone National Forest recognized this special area and laid out a nature trail system that will leave you a happy waterfall hiker—with additional benefits.

The trailhead, located on a turn in KY 3497, lends no indication of what lies below, in the valley of Dutch Branch. You join the Scuttle Hole Trail as it dips to quickly meet Dutch Branch in thick hemlock, mountain laurel, and rhododendron woods. The stream slides down a smooth rock channel backed by a parallel low cliff line. You are then cruising directly down the stream channel with cliff lines rising on both sides of the trail and creek, complemented with a little slide cascade!

Next thing you know the trail is taking you along the high cliff line over which Dutch Branch Falls makes its maneuver, free-falling 60 feet into a semicircular rock amphitheater. You cannot see the waterfall from here, but you can hear it. Hang on and you will get the opportunity to admire Dutch Branch Falls in its fullness. Ahead the Dutch Branch valley opens, and you can see this from the gorge rim.

Two streams meet to form a multifaceted cataract.

You then reach the junction to cut through the Scuttle Hole to the falls, but for now stay right, heading out to the panoramas. It isn't long before reaching the first developed overlook, marked with stonework and a fence. Gaze to the west, with the Dutch Branch valley to your left and the Rockcastle River arm of Lake Cumberland in the distance. Two more overlooks lie ahead, the last of which allows the most expansive view, including across the Rockcastle River embayment to sheer stone cliffs.

After backtracking you then drop through the Scuttle Hole, where stone steps take you through a break in the cliff line. Admire the geology while scuttling down toward Dutch Branch. Just ahead, listen for the first waterfall just below a trail bridge crossing a tributary of Dutch Branch. The Dutch Branch watershed is small, so this and the other spillers here can become trickles by late summer and fall. However, if the water is flowing you can circle below this 12-foot cataract framed in moss, rock, and rhododendron.

You then turn up Dutch Branch, bridging the stream near a small cascade, then ascend sharply, bordered by boulders on one side and Dutch Branch on the other, gurgling unseen amid its own boulders and thickets of rhododendron. Ahead a side trail leads to 60-foot Dutch Branch Falls, pirouetting from the high cliff circling the

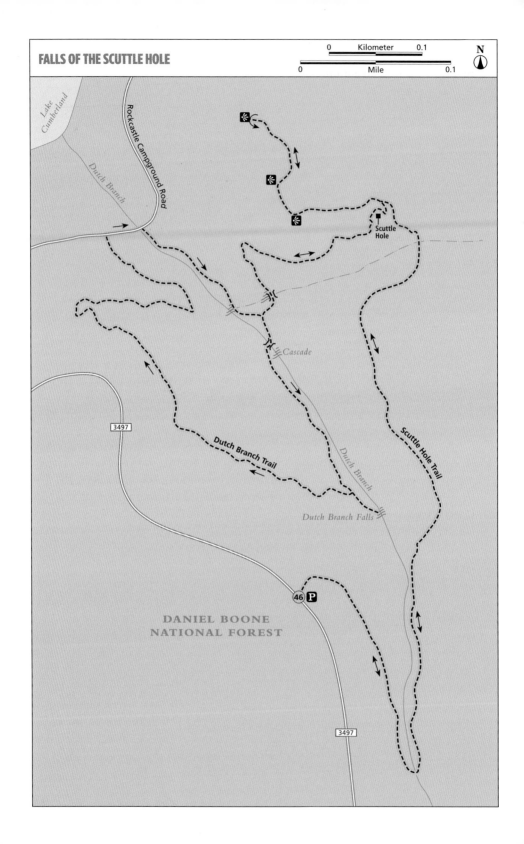

FALLS OF THE SCUTTLE HOLE

0 Kilometer 0.1
0 Mile 0.1

N

Lake Cumberland

Rockcastle Campground Road

Dutch Branch

Scuttle Hole

3497

Cascade

Dutch Branch Trail

Dutch Branch

Scuttle Hole Trail

Dutch Branch Falls

46 P

DANIEL BOONE
NATIONAL FOREST

3497

defile below. Dutch Branch Falls flows best from winter through spring and will reduce to a trickle in autumn.

Continue exploring the Dutch Branch valley, heading along a glorious cliff line rising overhead. The trail then switchbacks down to Rockcastle Campground, where Dutch Branch flows under the campground road. From here, climb the Dutch Branch Trail, passing an interesting cascade where Dutch Branch and a tributary merge.

After this, it is time to climb back through the Scuttle Hole and back to the trailhead, after enjoying not only waterfalls but also geological and visual highlights that demonstrate Kentucky hiking at its best.

Miles and Directions

0.0 Leave the Scuttle Hole trailhead on KY 3497. Join a singletrack path descending gently to Dutch Branch, swaddled in evergreens. Cross Dutch Branch and turn downstream as the creek flows along a low channel-like cliff line.

0.3 Come to the top of a high cliff line, the precipice from which Dutch Branch tumbles 60 feet into an overhanging, echoing amphitheater of rock. You can't see anything but the top of the falls from here. Keep hiking along the rim of the Dutch Branch gorge. Views open of the widening Dutch Branch valley.

0.6 Reach a trail intersection. For now, stay right toward the overlooks before returning to this intersection and visiting the waterfalls. Soon pass the first two developed overlooks.

0.8 Reach the final overlook. The Rockcastle River arm of Lake Cumberland opens before you, including cliffs above the embayment of Pole Bridge Branch. Savor the scenery then backtrack.

1.0 Descend through the Scuttle Hole on stone steps. Pass an inspiring rock house to the right of the trail.

1.1 Intersect the Dutch Branch Trail, which has come up from Rockcastle Campground. Turn left, climbing along Dutch Branch. Just ahead, span Dutch Branch near a small cascade and continue to climb.

1.2 Reach a trail intersection and head left toward Dutch Branch Falls on a spur trail. Ahead you will meet the amphitheater of stone into which Dutch Branch nosedives into a rock heap. Photograph the falls from different angles and walk behind the cataract before backtracking to the intersection.

1.3 Resume the Dutch Branch Trail, and hike in the shadows of a monumental cliff line. During leafless times, scan across the Dutch Branch valley to find the developed overlooks.

1.6 Descend from the cliff line on switchbacks.

1.8 Come to Rockcastle Campground. Walk just a few feet on the road to bridge Dutch Branch via culvert. Turn right and join the Dutch Branch Trail. Climb the narrow path in a steep vale to find a cascade where Dutch Branch and a tributary merge.

1.9 Come to a trail intersection. You were here before. From here, work your way up through the Scuttle Hole, now backtracking.

2.7 Arrive back at KY 3497 and the trailhead, completing the exciting hike.

47 Cascades of Bark Camp Creek

Bark Camp Creek features a well-known tier of cascades dropping 20 feet and also a pair of seasonal tributary falls. In addition to these spillers, the valley of Bark Camp Creek is one of the most stunning sites in the Bluegrass State, with everywhere-you-look beauty. You can turn the recommended out-and-back hike into a lollipop loop, availing a side trip to a trail shelter, a wildflower-filled flat, and another look at Bark Camp Creek, but it does require an unbridged crossing of the creek.

Waterfall height: In order, 40 feet, 45 feet, 20 feet

Waterfall beauty: 4

Distance: 5.2-mile out-and-back

Difficulty: Moderate

Hiking time: About 2.7 hours

Trail surface: Natural

Other trail users: None

Canine compatibility: Leashed pets allowed

Land status: National forest

Fees and permits: None

Maps: Daniel Boone National Forest, South Section; USGS Sawyer

Trail contact: Daniel Boone National Forest, London Ranger District, 761 S. Laurel Rd., London 40744; (606) 864-4163; www.fs.usda .gov/dbnf

Finding the trailhead: From exit 25 on I-75 near Corbin, take US 25W south for 4.7 miles and turn right onto KY 1193 north. Follow KY 1193 north for 4.6 miles, then continue straight on Bee Creek Road. Follow Bee Creek Road for 1.2 miles, then turn left onto FR 193. Follow FR 193 for 1.8 miles to reach the Bark Camp trailhead on your right at a curve before FR 193 spans Bark Camp Creek by culvert. GPS: N36° 54.282' / W84° 16.854'

The Hike

The cascades of Bark Camp Creek consist of a series of wide, tiered cataracts on lower Bark Camp Creek just prior to its confluence with the Cumberland River. Additionally, you will find a pair of tributary cataracts spilling over the rim of the Bark Camp Creek gorge, creating low-flow, high-drama spillers that add more waterfall beauty to a hike through a superlatively scenic valley. Being on the Cumberland Plateau, it is no surprise that you will enjoy an outstanding geological presence on the adventure. You will view colossal boulders in regal repose, pendulous bluffs flanking the stream valley, and rock houses sheltering forested flats. However, the abundance of rock adds difficulty to the hike, as you work your way through the stony maze.

You may want to extend your hike by making a loop that requires a bridgeless crossing of Bark Camp Creek. You can then take a side trip to the Bark Camp trail shelter and flowery flats along the Cumberland River. Next, you can return past Bark Camp Creek Cascades and complete the loop using a trail bridge to cross back over Bark Camp Creek.

The gorgeous scenery starts instantaneously. Curve downstream, entering a magical melding of flora, water, and geology. Cliff lines rise overhead, rhododendron forms green thickets, and bestilled boulders stand in and around Bark Camp Creek, adding its alluring flow. The path undulates its way through the attractive obstacle course, coming near and distant to Bark Camp Creek. Watch for deep pools creating potential swimming holes when you are near the creek, and scan for little yellow sand beaches and small wooded islands in the creek. The flow of Bark Camp Creek increases below the confluence with Grassy Branch. The trail wanders through a relatively large flat near this confluence.

Faucet Falls splashes beside the trail as you are walking along an overhanging cliff line with boulder rubble beneath it. Here an unnamed tributary of Bark Camp Creek makes a 40-foot straight drop over the cliff into a mix of rubble and vegetation. This seasonal stream can nearly dry up in late summer and autumn.

The waterfall known as Stairstep Veil lies just ahead. It is similar to Faucet Falls in that it also spills from a cliff line, along which you are walking. Stairstep Veil is also a

The famed ledges of Bark Camp Creek bathed in autumn glory.

Stairstep Veil bounces down ledges before making its free-fall.

low-flow cascade. However, there is a difference. Stairstep Veil, located along a curve of the cliff line, first tumbles in several short steps over stone ledges then makes the big dive from the cliff line, dropping a total of 45 feet. Stairstep Veil also makes a wider drop than Faucet Falls.

Beyond the two tributary falls, the hike winds westerly as Bark Camp Creek tries to find a seam to cut through the Cumberland Plateau. The Bark Camp Creek Trail meets the Sheltowee Trace at a metal hiker bridge. Here the Sheltowee Trace makes its crossing of Bark Camp Creek, while our hike stays on the north bank of the creek, as it has thus far. The former Sheltowee Trace bridge was below Bark Camp Creek Cascades and suffered from regular flood-caused washouts, but this replacement bridge is better located for long-term survival. It stands atop two boulders on either side of the creek, with an additional connecting bridge segment on the south side of the creek.

The trail winds through mountain laurel and thick tree cover along the creek. Look for lesser waterslides and rapids. Then the louder roar of Bark Camp Cascades rings into your ears. Here the three primary waterfall tiers—divided by pools—make their drop as Bark Camp Creek heads toward the Cumberland River. Flat rock slabs below and alongside the cascades make for easy hanging out and photography spots. It's a great place to linger.

A trail intersection is just beyond the cascades. Here the Sheltowee Trace Alternate Flood Route leaves right and the Sheltowee Trace keeps straight, onward down the Cumberland River. To the left, the old Sheltowee Trace bridge once went over Bark Camp Creek—look for the abutments. When Bark Camp Creek is at normal to low levels, you can cross the stream at the former bridge site and make a loop. If you can cross the creek, rejoin the Sheltowee Trace southbound to take a spur to Bark Camp trail shelter. The Adirondack-style wood shelter opens in front to a flat full of wildflowers in spring. An imposing cliff line rises behind the shelter.

From the shelter you can backtrack to the old bridge site and head up the south bank of Bark Camp Creek on the Sheltowee Trace, rising well above the stream before returning to the metal bridge then backtracking up Bark Camp Creek.

Miles and Directions

0.0 Leave the trailhead on FR 193. Hike westerly down the valley of Bark Camp Creek, flowing to your left. Black birch and hemlock rise overhead. Reach the first cliff line almost immediately.

0.4 Meet a rockfall arch. Here the Bark Camp Trail leads beneath a fallen boulder flanked by a cliff line and another boulder, creating a rock roof. Beyond there, shoot through a narrow passage betwixt a deep pool and a cliff.

0.9 Reach slim 40-foot Faucet Falls after walking along cliff lines and under a huge overhanging boulder.

1.1 Come to 45-foot Stairstep Veil, another low-flow waterfall that dances down stair-step ledges to then plummet onto sodden rocks.

CASCADES OF BARK CAMP CREEK

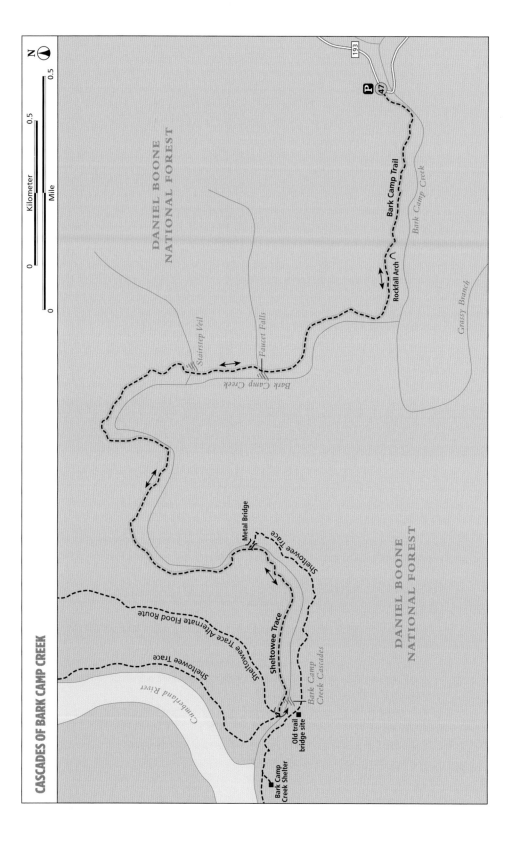

DANIEL BOONE
NATIONAL FOREST

DANIEL BOONE
NATIONAL FOREST

Stairstep Veil

Faucet Falls

Bark Camp Creek

Rockfall Arch

Bark Camp Trail

Bark Camp Creek

Grassy Branch

Metal Bridge

Sheltowee Trace

Sheltowee Trace

Sheltowee Trace Alternate Flood Route

Bark Camp Creek Cascades

Old trail bridge site

Bark Camp Creek Shelter

Cumberland River

193

47

P

N

Kilometer
0   0.5

Mile
0   0.5

2.2 Intersect the Sheltowee Trace at a bridge over Bark Camp Creek. Keep straight, not crossing the bridge.

2.6 Come to the primary tiers of the Bark Camp Creek Cascades to your left. Just ahead, reach a trail intersection. Here the Sheltowee Trace Alternate Flood Route leaves right while the Sheltowee Trace keeps straight. If you want to make a 5.8-mile lollipop loop, head left here, crossing at the site of the former Sheltowee Trace bridge, then visit Bark Camp shelter and return on the Sheltowee Trace. Otherwise, backtrack to the trailhead.

5.2 Arrive back at the trailhead, completing the waterfall hike.

48 Star Creek Falls, Dog Slaughter Falls

This gorgeous hike visits waterways big and small as well as waterfalls big and small. Start by hiking down the scenic Dog Slaughter Creek valley to visit iconic Dog Slaughter Falls, a 20-foot classic spiller ensconced within geological amazement for which the Daniel Boone National Forest is known. From there turn down the brawling Cumberland River on the Sheltowee Trace amid big trees, bigger boulders, and scrappy rapids to find delicate, ribbonlike, 70-foot Star Creek Falls and the Star Creek backcountry shelter.

Waterfall height: In order, 20 feet, 70 feet
Waterfall beauty: 5
Distance: 7.6-mile out-and-back
Difficulty: Moderate to difficult
Hiking time: About 4 hours
Trail surface: Natural
Other trail users: None
Canine compatibility: Leashed pets allowed

Land status: National forest
Fees and permits: None
Maps: Daniel Boone National Forest, South Section; USGS Cumberland Falls, Sawyer
Trail contact: Daniel Boone National Forest, London Ranger District, 761 S. Laurel Rd., London 40744; (606) 864-4163; www.fs.usda.gov/dbnf

Finding the trailhead: From exit 25 near Corbin, take US 25W south for 7.5 miles to KY 90. Veer right onto KY 90 west for 2.2 miles to reach FR 195. Follow FR 195 for 3 miles to the lower Dog Slaughter Creek Trail parking on your left heading downhill as FR 195 curves right. GPS: N36° 51.558' / W84° 17.986'

The Hike

This is a scenic waterfall hike through ruggedly beautiful terrain in the Daniel Boone National Forest. The trails are correspondingly challenging, especially as you negotiate cliff lines, bluffs, and boulder fields. Dog Slaughter Falls—20 feet of Kentucky pride—is a classic Bluegrass State spiller set in the wilds of the Cumberland River gorge, on a Cumberland River tributary of the same intriguing name.

Star Creek Falls is also on a tributary of the Cumberland River, though it has much lower flow than does Dog Slaughter Falls. However, Star Creek Falls is a dramatic tall fall, hurtling a full 70 feet from its stony heights, first down a stratified rock ledge then making a free-fall to land in a rock atrium. Star Creek Falls is a lesser-visited destination and requires a short bushwhack from the trail. However, watery noise will alert you to its presence and you can enjoy the falls without too much trouble.

The hike first follows South Fork Dog Slaughter Creek downstream in a richly wooded vale heavy with evergreens infiltrated with big mossy boulders, imposing cliff lines, and overhanging rock houses. North Fork Dog Slaughter Creek merges

Dog Slaughter Falls as seen through adjacent rhododendron thickets.

with South Fork to form Dog Slaughter Creek. The streamside scenery continues to be among Kentucky's finest landscapes. You'll curve along Dog Slaughter Creek then gain a top-down view of Dog Slaughter Falls as it spills over a rock rim. Don't approach the falls from here. For starters, you can't get much of a view, and secondly, it is a dangerous proposition. Continue with the trail as it cruises along a stone brow before cutting through a break in the cliff line to turn into the alcove where Dog Slaughter Falls can be viewed in its full glory. The pour-over spills from a horizontal rim into a dark plunge pool framed by an overhanging cliff and bordered by big boulders on one side and lesser rocks on the other. Photography angles are numerous and easy to reach. Linger a while before you head on.

The lower Dog Slaughter Creek valley is rugged to the extreme, to which the hike attests. Work over rocks and boulders to meet the Sheltowee Trace. You are now officially along the mighty Cumberland River. The Sheltowee Trace bridges Dog Slaughter Creek above an incredible boulder jumble through which the creek flows.

Begin cruising downstream along the Cumberland River, singing in broken shoals as it works around midstream boulders. This part of the riverbank faces southwest; therefore, oaks, dogwoods, and pines border the sandy trail. The vegetation changes to rhododendron, hemlock, and beech as the river curves to face northwest. You are still wandering a geological fairyland, including a picture-worthy rockfall arch.

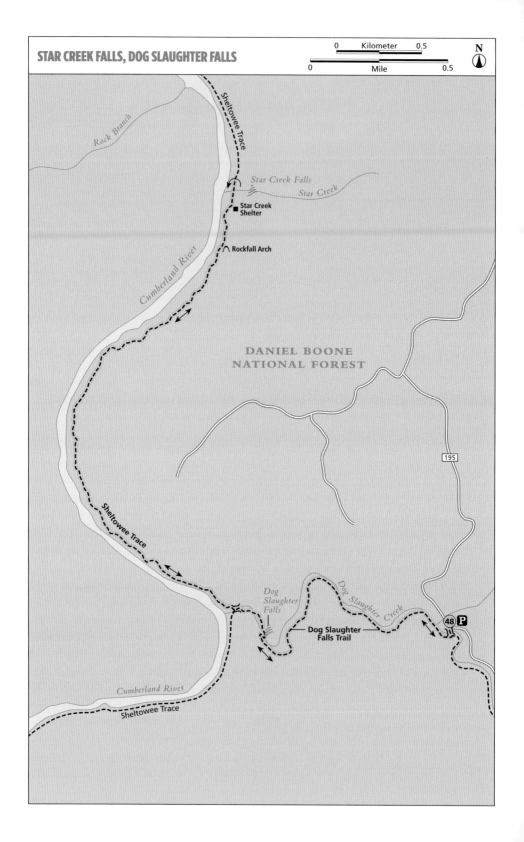

Kilometer

Mile

N

Rock Branch

Sheltowee Trace

Star Creek Falls

Star Creek

Star Creek Shelter

Rockfall Arch

Cumberland River

DANIEL BOONE NATIONAL FOREST

195

Sheltowee Trace

Dog Slaughter Falls

Dog Slaughter Creek

Dog Slaughter Falls Trail

48

P

Cumberland River

Sheltowee Trace

You will also pass the Star Creek trail shelter before reaching Star Creek Falls. The three-sided Adirondack–style camping refuge has a fire ring and is open in the front. This is a good break spot even if you are not backpacking. After passing the shelter, begin to seriously look for Star Creek Falls. Ahead, you will come to Star Creek (it crosses the trail). To your right, falling off a high rock ledge, pours forth Star Creek Falls. A manway leads to the base of the spiller, bucketing stage by stage over a stone face then free-falling to splash a rock field below. At low flows this cataract will be less impressive, but it makes a fine waterfall hike destination nonetheless. Enjoy your return trip among many an enchanting scene within the Daniel Boone National Forest.

Miles and Directions

0.0 Leave FR 195 then immediately drop to a streamside flat. Join a wood hiker bridge crossing South Fork Dog Slaughter Creek. Intersect the Dog Slaughter Falls Trail and turn right, heading downstream among boulders.

0.4 The Dog Slaughter Trail curves around a tributary. Cliff lines and rock shelters lie ahead as the trail undulates along Dog Slaughter Creek, where massive boulders lie in repose midstream.

0.7 Look down on a big pool bordered with kingly pillars.

1.1 Step over a tributary of Dog Slaughter Creek.

1.2 Grab a downhill view of Dog Slaughter Falls after making a big bend on Dog Slaughter Creek.

1.3 Come face to face with 20-foot Dog Slaughter Falls as it executes a curtain drop beneath a rock house. Soak in the scene then continue downstream.

1.4 Intersect the Sheltowee Trace and turn right to use an angled hiker bridge to cross Dog Slaughter Creek. From the bridge look toward the Cumberland River over a dreadful and chaotic boulder jumble, then head downstream along the crashing Cumberland.

2.2 The Sheltowee Trace bridges a small stream.

3.1 Come along a cliff line below which the trail travels for a full quarter-mile.

3.5 Hike beneath an unmistakable rockfall arch, where two boulders stand perched atop two larger boulders.

3.7 A very short spur leads right to the Star Creek shelter, an open-fronted wood structure complemented by a fire ring. The shelter faces the Cumberland River. Begin to listen for Star Creek Falls beyond the shelter.

3.8 Come to Star Creek and walk right up a manway a short distance to already audible and partly visible Star Creek Falls. Backtrack to the trailhead.

7.6 Arrive back at the trailhead, completing the hike.

49 Waterfalls of the Cumberland River Gorge

This hike takes you not only to two of Kentucky's most notable cataracts, but also to four other named waterfalls in the wild and beautiful Cumberland River gorge. The trek first leads to big, brawling Cumberland Falls, a popular area featuring several designated overlooks of the 65-foot "Niagara of the South." Continue down the Cumberland River gorge, where several lesser-known waterfalls set in a geological wonderland await. Finally, find Dog Slaughter Falls tucked away in a rugged vale, making its curtain spill into a stone-bordered pool.

Waterfall height: In order, 67 feet, 30 feet, 20 feet, 10 feet, 12 feet, 20 feet
Waterfall beauty: 5+
Distance: 7-mile out-and-back
Difficulty: Moderate to difficult
Hiking time: About 3.8 hours
Trail surface: Concrete on first half-mile, natural rest of way
Other trail users: None

Canine compatibility: Leashed pets allowed
Land status: State park
Fees and permits: None
Maps: Cumberland Falls State Resort Park; USGS Cumberland Falls
Trail contact: Cumberland Falls State Resort Park, 7351 KY 90, Corbin 40701; (606) 528-4121; www.parks.ky.gov/parks/resortparks/cumberland-falls

Finding the trailhead: From exit 25 on I-75 near Corbin, take US 25W south for 7.5 miles to KY 90. Turn right and take KY 90 west for 8.3 miles, turning right into the large Cumberland Falls parking area before the bridge over the Cumberland River. GPS: N36° 50.2620' / W84° 20.6157'

The Hike

Not only can you see an array of waterfalls on this hike, but also experience the famed "moonbow" created by Cumberland Falls. The spray rising from the waterfall creates a moonbow, purportedly one of only two moonbows in the world. This occurs when a full moon shines on the waterfall's mist and creates the phenomenon, like how the sun creates a rainbow during daytime, a regular occurrence at Cumberland Falls in and of itself. Where this hike starts—Cumberland Falls State Resort Park—specifies the monthly dates and times of the moonbows (cloud cover notwithstanding) on their website.

This hike takes the park's Moonbow Trail (with which the Sheltowee Trace runs in conjunction) from the visitor center area on KY 90 to view the Bluegrass State's most powerful cataract bellowing from a horseshoe-shaped sandstone rim. The trail then explores the state-designated portion of the Cumberland that is a Kentucky Wild River, and boy does it live up to that name. A plentitude of waterfalls spill near

Dog Slaughter Falls as seen from its pool.

the trail, culminating in the visual highlight that is Dog Slaughter Falls (not to mention it is also on the top 10 all-time Kentucky waterfall names list).

The beginning of the hike is busy and developed. Scores of people regularly stop at Cumberland Falls, and the large parking area demonstrates that. Wander past the visitor center, gift shop, and other amenities to shortly reach Cumberland Falls. Here the entire flow of the Cumberland River drops 67 feet in a 125-foot-wide horseshoe-shaped curtain. This spray and mist and noise and vigor make Cumberland Falls one of Kentucky's natural wonders.

Multiple overlooks deliver different vantages of the cataract—from above, beside, and below. A concrete trail takes you downriver to Lovers Leap. The sometimes crowded spot delivers the best view of the falls. The area is centered by a memorial to Kentucky native T. Coleman DuPont. Mr. DuPont purchased Cumberland Falls and the adjoining tracts to then donate the land to the Commonwealth of Kentucky, creating the state park. The big river, big falls, big bluffs, and big gorge combine to create a big-time panorama.

Beyond this overlook, the hike leaves the crowds behind. You are now cruising the bottoms of the designated Kentucky Wild River, where enormous boulders line the now-narrower watercourse, creating sporadic rapids. The rocky terrain makes for slow travel as cliff lines rise overhead. Rock House Falls adds to the trailside beauty with its low-flow 30-foot drop. In places the bluffs recede and the Moonbow Trail/Sheltowee Trace cuts through bottomland where sand beaches gather along the Cumberland and river birch trees spread their limbs. The next cataract is Anvil Falls, a 20-foot slide cascade that disappears into a boulder field.

Continue in geological wonderment of cliffs, rock houses—even a rockfall arch. Pass Veil Cascade ahead. The delicate, 10-foot, curtain-type fall drops directly beside the trail. Beyond here the hike scenery mixes beaches and bouldery fields as it curves with the curve of the Cumberland River. You can't miss Catfish Creek Cascades, as it is located uphill from where the Moonbow Trail/Sheltowee Trace crosses Catfish Creek on a wooden hiker bridge. Look up Catfish Creek for the cataract spilling 12 feet over a rock face, then caroming amid mossy boulders before flowing under the bridge upon which you stand. It takes a little work to photograph the spiller. This bridge roughly marks your entrance into the Daniel Boone National Forest.

The scenery stays first-rate as you enter the valley of Dog Slaughter Creek. Wind among immense boulders and under rockhouses to reach Dog Slaughter Falls, making a wide, curtain-type, 20-foot dive into an alluring big plunge pool. Boulders and other rock perches make for multiple photography vantages. It's a cool place to hang out. Allow plenty of time to backtrack. I guarantee you will see additional beautiful sights on your return trip, executing one of Kentucky's best all-around waterfall hikes.

Miles and Directions

0.0 Leave the large parking area on KY 90. Walk past the visitor center to quickly reach the first overlook of Cumberland Falls. From there, walk downstream to curve under a cliff line

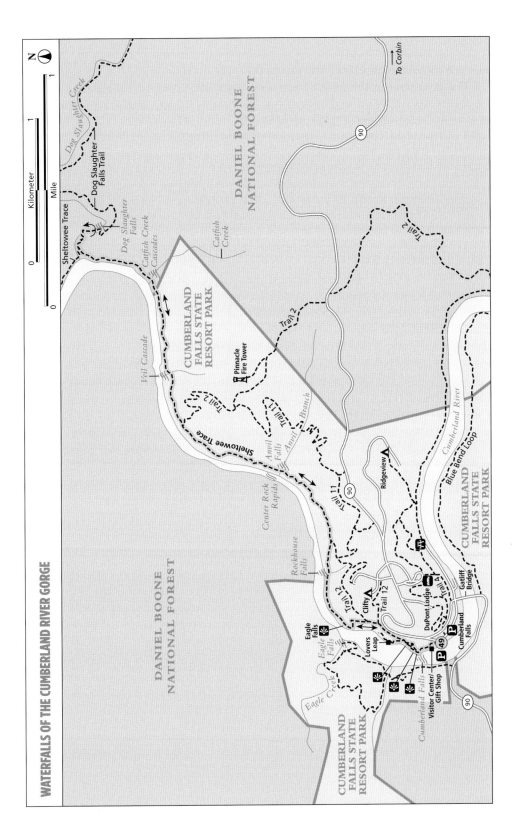

WATERFALLS OF THE CUMBERLAND RIVER GORGE

to a lower view of the falls. This viewpoint is close enough to the falls to get misted on. Resume downstream toward Lovers Leap view.

0.3 Reach Lovers Leap view. Enjoy the large-scale waterfall scene, then backtrack a little to pick up the Moonbow Trail/Sheltowee Trace. Pass a couple of quick intersections with Trail 12. Stay with the Moonbow Trail/ Sheltowee Trace.

0.7 A series of switchbacks and a staircase take you back to the Cumberland River bottoms. The crowds have been left behind. Ahead, look across the river for Eagle Falls. Course down the incredible Cumberland River gorge.

1.1 The trail splits right. Here the old abandoned part of the Sheltowee Trace once kept directly along the river. However, the current route goes underneath low-flow Rockhouse Falls, spilling 30 feet from the stone above. This is the first of the lesser falls between Cumberland Falls and Dog Slaughter Falls. Ahead, climb beyond a trail leading uphill into the park trail network before the Moonbow Trail/Sheltowee Trace returns back to the river, cruising bottoms and along bluffs.

1.6 Reach Anvil Falls, a 20-foot, low-flow slide cascade slipping down a ledge to disappear into a boulder field then flow as a creek under the trail. Just ahead, walk to a riverside boulder to see Center Rock Rapids, where the Cumberland loudly crashes white through a boulder jumble.

1.8 Walk under an immense rock house with a massive overhang.

1.9 Pass beneath a rockfall arch after dancing through boulders and a cliff line.

2.2 Reach a trail intersection. Here, Trail 2 leaves right. Keep on the Moonbow Trail/Sheltowee Trace.

2.5 Reach a delicate, 10-foot, curtain-type fall, Veil Cascade.

2.9 Cross a wooden bridge over Catfish Creek. Catfish Creek Cascades pours uphill above the bouldery part of the stream. Ahead, enter the Daniel Boone National Forest, leaving the state park and staying closer to the Cumberland River.

3.3 Turn right onto the Dog Slaughter Falls Trail. Dance among big boulders to enter the Dog Slaughter Creek valley.

3.5 Reach 20-foot Dog Slaughter Falls as it discharges over a stone rim into a boulder-bordered pool. Backtrack to the trailhead.

7.0 Arrive back at the trailhead, completing the hike.

50 Blue Bend Falls

This short trek at Cumberland Falls State Resort Park travels to one of the least heralded cascades in this waterfall-rich preserve. It starts at the popular Cumberland Falls parking area then crosses the Cumberland River on the Gatliff Bridge to join the Blue Bend Loop, a hiking trail traveling along the Cumberland River. The path explores the shoreline to reach a short spur to Blue Bend Falls, a 26-foot pour-over located in a narrow hollow. If the hike is too short, simply complete the 4.6-mile Blue Bend Loop, or visit many other nearby waterfalls at Cumberland Falls State Resort Park.

Waterfall height: 26 feet
Waterfall beauty: 3
Distance: 0.6-mile out-and-back
Difficulty: Easy
Hiking time: About 0.5 hour
Trail surface: Concrete at first, then natural
Other trail users: None
Canine compatibility: Leashed pets allowed

Land status: State park
Fees and permits: None
Maps: Cumberland Falls State Resort Park; USGS Cumberland Falls
Trail contact: Cumberland Falls State Resort Park, 7351 KY 90, Corbin 40701; (606) 528-4121; www.parks.ky.gov/parks/resortparks/cumberland-falls

Finding the trailhead: From exit 25 on I-75 near Corbin, take US 25W south for 7.5 miles to KY 90. Turn right and take KY 90 west for 8.3 miles, coming to the parking area for Cumberland Falls on your right just before KY 90 crosses the Gatliff Bridge over the Cumberland River. The parking area is very large. Park as close to the Gatliff Bridge as possible, away from the state park visitor center/gift shop. GPS: N36° 50.1938' / W84° 20.4411'

The Hike

This waterfall hike is located in the Blue Bend part of Cumberland Falls State Resort Park. This is also part of the Cumberland Falls State Park Nature Preserve. Rock houses, mossy boulders, and rare flora and fauna are protected within the 1,294-acre preserve. In the preserve you will also find wildflowers in spring, alluring riverside habitats—and waterfalls within this sanctuary of Bluegrass State splendor established in 1983.

Blue Bend Falls is located on an unnamed tributary of the Cumberland River, just upstream of Cumberland Falls and the Gatliff Bridge. The hike to Blue Bend Falls is straightforward. After parking at Cumberland Falls near the Gatliff Bridge, walk to KY 90 and the Gatliff Bridge. Carefully cross the river on the road bridge. Just after crossing the Cumberland River, you pick up the Blue Bend Loop, a singletrack hiking trail heading up the right bank of the river.

Looking up the hollow from which Blue Bend Falls makes its dive.

The Cumberland River is over 200 feet wide here and descending fast in shoals and rapids, precursors to Cumberland Falls below. The Blue Bend Loop wanders through lush woods with magnolia trees aplenty. After climbing a bit, the trail dips to the unnamed tributary where Blue Bend Falls is found. You will be able to hear and see the falls from the hiker bridge crossing the unnamed creek.

From the bridge, follow a user-created trail a short distance upstream to Blue Bend Falls. This low-flow cataract is at its best from winter through spring. Here the stream discharges 26 feet over a two-layered rock ledge into a crumby pile of rock. The upper drop is higher and wider, around 20 feet, then the stream makes a narrower 6-foot-or-so drop over a second ledge. Beyond the lower fall, the creek reforms then flows under the hiker bridge and on to the Cumberland River.

After visiting Blue Bend Falls, you can continue the Blue Bend Loop, returning after 4 more miles to KY 90 a little west of the Gatliff Bridge, or make the hike to nearby Eagle Falls and Cumberland Falls.

Miles and Directions

0.0   Leave the Cumberland Falls parking area. Walk to KY 90 then head south on the road, crossing the Gatliff Bridge over the Cumberland River.

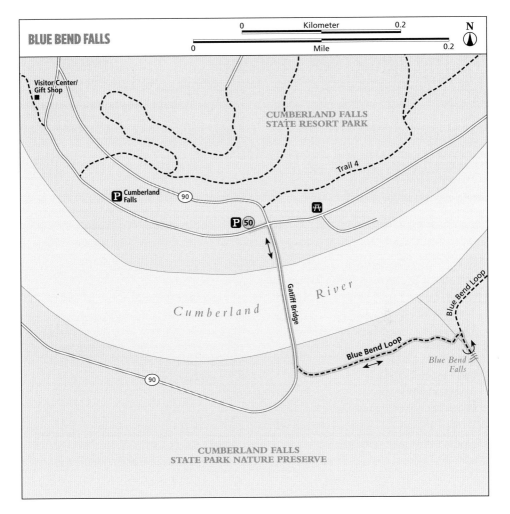

CUMBERLAND FALLS STATE RESORT PARK

Trail 4

Cumberland Falls

90

Visitor Center/ Gift Shop

Gatliff Bridge

Blue Bend Loop

Cumberland River

Blue Bend Loop

Blue Bend Falls

90

CUMBERLAND FALLS STATE PARK NATURE PRESERVE

0.1 Leave KY 90 left, joining the Blue Bend Loop (no parking here). Enter woods with the Cumberland River to your left. Climb away from the river a bit then descend.

0.3 Reach the wood hiker bridge over the unnamed stream forming Blue Bend Falls. Turn up the user-created trail to reach 26-foot Blue Bend Falls. Backtrack to the trailhead.

0.6 Arrive back at the trailhead, completing the hike.

51 Eagle Falls, Cumberland Falls, Eagle Creek Cascade

One of Kentucky's finest waterfall hikes, this triple waterfall adventure is exciting from the first step to the last. Powerful, thunderous, 67-foot Cumberland Falls; noble 40-foot Eagle Falls; and under-visited 10-foot Eagle Creek Cascade are served on the waterfall menu, along with vistas of the Cumberland River and its gorge enhancing the experience. First, see Cumberland Falls, a river-wide horseshoe-shaped cataract of muscle, mist, and magnificence. Trace cliff lines above the Cumberland River to reach river bottom, where Eagle Falls dives into a boulder-bordered pool. Walk up the rugged Eagle Creek watershed to find Eagle Creek Cascade and wooded hills. The balance of the hike loops you back to the trail, with a side trip to a historic overlook.

Waterfall height: In order, 67 feet, 40 feet, 10 feet

Waterfall beauty: 5

Distance: 2.2-mile lollipop loop with spurs

Difficulty: Moderate

Hiking time: About 1.3 hours

Trail surface: Natural

Other trail users: None

Canine compatibility: Leashed pets allowed

Land status: State park

Fees and permits: None

Maps: Cumberland Falls State Resort Park; USGS Cumberland Falls

Trail contact: Cumberland Falls State Resort Park, 7351 KY 90, Corbin 40701; (606) 528-4121; www.parks.ky.gov/parks/resortparks/cumberland-falls

Finding the trailhead: From exit 25 on I-75 near Corbin, take US 25W south for 7.5 miles to KY 90. Turn right and take KY 90 west for 8.4 miles, bridging the Cumberland River just above Cumberland Falls. From the bridge continue on KY 90 for 0.3 mile to reach the Eagle Falls trailhead on your right. GPS: N36° 50.210' / W84° 20.733'

The Hike

For a short hike of only 2.2 miles, you will find this trek challenging. The short distance, however, gives it a moderate rating. While chasing waterfalls you will climb and descend hills, use staircases, walk steps, and pick your way along sandy shores and boulder gardens. Do not be dissuaded—anyone can execute the hike with adequate time. Allow yet additional time to take pictures and videos of this trio of first-rate cataracts.

From the trailhead, the hike quickly saddles alongside the Cumberland River, just a short distance upstream of Cumberland Falls. The track squeezes past cliffs then climbs. Cumberland Falls is below, obscured by trees. Climb past an overlook, then join another cliff line where incredible upriver views of Cumberland Falls are among the finest vistas in the entire state. Here, Cumberland Falls brews up a 67-foot-high,

Majestic Cumberland Falls is the most powerful rumbler in the Bluegrass State.

125-foot-wide, hurtling vertical plunge, collapsing in spiraling spray. One look and you will see why Cumberland Falls is known as the "Niagara of the South."

Beyond here you begin the loop portion of the hike amid rugged terrain inside the gorge of the Cumberland, finally dipping to reach the Cumberland River, aided by steps and stairwells. The river bottom is uneven but picturesque. The path courses through boulders, sandbars, and brush before reaching 40-foot Eagle Falls. View Eagle Creek free-falling from a rock lip into a boulder-bordered basin. These rocks allow for multiple photography vantages of the spiller. Below the waterfall plunge pool, Eagle Creek gurgles through boulders then makes one last 6-foot drop before giving its waters up to the Cumberland River.

Explore Eagle Falls and the adjacent beach on the Cumberland River before backtracking to the loop portion of the hike where Eagle Creek dashes among rocks below rhododendron, evergreens, and ferns. Ahead, find Eagle Creek Cascade—a 10-foot angled slide fall, pouring over a slab of stone before ending in a final, vertical descent—on a bend in Eagle Creek.

The loop part of the hike shortly leaves Eagle Creek and climbs past a rock overhang en route to a hilltop. From here the trail dips along a hollow to finish out the circuit. At this point you can backtrack straight to the trailhead or take the spur to the historic overlook with the Civilian Conservation Corps (CCC) gazebo. The

Eagle Falls drops 40 feet into its boulder-bordered plunge pool.

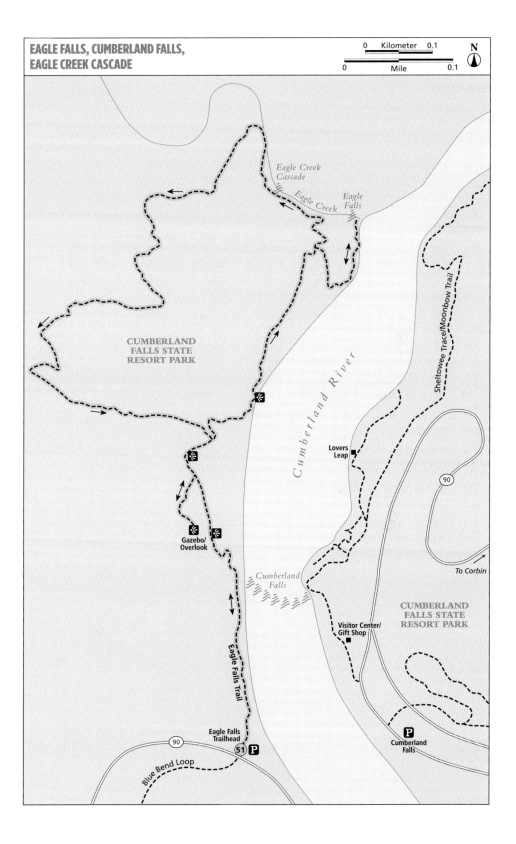

0   Kilometer   0.1

0   Mile   0.1

N

*Eagle Creek
Cascade*

Eagle Creek

*Eagle
Falls*

Sheltowee Trace/Moonbow Trail

CUMBERLAND
FALLS STATE
RESORT PARK

Cumberland River

Lovers
Leap

90

*Gazebo/
Overlook*

To Corbin

*Cumberland
Falls*

CUMBERLAND
FALLS STATE
RESORT PARK

Visitor Center/
Gift Shop

Eagle Falls Trail

Eagle Falls
Trailhead

90

51   P

Blue Bend Loop

P
Cumberland
Falls

CCC was a government works organization employing young men during the Great Depression of the 1930s, and they developed many of the trails and facilities here at Cumberland Falls State Resort Park. The overlook and gazebo are a fitting tribute to those men of yesteryear.

Miles and Directions

0.0   Join the Eagle Falls Trail, leaving KY 90 and working downstream. Pass warning signs about being swept over Cumberland Falls, which is already audible.

0.1   The trail comes fast against a dripping cliff line. Climb well above Cumberland Falls.

0.2   Squeeze under a rock overhang then reach a view of the Cumberland River gorge, downriver of the falls.

0.3   Reach a spur trail to a historic overlook of the Cumberland River gorge, complete with a gazebo constructed by the CCC in the 1930s. For now, keep straight with the Eagle Falls Trail, soon passing an incredible overlook of Cumberland Falls.

0.4   Step over a stream and come to the loop portion of the Eagle Falls Trail. Stay right here, continuing downstream along the Cumberland River. Stop by a second Cumberland Falls overlook ahead.

0.6   Reach another trail intersection. Head right here on the spur to Eagle Falls. Metal, stone, and wood steps lead down to the river bottom.

0.7   Come to 40-foot Eagle Falls. Here, the cataract pours curtain-style into a plunge pool bordered by boulders. Backtrack to the loop portion of the hike.

0.8   Resume the loop, now heading up Eagle Creek.

0.9   Reach Eagle Creek Cascade, a 10-foot slide fall located on a bend in Eagle Creek.

1.1   Pass by a rock shelter littered with stone debris.

1.3   Top out on a hill. Walk among pines and oaks before descending into a moist hollow.

1.5   Come alongside a Cumberland River tributary.

1.7   Finish the loop portion of the hike. Backtrack.

1.8   Head right up wooden steps aplenty to reach an overlook and a wooden gazebo built by the CCC. Backtrack to the trailhead.

2.2   Arrive back at the trailhead, completing the hike.

52 Yahoo Falls, Roaring Rocks Cataract

This hike amid a nest of nature trails takes you to Kentucky's highest waterfall—Yahoo Falls—plus a few other highlights, including Roaring Rocks Cataract, set inside the Big South Fork National River and Recreation Area. First, walk to the base of the 113-foot-high spiller that is Yahoo Falls, then circle past veiled Roaring Rocks Cataract. Climb to the rim of the cliff line over which Yahoo Falls spills, gaining top-down views of Yahoo Falls before returning to the trailhead.

Waterfall height: In order, 113 feet, 30 feet
Waterfall beauty: 5
Distance: 1.3-mile lollipop loop with a spur
Difficulty: Easy
Hiking time: About 1 hour
Trail surface: Mostly natural
Other trail users: None
Canine compatibility: Leashed pets allowed

Land status: National river and recreation area
Fees and permits: None
Maps: National Geographic #241 Big South Fork; USGS Nevelsville
Trail contact: Big South Fork National River and Recreation Area, 4564 Leatherwood Rd., Oneida 37841; (423) 286-7275; www.nps.gov/biso

Finding the trailhead: From the intersection of KY 700 and US 27 just north of Whitely City, take KY 700 west for 3.9 miles and turn right onto Yahoo Falls Road. Follow it for 1.5 miles to reach a restroom and parking area for Yahoo Falls at the lower end of the parking area loop road. The trail starts on your right. GPS: N36° 46.424' / W84° 31.455'

The Hike

Yahoo Falls is located in a nest of nature trails at what is known as the Yahoo Falls Scenic Area, part of the Big South Fork National River and Recreation Area. This is a scenic designation–worthy parcel of the Bluegrass State, some of the best of the best, where nature's splendor is concentrated in one spot.

There's only one little problem—the mazelike network of trails can be confusing. But even if you get lost (if you are a man, of course, you won't be lost, you will just be briefly "turned around"), you will see some of the sights for which the area is known: the overlook of the Big South Fork, metal stairs descending a cliff, an immense rock house occupied by aboriginal Kentuckians, a garden of massive boulders, and, of course, the waterfalls themselves. Ambitious hikers can also make a side trip to Yahoo Arch, a stone span located on a spur trail linking to the Yahoo Falls Scenic Area.

Your best bet to stay with your position is to study the map in this guide and take a picture of the map at the trailhead with your phone. And even if you don't follow this hike exactly, you will find the waterfalls quite rewarding—after all, Yahoo Falls is Kentucky's highest cataract.

Leave the trailhead on the signed path toward Yahoo Falls. Soon take the short spur left to an overlook of the Big South Fork. Here the river bends left near its confluence with Yahoo Creek. Enjoy this perspective then reach the loop portion of the hike. Here you descend an incredible metal stairwell down a steep bluff. Once at the base of the cliff line, begin heading toward Yahoo Falls, echoing in the immense semicircular rock house ahead, below which grows junglesque flora. Aboriginals used this considerable rock house in pre-Columbian days.

Yahoo Falls makes its long dive from an overhanging ledge, a slender curtain of white landing on rocks before gathering in a shallow pool. The 113-foot falls and enormous shelter fashion an outstanding waterfall picture. The official trail leads beneath the rock house and behind Yahoo Falls, then works behind a boulder jumble. Waterfall photography angles open all along the trail and in front of the falls. Work your way to Yahoo Creek, where gargantuan boulders seem to block the trail. The path keeps upstream on the creek, squeezing amid the boulders.

The walking becomes easy again as you cruise up along Yahoo Creek then come to Roaring Rocks Cataract. The 30-foot faucet-like waterfall dashes through a boulder garden, mostly obscured by thickets of rhododendron, making it very difficult to photograph, yet is a splendid sight to see nonetheless.

Ahead, work your way past the side trail to Yahoo Arch (a worthy 0.8-mile one-way side trip), then carefully walk along the cliff line above Yahoo Falls. Three designated overlooks give you a chance to safely look down into the chasm below, where Yahoo Falls sings its watery song, echoing off the chasm walls below. A bridge leads over the stream forming Yahoo Falls. One last top-of-the-rim overlook of Yahoo Falls awaits. Beyond there, the loop concludes. Make the short backtrack to the trailhead, where restrooms are available. The Yahoo Falls area also offers additional trails such as the Sheltowee Trace and scattered picnic sites with tables. After the hike you will understand why it is dubbed Yahoo Falls Scenic Area.

Miles and Directions

0.0 Leave the trailhead parking area toward Yahoo Falls. Shortly reach a spur trail leading left to an overlook of the Big South Fork, at this point usually backed up as uppermost Lake Cumberland.

0.2 Come to a trail junction and the loop portion of the hike. Turn left here, aiming for the base of Yahoo Falls. Ahead, a long set of metal stairs lead you below a sheer bluff.

0.3 A spur trail heads left to the Sheltowee Trace. Our hike keeps straight, running along the base of the cliff line from which Yahoo Falls drops.

0.4 Come to 113-foot Yahoo Falls, the centerpiece of an enormous rock house that has to be seen to be comprehended. Steps lead to the splashy shallow pool of the long, narrow cataract. Circle behind Yahoo Falls and around the rock house to next turn left at an intersection, descending away from the cliff line. A short switchback leads you to still another trail junction. The trail leading left bridges the creek of Yahoo Falls. However, this hike turns right up Yahoo Creek.

Yahoo Falls at 113 feet is Kentucky's highest waterfall.

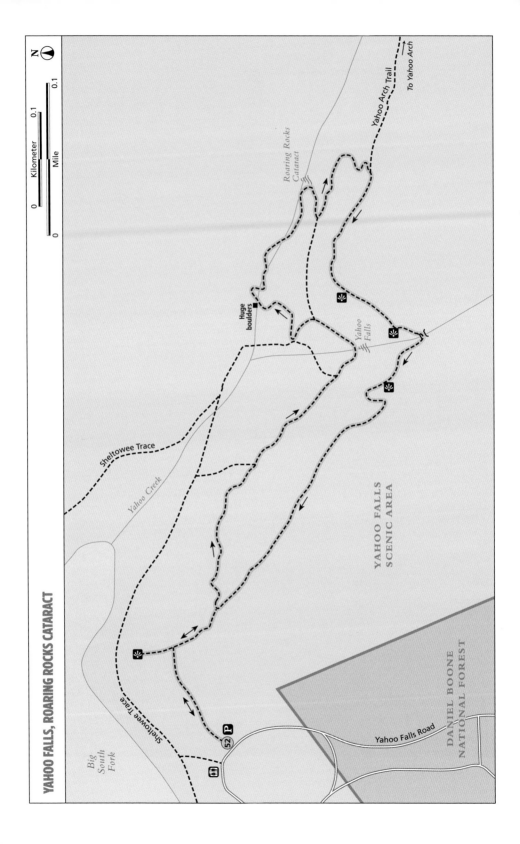

YAHOO FALLS, ROARING ROCKS CATARACT

Roaring Rocks Cataract

Yahoo Arch Trail

To Yahoo Arch

Huge boulders

Yahoo Falls

Sheltowee Trace

Yahoo Creek

YAHOO FALLS SCENIC AREA

Big South Fork

Sheltowee Trace

52

Yahoo Falls Road

DANIEL BOONE NATIONAL FOREST

N

Kilometer

Mile

0.1

0.1

0.5 The trail seemingly dead-end at big boulders on Yahoo Creek. Work your way upstream of the boulder field, crisscrossing Yahoo Creek.

0.6 Come to Roaring Rocks Cataract. The 30-foot faucet spiller dances through boulders and rhododendron. Cross Yahoo Creek beyond the falls, and come to a cliff line and trail intersection. Turn left here and climb.

0.7 Come to yet another intersection. Here the Yahoo Arch Trail leads left 0.8 mile to Yahoo Arch and makes a worthy side trip. Our hike heads right to cruise the cliff line above Yahoo Falls, passing two overlooks.

0.9 Cross the creek of Yahoo Falls and pass one last overlook of the falls below. Continue back toward the trailhead.

1.1 Complete the loop portion of the hike and begin backtracking toward the trailhead.

1.3 Arrive back at the trailhead, completing the hike.

53 Falls of Jones Branch, Yahoo Falls

On this hike—if the water is up—you will see a slew of waterfalls, including Kentucky's highest cataract: 113-foot Yahoo Falls. The hike leaves Alum Fork Campground and passes a pair of spillers on Jones Branch, then three other cataracts, all with their own personality. Culminate the waterfall quest with a trip to Yahoo Falls, with its magnificent and historic rock house. The initial part of the walk takes you along the Big South Fork gorge, passing side streams that create the falls. The last part enters the Yahoo Falls Scenic Area, with a nest of nature trails and other highlights to extend your exploration if you so choose.

Waterfall height: In order, 12 feet, 14 feet, 16 feet, 40 feet, 30 feet, 113 feet
Waterfall beauty: 5
Distance: 3.8-mile out-and-back
Difficulty: Moderate
Hiking time: About 2 hours
Trail surface: Natural
Other trail users: None
Canine compatibility: Leashed pets allowed

Land status: National river and recreation area
Fees and permits: None
Maps: National Geographic #241 Big South Fork; USGS Nevelsville
Trail contact: Big South Fork National River and Recreation Area, 4564 Leatherwood Rd., Oneida 37841; (423) 286-7275; www.nps .gov/biso

Finding the trailhead: From the intersection of KY 700 and US 27 just north of Whitely City, take KY 700 west for 5.4 miles to reach the left turn into Alum Ford Campground. Park on the right shoulder of KY 700 here. (**Note:** If you continue on KY 700, it soon dead-ends at the Alum Ford boat ramp on the Big South Fork.) The Sheltowee Trace leaves on your right. GPS: N36° 45.935' / W84° 32.695'

The Hike

It is surprising that this segment of the Sheltowee Trace doesn't receive more accolades. Starting at the Big South Fork National River and Recreation Area's Alum Ford Campground, the Sheltowee Trace makes its way down the declivitous valley of the Big South Fork, with its everywhere-you-look beauty—and numerous waterfalls formed by tributary streams tumbling down to the Big South Fork.

If the water is up, you will see no less than five waterfalls, and that is before you find the coup de grâce: Yahoo Falls, generally accorded the laurels of being Kentucky's highest cataract at 113 feet. Furthermore, the first five falls all present a different picture of a Kentucky cataract. The falls of Jones Branch flow wide and curtain-like off a rock rim, and the next waterfall spills in a veil then slaloms through a boulder field. The waterfall after that makes a 40-foot play dropping in stages, stair-stepping

Yahoo Falls in late winter, fringed with ice at its base.

downward amid lush vegetation. The last of the five spillers before Yahoo Falls makes a tall, slender, and misty 30-foot descent from a vertical stone face.

And then you reach the Yahoo Falls Scenic Area, a nest of nature trails that allow visitors to view Kentucky's tallest spiller from multiple angles. If you want to extend your hike, explore the trails and perhaps visit two more highlights: 30-foot Roaring Rocks Cataract, a pour-over enshrouded in rhododendron, and Yahoo Arch, a natural bridge about a mile farther up-trail.

Solitude will be found between Alum Ford Campground and Yahoo Falls Scenic Area, but you will have company around Yahoo Falls, since a parking area is located close to it and the scenic area is popular with casual trail trekkers.

Our hike starts at Alum Ford, so named because the locale was once used as a seasonal crossing of the Big South Fork in the days before bridges spanned the river. Today the area is managed by the National Park Service and features a boat ramp at the old ford site and an intimate six-site campground where I have overnighted many a time. Consider incorporating a campout at Alum Ford with this hike—you are close enough to crawl from the trailhead to the campground!

Leaving Alum Ford, the Sheltowee Trace winds among stone-pocked hardwood slopes—heavy with sweetgum—above the Big South Fork and below KY 700, the Alum Ford access road. The trail is well marked and easy to follow, but you will undoubtedly notice old roadbeds and tracks along the slopes.

After a half-mile, you have turned into Jones Branch. Here you will find the first two cataracts. Upper Jones Branch Falls is above the trail and emerges from a V-shaped hollow to dive off a shelf about 12 feet, a little less wide than tall. In exploring this squarish fall, you will see crumbled coal all about, from a mine just upstream. Find Lower Jones Branch Falls after crossing Jones Branch and working your way down toward the Big South Fork. This cataract spills about 14 feet from an overhanging, symmetrical, semicircular ledge, then pushes through a rocky streambed onward to deliver its waters to the Big South Fork.

Beyond Jones Branch, continue meandering down the Big South Fork valley to reach the second stream and another curtain-type fall, followed by a dance through rocks. This 16-foot spiller requires no off-trail scrambling to photograph—and you can't miss it. The hike keeps down along the Big South Fork. At this point the river is seasonally backed up as the backwaters of Lake Cumberland, thus may be stilled.

The hiking is easy, with little vertical variation. You soon meet the third stream. Not surprisingly, it has yet another cataract. This 40-foot spiller drops in stages and although impressive, much of it can be obscured by vegetation, making it difficult to photograph. Past this 40-footer, rock palisades rise to your right and you soon enter the Yahoo Falls Scenic Area, marked by a trailside No Hunting sign. A tall, low-flow, ephemeral waterfall greets you. This 30-foot force of water spatters over a stone wall, at the base of which stands a boulder garden. This waterfall has the smallest watershed and is the first to run dry.

Lower Jones Branch Falls froths white from a tan stone lip.

Fear not, for you are turning into Yahoo Creek and the astonishing Bluegrass State beauty that awaits. Finding Yahoo Falls amid the nature trails is easy—just keep going to the waterfall noise and keep the steep rock wall to your right. And then Yahoo Falls appears, making its lofty faucet-type dive from one of the biggest rock houses in Kentucky, and that is saying a lot. Everything around Yahoo Falls is on a grand scale, and you will probably be tempted to further explore the Yahoo Falls area. Check out Roaring Rocks Cataract, Yahoo Arch, and the top-down vista of Yahoo Falls. Hopefully you won't get caught in the spiderweb of trails found here . . .

Miles and Directions

0.0 From the roadside parking across from the entrance road to Alum Ford Campground, walk back up KY 700 just a short distance to join the Sheltowee Trace, heading northeast. Roll through sweetgum and beech on a slope. Watch for old roadbeds potentially leading you astray.

0.5 Reach Jones Branch and a pair of waterfalls. Upper Jones Branch Falls is above the trail spilling 12 feet from a rock shelf, whereas Lower Jones Branch Falls tumbles 14 feet from a curved ledge below the trail. To most easily access Lower Jones Branch Falls, stay with the Trace, crossing Jones Branch, and then descend along the streamside hill.

0.7 Turn into the second tributary, this one unnamed, to find another waterfall. This aquatic surge makes a wide curtain-like dive over an irregular stone face, then bounces through

FALLS OF JONES BRANCH, YAHOO FALLS

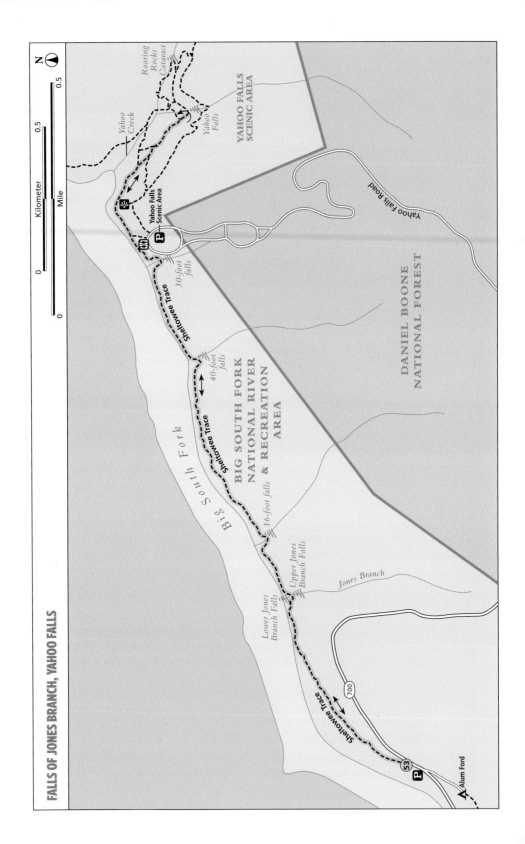

N

Roaring Rocks Cataract

Yahoo Creek

Yahoo Falls

YAHOO FALLS SCENIC AREA

Yahoo Falls Scenic Area

Kilometer

Mile

Sheltowee Trace

30-foot falls

Yahoo Falls Road

DANIEL BOONE NATIONAL FOREST

40-foot falls

Sheltowee Trace

BIG SOUTH FORK NATIONAL RIVER & RECREATION AREA

Big South Fork

16-foot falls

Upper Jones Branch Falls

Jones Branch

Lower Jones Branch Falls

700

Sheltowee Trace

53

Alum Ford

rocks to flow across the Sheltowee Trace. This 16-foot waterfall is easy to access and photograph from the trail.

0.9 The Sheltowee Trace squeezes between boulders. Continue rolling through woods.

1.2 Find yet another waterfall after reaching the next tributary. Here the 40-foot cascade plunges in stages amid heavy vegetation just upstream of the trail. Note the enchanting shorter slide cascade below the trail crossing of the stream.

1.4 Reach a trail intersection and waterfall. Here a spur trail leads right up to the Yahoo Falls parking area. Stay straight and cross a bridge at a low-flow 30-foot waterfall spilling from a high stone wall into a boulder garden. Beyond here, hike along high cliff lines then turn into the Yahoo Creek valley.

1.7 Come to yet another intersection. Here the Sheltowee Trace splits down and to the left, aiming for points north. We, however, keep straight and head for Yahoo Falls on an unnamed nature trail. Keep going toward the noise of Yahoo Falls and keep the high cliff line to your right, ignoring other nature trails.

1.9 Reach the base of 113-foot Yahoo Falls and the immense, culturally and historically significant rock house around it. This waterfall is worth viewing from multiple angles and perspectives. From here you can backtrack or delve into the nest of nature trails that allow views of Yahoo Falls from all angles.

3.8 Arrive back at the Alum Ford trailhead, completing the hike.

54 Julia Lynn Falls, Princess Falls

This fun little trek to two completely different waterfalls starts at a place known as Yamacraw. Here, join Kentucky's master path—the Sheltowee Trace—running deep in the valley of the Big South Fork. Find Julia Lynn Falls up a side hollow, making its narrow but uniform drop from a ledge overhanging a rock house. Enjoy the cataract from multiple angles before turning up the Lick Creek valley where you find unusual Princess Falls, making its very wide descent just as Lick Creek makes a bend. Numerous viewing positions and a large plunge pool add to the enjoyment of Princess Falls. The walking is mostly level, making for an easy trek.

Waterfall height: In order, 25 feet, 18 feet
Waterfall beauty: 4
Distance: 2.6-mile out-and-back
Difficulty: Easy
Hiking time: About 1.5 hours
Trail surface: Natural
Other trail users: None
Canine compatibility: Leashed pets allowed

Land status: National river and recreation area
Fees and permits: None
Maps: National Geographic #241 Big South Fork; USGS Barthell
Trail contact: Big South Fork National River and Recreation Area, 4564 Leatherwood Rd., Oneida 37841; (423) 286-7275; www.nps.gov/biso

Finding the trailhead: From Whitley City, take US 27 south to KY 92. Turn right and head west on KY 92 for 7.9 miles, then turn right into the Yamacraw Day Use Area on the right just before KY 92 bridges the Big South Fork. GPS: N36° 43.5276' / W84° 32.5768'

The Hike

This is a fun and easy day hike in the valley of the Big South Fork visiting two completely dissimilar waterfalls. Deep in the bowels of the gorge of the Big South Fork, KY 92 leads to a bridge crossing at a place called Yamacraw. Like many abandoned communities in southeastern Kentucky, Yamacraw was once the site of a mining operation and railroad. The railroad line bridged the Big South Fork a little south of where the current KY 92 crosses the river. The rail line was shut down in 1949, and not surprisingly the post office was shuttered a year later. The Yamacraw mine's run was from 1910 to 1958.

Now all we are left with is a name and story—and a place to start a waterfall hike. The Sheltowee Trace passes through the gorge of the Big South Fork here, and we follow Kentucky's longest and wildest trail along the big and brawling river. The path here is well marked and maintained and is part of a short nature trail loop leaving from Yamacraw. Here you parallel the Big South Fork, following it downstream, well above the waterway, shaded by a host of hardwoods such as beech and oak, along with rhododendron, ever-present in the cool, shady streamside woods of the Big

South Fork National River and Recreation Area as well as the Daniel Boone National Forest.

It isn't long before the short nature trail—the Yamacraw Loop—splits left to circle down to the river. The Sheltowee Trace keeps down the Big South Fork gorge, turning east, tracing the curves of the river. The path comes to the banks of the Big South Fork and joins a long-forgotten roadbed. Dripping cliff lines rise to your right, and small springs dribble across the path.

You won't miss Julia Lynn Falls, visible from the trail. The noisy cataract makes a uniform dive from a horizontal ledge, worn a little on the top but incredibly straight on its lower edge. A deep rock house forms behind the tumbler as it free-falls 25 feet, quickly gathers in no pool of consequence, and flows on over a stone bed, crossing the trail and emptying into the Big

Julia Lynn Falls as seen from the Sheltowee Trace.

South Fork. The arrow-straight drop of Julia Lynn Falls is its most singular feature. Approaching the cataract is a simple matter of meandering among some mossy boulders and investigating it up close as well as its rock house. Since Julia Lynn Falls has a small watershed, the waterfall tends to run poorly from summer through autumn. If coming during that time, try to visit after rainy periods, or better yet, come during the winter and spring.

The next waterfall—Princess Falls—is one of your better year-round cataracts in these parts. However, before reaching that big and wide spiller, you continue up the vale of the Big South Fork, rich with wildflowers in spring. Big boulders and river birch are found along the path. You'll cross a small stream as the valley of Lick Creek opens to your right. This area can be a bit confusing, as illegal ATVs from adjacent private parcels have historically plagued the locale, creating bootleg trails.

The Sheltowee Trace turns into sycamore-rich flats along Lick Creek to reach a trail intersection. Here the Sheltowee Trace splits left to bridge Lick Creek, while an old roadbed—sometimes used by ATVs—leaves right and uphill. Between these two paths, the signed, singletrack Lick Creek Trail keeps up the Lick Creek valley. Join the Lick Creek Trail, snaking among mossy boulders and tall trees.

And then Princess Falls appears in all its magnificence, tumbling 18 feet over a ledge easily three times as wide as it is tall, quite the opposite of Julia Lynn Falls. You

Morning light of winter spills on Princess Falls.

can admire this cascade from different perspectives, one of which is getting down to the plunge pool, where an overhanging ledge stretches alongside the pool. You can get under the ledge or at lower water levels walk around on sandbars next to the copious plunge pool. Interestingly, the actual Lick Creek Trail travels atop this over-hanging ledge. The elevated perch delivers yet another perspective, as does the view of the falls from a nearby campsite by the plunge pool.

These two spillers give you an idea of the many shapes and forms Kentucky waterfalls can take. If you still desire more waterfalls, head on up to Lick Creek Falls and Lower Lick Creek Falls, about a mile and a half up Lick Creek. Otherwise, back-track to the Yamacraw trailhead, passing Julia Lynn Falls one more time. Additionally, you could complete the short Yamacraw Loop on your way back, passing a few little shoals and walking along the river before reaching a lower alternate parking area, then completing the nature trail with a very short road walk.

Miles and Directions

0.0   Start the hike as the Sheltowee Trace leaves from the upper end of the small Yamacraw Day Use Area, at the point where the access road bends left to pass under the KY 92 bridge. Head northeast on the singletrack Sheltowee Trace. Quickly pass under a power line clearing.

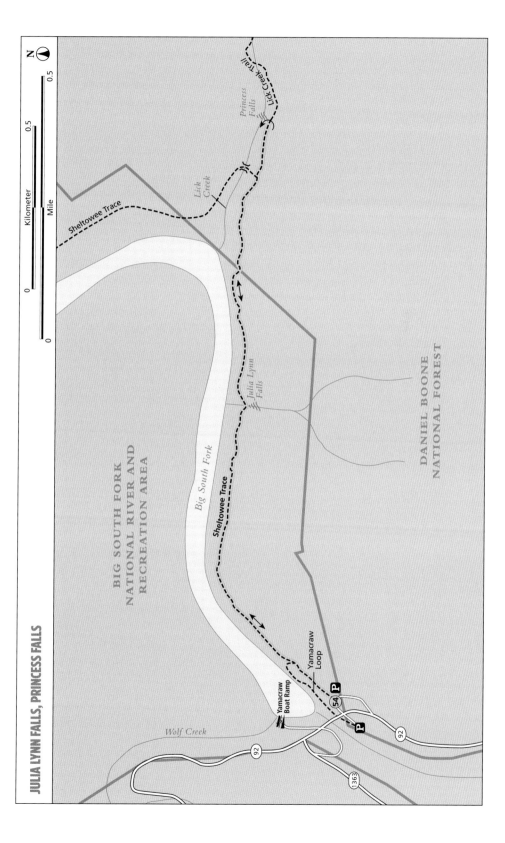

JULIA LYNN FALLS, PRINCESS FALLS

Princess Falls

Lick Creek Trail

Lick Creek

Sheltowee Trace

BIG SOUTH FORK
NATIONAL RIVER AND
RECREATION AREA

Julia Lynn
Falls

Big South Fork

Sheltowee Trace

DANIEL BOONE
NATIONAL FOREST

Yamacraw
Loop

Yamacraw
Boat Ramp

Wolf Creek

92

54

P

P

92

363

N

Kilometer
0   0.5
Mile
0   0.5

0.1 Reach a small creek and a trail intersection. Here the Yamacraw Loop nature trail descends by tight switchbacks along the small creek then turns up the Big South Fork, making a 0.4-mile loop. We stay straight with the Sheltowee Trace, eventually curving to the east, tracing the bend of the river.

0.7 Come to the outflow of Julia Lynn Falls as it crosses the Sheltowee Trace. From here, walk about 120 feet up the stream to reach the 25-foot pour-over, visible from the trail. Check out the falls and the rock house. Note the uniform descent of Julia Lynn Falls, making a vertical dive from its ledge.

1.0 Step over a small stream just before fully turning into the Lick Creek drainage.

1.2 Come to a trail intersection. Here the Sheltowee Trace descends left to a bridge over Lick Creek, while an old roadbed used as a bootleg ATV trail leaves uphill to the right. However, you join the signed Lick Creek Trail, running between the old roadbed and the Sheltowee Trace. Follow the singletrack path up along Lick Creek.

1.3 Reach Princess Falls. Here a short path descends to the base of the wide waterfall, where the entirety of Lick Creek spills over a broad ledge just as the creek is making a big turn. A long overhanging ledge stands downstream of the falls, beside a huge plunge pool, while a campsite lies below the falls on the far side of the trail. The campsite is impossible to reach dry-footed at higher flows. Explore the falls some more by heading up the Lick Creek Trail a bit. Backtrack to the trailhead.

2.6 Arrive back at the Yamacraw trailhead, completing the hike.

55 Princess Falls, Lick Creek Falls, Lower Lick Creek Falls

This waterfall adventure leads to three gorgeous yet disparate cataracts in one beautiful valley—and undertakes an interesting trip along the way. The hike includes metal ladders, unique rock houses, creek crossings, and everywhere-you-look beauty. Lower Lick Creek Falls, Lick Creek Falls, and Princess Falls will all captivate your attention and make the trip worthwhile.

Waterfall height: In order, 16 feet, 40 feet 18 feet
Waterfall beauty: 5
Distance: 7.4-mile out-and-back with spur
Difficulty: Moderate to difficult
Hiking time: About 4.2 hours
Trail surface: Natural
Other trail users: None
Canine compatibility: Leashed pets allowed

Land status: National forest
Fees and permits: None
Maps: Daniel Boone National Forest, South Section; USGS Whitely City, Barthell
Trail contact: Daniel Boone National Forest, Stearns Ranger District, 3320 US 27 North, Whitley City 42653; (606) 376-5323; www.fs.usda.gov/dbnf

Finding the trailhead: From traffic light #4 on US 27 at the intersection with KY 478 in Whitley City, head west on KY 478 for 0.1 mile, then turn left on KY 1651 south. Follow it for 1 mile and turn right onto Ranger Road. Follow Ranger Road just a short distance to reach a gravel parking area on your right, between two houses. GPS: N36° 42.899' / W84° 28.857'

The Hike

Simply put, this is yet another top-notch Kentucky waterfall hike. Located within the confines of the Daniel Boone National Forest just outside of Whitley City, the trek visits three major waterfalls: Lower Lick Creek Falls, Lick Creek Falls, and Princess Falls. The three distinctly dissimilar cataracts are situated within the gorgeous Lick Creek valley, where the blue-green stream courses among massive boulders and the trail uses ladders to descend cliff lines and then stone steps to curve under a massive rock house that will certainly grab your attention.

The waterfalls themselves hold their own and more in the beauty department. Lower Lick Creek Falls is an unusual cataract. It makes an angled stair-step descent— nothing unusual about that—but it is the massive boulder perched atop the pour-over that makes the spiller stand out. Lick Creek Falls is a slender free-faller parachuting 40 feet from a cut in an overhanging stone lip enveloped in a sandstone rock house. Princess Falls is altogether different from the other two cascades. Located on Lick Creek itself (the other two are on a tributary of Lick Creek), Princess Falls is situated on a bend in the stream. Here, Lick Creek flows over an extended rock slab then

Lick Creek Falls plummets into an overhanging stone cathedral.

makes an abrupt right turn, spilling 18 feet over a 45-foot-wide ledge into a sizable pool, creating one broad curtain fall.

The wildness of the hike is belied by its beginning, starting on the edge of Whitley City. Hiking through ridgetop pines and oaks, it isn't long before you leave civilization behind to enter the gorge of Lick Creek, using the aforementioned metal ladders to descend cliff lines. And the excitement continues when you curve under a stone-littered rock house of impressive proportions. The whole scene is ethereal. Furthermore, when the rains have been falling, the rock house has a slender spiller of its own.

You then reach Lick Creek itself, working downstream in a classic eastern Kentucky landscape of big boulders, cliff lines, and rich woods. It isn't long before you are turning up another tributary of Lick Creek, to visit Lower Lick Creek Falls and Lick Creek Falls. These two spillers are perhaps misnamed since they are not on Lick Creek itself. Names aside, the two falls are worth the side trip and offer exciting photography opportunities.

A trip along a dripping cliff line ends in the grotto from which Lick Creek Falls makes its 40-foot dive. The cliff walls are stained in iron and along with other colored rock add a tinted splash to the waterfall. It is not tough to move about the falls to regard the white spray from different perspectives.

Now, on to Princess Falls. A short backtrack followed by a trail split and rock-hop gets you heading down Lick Creek past big pools and scads of rhododendron. A few manageable creek crossings lie ahead, then you'll come to a campsite near a tributary of Lick Creek before reaching a stream curve and Princess Falls. If you stay with the trail, you can then drop below 18-foot Princess Falls from the bottom. If the water is up, expect to get your feet wet wrangling around below the falls. Nonetheless, Princess Falls can be viewed from 360 degrees, allowing you to fully appreciate the wider-than-long cataract that flows into a large plunge pool bordered by a campsite.

From here you can simply take the Lick Creek Trail directly back to the trailhead, avoiding the spur to Lower Lick Creek Falls and Lick Creek Falls. However, it will be rewarding to experience a second time the ethereal rock house and ladders climbing the cliff lines on your way back.

Many hikers erroneously bypass Lower Lick Creek Falls.

PRINCESS FALLS, LICK CREEK FALLS, LOWER LICK CREEK FALLS

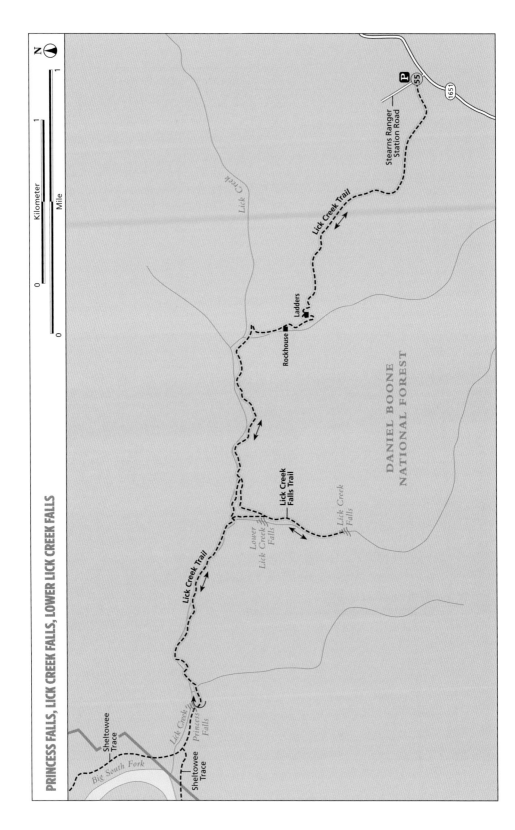

N

Kilometer

Mile

0   1

Lick Creek

Stearns Ranger Station Road

P

55

1651

Lick Creek Trail

Ladders

Rockhouse

Lick Creek Falls Trail

Lower Lick Creek Falls

Lick Creek Falls

Lick Creek Trail

DANIEL BOONE NATIONAL FOREST

Sheltowee Trace

Lick Creek Tr.

Princess Falls

Sheltowee Trace

Big South Fork

Miles and Directions

0.0 Leave the trailhead and look left for the trail sign and pole gate. Pass by the pole gate and walk along the wood's edge near a private house to your left. Pick up the Lick Creek Trail, at this point a doubletrack path running along the Daniel Boone National Forest boundary.

0.1 Stay right with the Lick Creek Trail, descending.

0.3 Pass under a power line.

0.9 Begin descending from the uplands.

1.2 Descend the first of two metal ladders, whereby hikers can safely scale a pair of sheer cliff lines. Dip to come along an unnamed tributary of Lick Creek.

1.4 The trail curves under a gigantic rock house scattered with fallen boulders and with a very low-flow fall. Take the stone steps between boulders and beneath the overhang of nothing but rock.

1.6 Reach Lick Creek and turn downstream. The creek flows to your right among midstream boulders shaded by tall trees.

2.3 Head left on the Lick Creek Falls Trail. Turn up an unnamed feeder stream, and join a slope well above Lick Creek.

2.5 Come to another signed trail intersection. Stay left toward Lick Creek Falls. Listen for Lower Lick Creek Falls, a 16-foot cataract complemented by a hanging boulder. There is no easy way to reach the falls. To reach it, scramble steeply downhill to your right. Approach it from the lower end of the falls then head upstream. Here you will face the falls, with the imposing boulder standing atop the angled, widening white cataract descending in increments before gathering in a shallow, sandy pool.

2.8 Reach 40-foot Lick Creek Falls, pouring into a stone amphitheater. Backtrack to the intersection.

3.1 Head left at the signed junction where you were earlier. Descend toward Lick Creek.

3.3 Return to the Lick Creek Trail after crossing Lick Creek just upstream of a huge boulder. When the water is up, this crossing may be a ford. Once on the Lick Creek Trail, head left, westerly, downstream.

3.7 Make a more difficult crossing of Lick Creek. Keep down the left-hand bank of the stream.

4.0 Come to a pair of creek crossings. You can make these two crossings, but a user-created trail sneaks along on the left-hand bank and avoids them. If you do make these crossings, note the illegal ATV trail coming in from the north bank.

4.1 Reach Princess Falls after passing through a campsite near a tributary stream entering from the left. Backtrack toward the trailhead.

4.9 Keep straight beyond the trail intersection with a path leading right for Lick Creek Falls.

5.1 Pass the second intersection leading right to Lick Creek Falls. Keep straight on the Lick Creek Trail.

5.8 Turn right away from Lick Creek.

6.2 Pass under the otherworldly rock house, then come to the metal ladders ascending cliff lines. Continue backtracking

7.4 Arrive back at the trailhead, completing the waterfall hike.

56 Blue Heron Falls, Upper Blue Heron Falls

If you catch these waterfalls during the wet season, you will be in for a treat. And even if Blue Heron Falls is flowing a little slow, the surrounding scenery will reward you nonetheless. This hike starts at historic Blue Heron, a former mining community restored by the National Park Service. From there, walk along the Big South Fork past a rip-roaring rapid known as the Devils Jump. Beyond the rapid, climb to an old railroad grade and follow it to meet Blue Heron Falls. The main cataract drops about 20 feet then flows across the trail and makes a long slide before flowing into the Big South Fork. Above it, Upper Blue Heron Falls makes its dive over a rock rim. Allow time to explore the Blue Heron outdoor museum before or after your hike.

Waterfall height: In order, 45 feet, 50 feet
Waterfall beauty: 5
Distance: 1.9-mile lollipop loop
Difficulty: Easy
Hiking time: About 1.2 hours
Trail surface: Natural
Other trail users: Equestrians, bicyclists on part of the trail
Canine compatibility: Leashed pets allowed

Land status: National river and recreation area
Fees and permits: None
Maps: National Geographic #241 Big South Fork; USGS Barthell
Trail contact: Big South Fork National River and Recreation Area, 4564 Leatherwood Rd., Oneida 37841; (423) 286-7275; www.nps .gov/biso

Finding the trailhead: From Whitley City, take US 27 south to KY 92. Turn right and head west on KY 92 for 1.2 miles, then veer left on KY 1651. Follow KY 1651 for 1 mile to reach KY 742. Make a sharp right here, and follow KY 742 for 8.1 miles to its dead end at the Blue Heron former mining community and outdoor museum, boat ramp, and trailhead. Drive all the way to the boat ramp parking area and park down here. Join the Blue Heron Loop where it leaves from the upper end of the boat ramp. GPS: N36° 40.098' / W84° 32.821'

The Hike

The stream that forms Blue Heron Falls has a small watershed as it flows from a narrow ridgetop down to the Big South Fork. The lowermost portion of this drainage is very steep—and that is what creates the waterfalls. Interestingly, when the nearby mining community of Blue Heron was in its heyday, the mine company probably thought of these waterfalls as an impediment and potential hazard. See, one of the many rail lines spurring from Blue Heron cut directly through Blue Heron Falls, and this flowing water could have undermined the tracks. Furthermore, when you get to Blue Heron Falls, you will also see a barred mineshaft directly next to the cataract. Again, the flowing water could have threatened the mineshaft.

Blue Heron Falls pitches forth into the gorge of the Big South Fork.

Today, however, Blue Heron is part of the Big South Fork National River and Recreation Area, and the site of Blue Heron is now an outdoor museum. And hikers like us have an appreciation for waterfalls in all their glory rather than seeing them as problematic. Furthermore, railroad tracks that once transported coal from the mines to the processing area are now used as trails. You will be following an old rail line for part of this hike.

The waterfall adventure starts near the Blue Heron boater access near the Big South Fork. The hike then joins the Blue Heron Loop, a hiker-only trail that runs among the massive boulders and big trees flanking the Big South Fork. The trail presents a close look at the gorge, where rock bluffs rise hundreds of feet from the water. You will then reach a hazardous rapid in the river known as the Devils Jump. It consists of a mid-river boulder jumble that requires skilled paddling to navigate. In my early days of paddling, this rapid flipped me and I only made it through unscathed once. Nowadays, I use the portage trail that runs around it on the southeast bank (our hike is on the northwest bank).

If you come here when the water is up—and that is when you should see Blue Heron Falls—the Big South Fork will be flowing bold and possibly muddy. And the Devils Jump will be roaring loud, echoing off the walls of the gorge. The trail takes you close to the rapid and then continues upstream before switchbacking uphill through a partly forested area of mine tailings. You will then join the Lee Hollow Loop, a trail open to bicyclers, equestrians, and hikers. The Lee Hollow Loop follows an old railroad bed and takes you to Blue Heron Falls. Here the upper half of Blue Heron Falls spills over layered strata then dances down a vertical face onto the trail, before surging onward down a concreted channel to the Big South Fork. Oddly, the concrete channel looks natural at first glance, and at second glance. The barred mine-shaft stands directly to the left of the falls as you face it.

Upper Blue Heron Falls spills about 60 yards upstream of the lower falls. It makes a classic Kentucky ledge dive from a rock rim then gently flows before spilling as Blue Heron Falls. You have to climb some to reach Upper Blue Heron Falls. Just remember, to best enjoy these cataracts come during the winter or spring since the stream has a small watershed.

Miles and Directions

0.0 While standing at the top of the Blue Heron boater access near the Big South Fork, join the Blue Heron Loop, hiking east with the Big South Fork to your right. Soon a spur leads left to the Lee Hollow Trail. Keep straight on the hiker-only Blue Heron Loop as it narrows to a singletrack path under sycamores.

0.2 Bridge a streamlet amid cane. Look for huge boulders along the trail, in the woods and in the river.

0.5 A sign alerts you to the Devils Jump rapid, roaring to your right. The water noise signals you also. High bluffs rise across the river.

0.6 Bridge a seasonal stream and enter a reclamation area where mine tailings were piled.

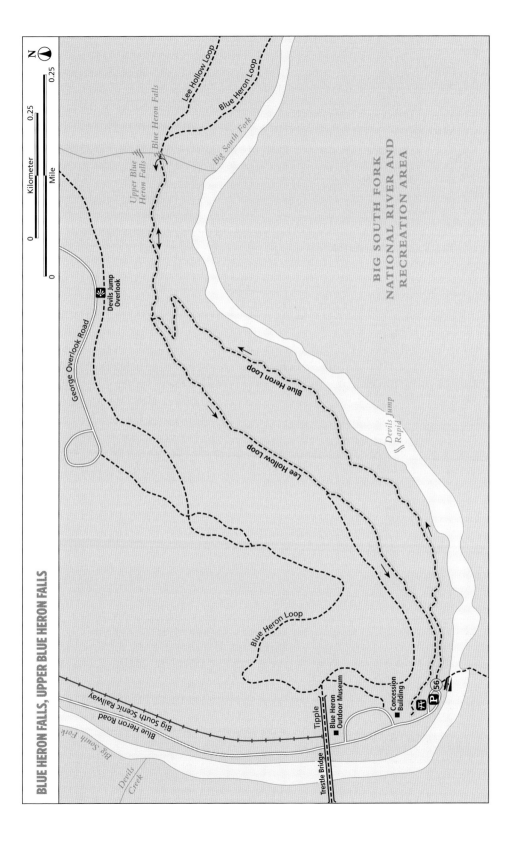

BLUE HERON FALLS, UPPER BLUE HERON FALLS

BIG SOUTH FORK
NATIONAL RIVER AND
RECREATION AREA

Blue Heron Road

Big South Fork Scenic Railway

Big South Fork

Devils Creek

Trestle Bridge

Tipple

Blue Heron Outdoor Museum

Concession Building

George Overlook Road

Devils Jump Overlook

Upper Blue Heron Falls

Blue Heron Falls

Big South Fork

Lee Hollow Loop

Blue Heron Loop

Blue Heron Loop

Lee Hollow Loop

Blue Heron Loop

Devils Jump Rapid

N

Kilometer

0   0.25

Mile

0   0.25

0.7 Climb through the tailings area, following the trail signs as the path crosses an old roadbed.

0.8 Come to a trail intersection after ascending steep log steps, and join a railroad grade right. Here the Blue Heron Loop and Lee Hollow Trail run conjunctively on a piney slope. Look down on the river and bluffs and the reclamation area. Pass a barred mineshaft to the left of the trail.

1.0 Come to Blue Heron Falls as it spills above the trail. Note the barred mineshaft next to the falls. The slide cascade shoots below the trail, while Upper Blue Heron Falls makes its drop over a ledge well above the path. Backtrack to the intersection.

1.2 Return to the intersection where you were earlier. This time stay with the Lee Hollow Loop, still on the railroad grade.

1.9 Arrive back at Blue Heron near the picnic shelters and the old schoolhouse, part of the Blue Heron outdoor museum.

57 Dick Gap Falls, Big Spring Falls

Start this waterfall extravaganza at a fascinating place known as Blue Heron, where a historical outdoor mining camp museum grabs your attention. The hike leads you across the Big South Fork on a trestle bridge from the former mine, then you ascend past bluffs up to an overlook of the Big South Fork gorge. Next, visit misty Dick Gap Falls and other cascades along that stream, then trace an old railroad grade along the Big South Fork to see tall and slender Big Spring Falls, deep in a mountain hollow.

Waterfall height: In order, 45 feet, 15 feet, 20 feet, 20 feet, 6 feet, 70 feet
Waterfall beauty: 4
Distance: 7.8-mile out-and-back
Difficulty: Moderate
Hiking time: About 4 hours
Trail surface: Almost all natural
Other trail users: None
Canine compatibility: Leashed pets allowed

Land status: National river and recreation area
Fees and permits: None
Maps: National Geographic #241 Big South Fork; USGS Barthell
Trail contact: Big South Fork National River and Recreation Area, 4564 Leatherwood Rd., Oneida 37841; (423) 286-7275; www.nps .gov/biso

Finding the trailhead: From Whitley City, take US 27 south to KY 92. Turn right and head west on KY 92 for 1.2 miles, then veer left on KY 1651. Follow KY 1651 for 1 mile to reach KY 742. Make a sharp right here, and follow KY 742 for 8.1 miles to its dead end at the Blue Heron former mining community and outdoor museum, boat ramp, and trailhead. Start the hike near the concession building on your left after driving under the trestle bridge over the Big South Fork. GPS: N36° 40.159' / W84° 32.848'

The Hike

This is a rewarding hike to some fine waterfalls complemented by non-waterfall highlights. Try to make an entire day of it, hiking to the waterfalls and exploring the Blue Heron area, once a thriving mining community and now preserved as a unique outdoor museum, as well as picnicking and even staying at nearby Blue Heron Campground, all a part of the Big South Fork National River and Recreation Area.

Before you come here for the waterfalls, however, know that the spillers are seasonal—winter and spring are the best times to catch them in full glory. And when the water is really flowing, you will find "bonus" seasonal cataracts in addition to Dick Gap Falls and Big Spring Falls. However, in summer and autumn, these waterfalls can disappoint.

From 1937 until it was shuttered in 1962, the Blue Heron Mine operated here in a flat beside the Big South Fork, a part of the Stearns Coal and Lumber Company. During three-odd decades, the coal mining and processing operation was the centerpiece of a virtually self-contained community that offered employees everything from a place to live to a church to worship in and a school to learn. Several hundred miners and their families called this deep valley on the banks of the Big South Fork home, amid the maze of hills and hollows that are the Cumberland Mountains. Once bustling and noisy, now the only sounds you hear are the murmurs of the Big South Fork and birdsong echoing through the gorge. When Blue Heron was closed in 1962, the Stearns Coal and Lumber Company took about everything they could cart off by train—and then some.

After the Big South Fork National River and Recreation Area was established in 1974, the restoration and interpretation of Blue Heron began. The mining tunnels and tracks and graded building sites were still here, and the Park Service set about integrating them into an outdoor museum. They constructed metal shells of the old buildings where they once stood (originally sized and shaped), replete with accompanying photos and audio recordings of former citizens of Blue Heron, who told of their experiences from the daily mining activities and women's life in the community to courting and visiting the general store. A series of interpretive trails takes you from building to building, where you see life at it was during the mining community's heyday in the 1950s.

I have come here time and again and never cease to enjoy touring Blue Heron. Please allow time to visit it in addition to your hike. You will be hard-pressed not to look around, since the beginning of our waterfall hike takes you into the heart of the tour, where you come near one of the old mine shafts, then cross the trestle bridge over the Big South Fork. The views from the trestle will excite—here you can gaze down on the rolling Big South Fork and the site of Blue Heron bordered by a resplendent rising forest broken by sandstone outcrops that define this slice of ol' Kentuck'.

Once across the trestle, the hike joins the Kentucky Trail, following a railroad grade astride the Big South Fork. The track then turns into cliffy Three West Hollow, cut by a stream. Curve around a cliff line before climbing a rock wall using steep wooden stairs flanked by rhododendron. You are now in uplands, 300 feet above the Big South Fork. After cruising the rim of the gorge, emerge at Catawba Overlook. Here you peer down at Blue Heron, the bridge over the Big South Fork, the Devils Jump—a river rapid that's flipped me a few times—and at the cliff lines across the waterway. The panorama lends perspective to the isolation of Blue Heron.

The hike bisects Dick Gap, a once-large cleared area, now almost completely reforested. Descend by the remains of an old chimney as you make your way down the unnamed stream of Dicks Gap Falls. A spur trail leads to the 45-foot wet-weather waterfall, cascading over a rock slab, sliding down before free-falling into a sandy pool beneath a rock overhang, all wrapped in swaying rhododendron. A lesser companion fall spills to the right of Dick Gap Falls from the same cliff. The Kentucky Trail continues its pattern of going on and off old roads and paths, but the track is well marked. If you go down the wrong old road, a blown-down tree or grown-over brush will soon block your way.

Dick Gap Falls makes its two-ledge gambit.

When the water is up an avid waterfaller will find better cataracts on the stream of Dick Gap Falls than Dick Gap Falls itself. However, to see them up close, you have to scramble off the Kentucky Trail a bit. A noteworthy 15-foot tumbler lies along the descent to a railroad grade, while yet another praiseworthy waterfall is found near where the stream of Dick Gap Falls gives its waters up to the Big South Fork.

The Kentucky Trail then picks up a level railroad grade, once again cruising along the Big South Fork. Here you pass another fall after an unnamed stream emerges from a trailside culvert to tumble downslope. The hike then enters Big Spring Hollow, a deep, cool cleft in the gorge. Here you leave the Kentucky Trail for a spur path leading to a designated overlook of Big Spring Falls. The dramatic 70-foot pour-over starts its plunge as a narrow gush of white, only to splash and widen on an angled rock face then scatter outward over a rock house into a sea of evergreen. Determined waterfall photographers can expect to earn their photos if they hope to get unusual shots of these spillers. And if the water is down, save your trip for another day.

Miles and Directions

0.0 While standing near the concession building with the trestle bridge to your left, join the asphalt path leading uphill to the left.

0.1 Reach the east end of the trestle bridge amid other nature trails near the Sand House. Cross the trestle bridge over the Big South Fork. Enjoy views of the Blue Heron community, the river, and the gorge.

0.4 Come to a trail intersection at the end of the bridge. Head left on the Kentucky Trail, tracing a former railroad grade with the river to your left. The walking is easy. Watch for the wheels and platform of an old mining railcar to your left. Beech and oaks rise overhead. Turn into Three West Hollow. Boardwalks help you over wet sections.

0.7 Cross the stream of Three West Hollow on a hiker bridge. Shortly turn back toward the Big South Fork, crossing another hiker bridge then coming along a cliff line.

1.2 Reach and climb steep steps, surmounting a cliff line.

1.3 Come to a trail intersection. Here a horse trail descends left to a ford of the Big South Fork at Blue Heron. Stay straight and climb, immediately reaching a second intersection with a spur going right to Dick Gap Overlook. Head left here, still on the Kentucky Trail, toward Catawba Overlook, walking through oaks and mountain laurel in uplands.

1.8 Come to the short spur leading left to Catawba Overlook. The view encompasses the Big South Fork gorge, trestle bridge, Blue Heron, and Devils Jump. Continue on the Kentucky Trail.

2.0 Pass through formerly grassy Dicks Gap. Descend.

2.1 Look for the remains of an old chimney on trail right. Ahead, step over the stream of Dick Gap Falls on a boardwalk.

2.2 Step over a short, strange bridge surmounting a fallen log.

2.3 Wooden steps take you down a low cliff line.

2.4 Split left at the spur to Dick Gap Falls. Soon reach the 45-foot discharge, nestled in rhododendron. The area below the falls is very mushy. Resume the Kentucky Trail, passing other cascades and cataracts along the stream of Dick Gap Falls.

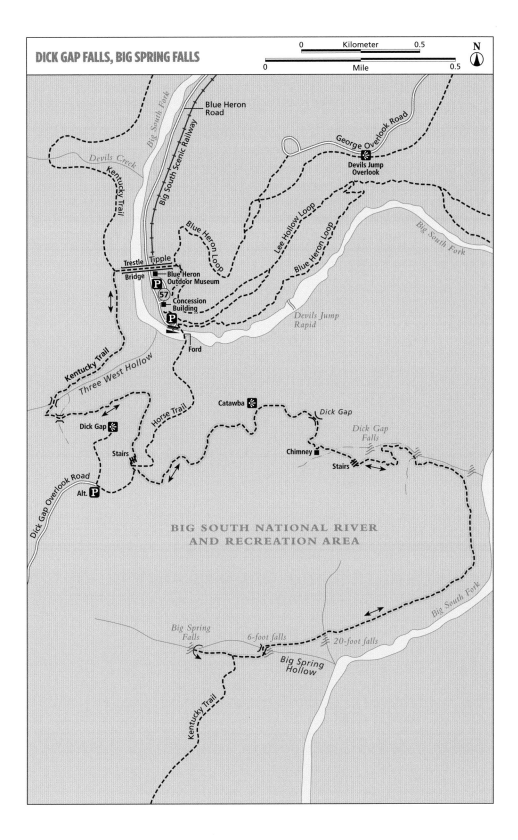

DICK GAP FALLS, BIG SPRING FALLS

0   Kilometer   0.5

0   Mile   0.5

N

Big South Fork

Blue Heron Road

Devils Creek

Kentucky Trail

Big South Scenic Railway

George Overlook Road

Devils Jump Overlook

Big South Fork

Blue Heron Loop

Lee Hollow Loop

Blue Heron Loop

Trestle   Tipple

Bridge

P

Blue Heron Outdoor Museum

57

Concession Building

P

Ford

Devils Jump Rapid

Kentucky Trail

Three West Hollow

Horse Trail

Catawba

Dick Gap

Dick Gap Falls

Dick Gap

Chimney

Stairs

Stairs

Alt. P

Dick Gap Overlook Road

BIG SOUTH NATIONAL RIVER
AND RECREATION AREA

Big South Fork

Big Spring Falls

6-foot falls

20-foot falls

Big Spring Hollow

Kentucky Trail

2.8 The Kentucky Trail curves right, joining a level railroad grade. Head upstream with the Big South Fork to your left.

3.4 The former grade passes over a stream. Below you, the bridged stream emerges from a culvert, creating a white tumbling cataract of about 20 feet. Turn into Big Spring Hollow.

3.6 Watch for a 6-foot horseshoe fall just before coming to the bridge over the stream of Big Spring Hollow. You won't miss the huge concrete building foundation to your left, just beyond the bridge. Delve deeper into the hollow.

3.7 Come a trail intersection. Here the Kentucky Trail splits left. We stay right on the spur to Big Spring Falls, well away from the creek below.

3.9 Come to the overlook of 70-foot Big Spring Falls. Here the overspill makes a slender dive from a rock precipice then splashes off a rock face, widening then splattering into a sea of rhododendron below. The base of the falls is difficult to access. Backtrack to the trailhead.

7.8 Arrive back at Blue Heron and the trailhead, completing the adventurous waterfall hike.

58 Dardy Falls

This is an unsung hike to an unsung waterfall at the Big South Fork National River and Recreation Area. Start the hike near two popular nature trails—Bear Creek Overlook and Split Bow Arch—to join the wide and easy-to-follow Cotton Patch Loop. It leads into the greater Bear Creek drainage to find Dardy Branch, where a white curtain of water spills into a lush glen. If you visit when the water is boldly flowing, you will be surprised this attractive cataract is not more heralded.

Waterfall height: 17 feet
Waterfall beauty: 4
Distance: 4.4-mile out-and-back
Difficulty: Moderate
Hiking time: About 2.1 hours
Trail surface: Natural
Other trail users: None
Canine compatibility: Leashed pets allowed

Land status: National river and recreation area
Fees and permits: None
Maps: National Geographic #241 Big South Fork; USGS Barthell, Oneida North
Trail contact: Big South Fork National River and Recreation Area, 4564 Leatherwood Rd., Oneida 37841; (423) 286-7275; www.nps.gov/biso

Finding the trailhead: From Whitley City, take US 27 south to KY 92. Turn right and head west on KY 92 for 1.2 miles, then veer left on KY 1651. Follow KY 1651 for 1 mile to reach KY 742. Make a sharp right here, and follow KY 742 for 3.1 miles to turn left onto Bear Creek Road/Ross Road. Follow it for 2 miles, then turn right and make a slight right at the signed turn for Bear Creek Scenic Area. Stay with this road for 0.4 mile, then turn left again, following the signs for Bear Creek Scenic Area. Continue for 1.1 miles to reach the Bear Creek Scenic Area parking, with restrooms, on your right. This is not the trailhead. Continue for 0.2 mile beyond this parking area to the next parking area on your right. This is the trailhead, a large gravel parking area with horse hitching posts. GPS: N36° 37.514' / W84° 31.598'

The Hike

Overshadowed by two nearby scenic nature trails as well as other waterfalls at Big South Fork National River and Recreation Area, Dardy Falls is off the radar, and it should not be. Tucked away in a corner of the park fast against the Tennessee state line, Dardy Falls is reached via the Cotton Patch Loop, a multiuse trail shared by equestrians, bicyclers, and hikers. The Cotton Patch Loop circles the lower Bear Creek watershed and its tributaries, including Dardy Branch.

Dardy Falls is tucked away in a deep, verdant ravine, making its dive over a ledge into an impressive plunge pool. Although the falls is clearly audible (and partly visible) from the trail, too few make their way down for a close look at the curtain-type spiller.

The hike is a good one, too, using well-maintained doubletrack trails throughout. It is primarily used by equestrians. The hardest part of the affair may be finding the correct trailhead. From the correct parking area, you start on the Bear Creek Loop, rising

Dardy Falls is one of Kentucky's unsung waterfalls.

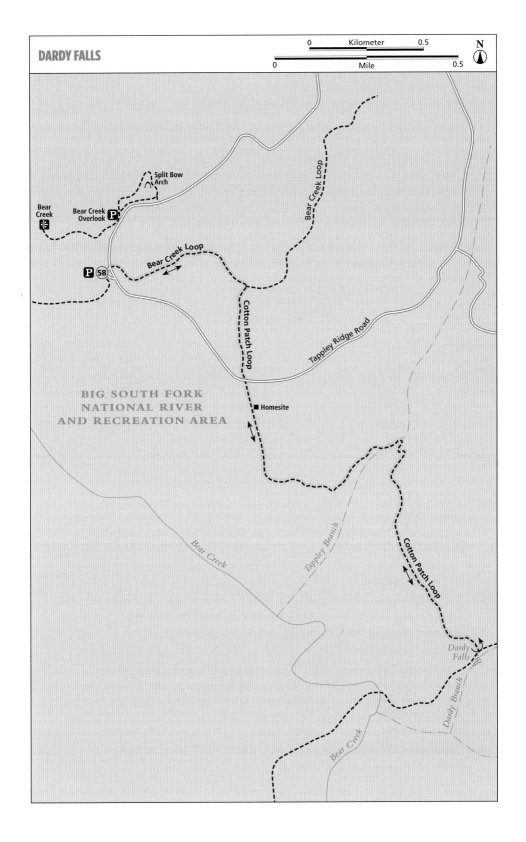

DARDY FALLS

0   Kilometer   0.5

0   Mile   0.5

N

Split Bow
Arch

Bear
Creek

Bear Creek
Overlook

P

P 58

Bear Creek Loop

Bear Creek Loop

Cotton Patch Loop

Tappley Ridge Road

BIG SOUTH FORK
NATIONAL RIVER
AND RECREATION AREA

Homesite

Bear Creek

Tappley Branch

Cotton Patch Loop

Dardy
Falls

Dardy Branch

Bear Creek

through ridgetop hardwoods on the Cumberland Plateau. The hike quickly joins the Cotton Patch Loop. The doubletrack path rolls through an old homesite—nearly grown over—where you may spot metal artifacts (please leave them for others to discover).

Beyond the homesite, the hike drops into Tappley Branch, a cool, rocky vale hosting the perennial stream. If the water is up, you have to be nimble-footed to cross the bridgeless creek. The Cotton Patch Loop rises steeply back to the Cumberland Plateau, crossing the divide between Tappley Branch and Dardy Branch. Finally, enter the hollow of Dardy Branch, curving to the waterway. A pair of trail signs (not mentioning the falls) and the noise of Dardy Branch spilling into the deep glen below alert you to the falls. A faint trail drops to the pour-over. The distance is neither too great nor too steep.

A close-up view at Dardy Falls shows an 8-foot-wide curtain of white vertically collapsing 17 feet from an undercut rock rim, then gathering in a big emerald pool before pushing downstream. Rhododendron, moss, and hemlock add a frame of green. If you have extra time, rather than backtracking a couple of miles to the trailhead, continue 8 miles through mostly uplands but also crossing Bear Creek twice, once near the Big South Fork, to complete the Cotton Patch Loop. Also while here, definitely make the short walks to Bear Creek Overlook and Split Bow Arch. You pass their trailhead just before reaching the trailhead for this hike.

Miles and Directions

0.0 From the parking area, cross the road and leave easterly on the Bear Creek Loop. Look for the sign stating "Bear Creek Horse Camp 2.4 miles." Cruise through upland hardwoods on a doubletrack trail, climbing. A different, incorrect leg of the Bear Creek Loop leaves southwest from the same parking area, dropping sharply to Bear Creek.

0.5 Come to a trail intersection. Here the Bear Creek Loop leaves left. We turn right, joining the Cotton Patch Loop, also a doubletrack trail. Head south, descending.

0.7 Cross gravel Tappley Ridge Road. Just ahead, enter a brushy area that was formerly a farm before the Big South Fork National River and Recreation Area was established. See if you can spot some leftover relics from the days when this was someone's home. The track is level and the hiking is easy.

1.0 Leave the plateau and begin dropping toward Tappley Branch. Enter a dark, cliff-lined hollow rich with evergreens.

1.4 Cross Tappley Branch without benefit of footbridge. If the water is up, you may have to ford, but that means Dardy Falls will be lively. Steeply climb away from the stream.

1.7 Return to upland oak woods dividing Tappley Branch from Dardy Branch.

2.0 Descend toward Dardy Branch.

2.2 Reach a signed intersection. Here a user-maintained trail leaves left to exit the park; therefore, signs have been placed to keep trail trekkers apprised of their whereabouts. This is also the location of Dardy Falls. You can hear the cataract from this point, and if you walk a little farther, you can peer over the edge of a cliff line at the falls. A faint path drops to Dardy Falls from the signs. After exploring the falls, backtrack to the trailhead.

4.4 Arrive back at the trailhead, completing the waterfall hike. While here, make the short walks to Bear Creek Overlook and Split Bow Arch.

59 Marks Branch Falls

Marks Branch Falls is the centerpiece of this rewarding loop hike that also takes you by a natural arch as well as another unnamed waterfall. Start your hike atop Divide Ridge, then drop into the geological wonderland of Marks Branch to see 80-foot Marks Branch Falls plunge into a reverberating rock house. Make multiple crossings of Marks Branch amid massive boulders to come near Rock Creek. The hike climbs from there, passing an unnamed 15-foot cataract before finding a high cliff line. Continue climbing to meet Gobblers Arch, a natural rock span, before completing the loop.

Waterfall height: In order, 80 feet, 15 feet
Waterfall beauty: 5
Distance: 6.1-mile loop
Difficulty: Moderate
Hiking time: About 3.5 hours
Trail surface: Natural
Other trail users: None
Canine compatibility: Leashed pets allowed

Land status: National forest, national recreation area
Fees and permits: None
Maps: National Geographic #241 Big South Fork; USGS Barthell SW, Bell Farm
Trail contact: Daniel Boone National Forest, Stearns Ranger District, 3320 US 27 North, Whitley City 42653; (606) 376-5323; www.fs.usda.gov/dbnf

Finding the trailhead: From the intersection of US 27 and KY 92 just south of Whitley City, take KY 92 west for 6.5 miles and turn left on KY 1363, just after bridging the Big South Fork River at Yamacraw. Follow KY 1363 for 11 miles to a T-intersection and the end of the blacktop. Turn left on Bell Farm Road and follow it 0.1 mile, then turn right on Peters Mountain Road/FR 139 and follow it 4.2 miles to the Peters Mountain trailhead, where parking is across the road in the Big South Fork National River and Recreation Area. The Peters Mountain trailhead has a picnic table and restrooms. GPS: N36° 37.433' / W84° 41.384'

The Hike

This waterfall hike explores a lesser-visited section of the Daniel Boone National Forest. However, after seeing Marks Branch Falls and the surrounding scenery, you will wonder why it is not more visited. Not only do you get to admire the 80-foot spiller that is Marks Branch Falls, but also enjoy another waterfall, a cliff-top view, and Gobblers Arch, a natural stone bridge tucked away in the national forest. However, there is a potential price to pay—the loop requires 17 creek crossings. During winter and early spring you may find it difficult to do this hike dry-shod, but during summer and fall agile trail trekkers will return to the trailhead with their shoes and socks dry.

The hike starts at the Peters Mountain trailhead on Divide Road. Divide Road separates the Daniel Boone National Forest to the west and north from the Big South Fork National River and Recreation Area to the east and south. The waterfall hike uses the Sheltowee Trace—Kentucky's master path running more than 300 miles through the state—southbound. Tread a slender footpath, working your way through transitioning woods into the Marks Branch watershed.

Rhododendron cloaks Marks Branch when you come upon it after a half-mile. The stream is already falling in small but noisy rapids, while the trail itself is bordered in evergreens. Ahead, skirt the top of Marks Branch Falls as it recklessly plummets from a cliff line into a stone auditorium. The trail finds a route down the cliff line, leading you to a face-on encounter with the slender, superlative spiller. Here, Marks Branch pours from a cliff line, an 80-foot straight drop splashing onto a sandy landing pad, framed by mineral-tinted rock. After gathering again, Marks Branch makes a serpentine flow into a riot of vegetation then courses onward toward Rock Creek to give up its waters.

Beyond Marks Branch Falls, the Sheltowee Trace courses directly down Marks Branch, crossing the stream again and again while passing huge, moss-covered boulders standing in and out of the water. Rhododendron finds its place amid the birch, tulip trees, and hemlocks on land. Long, gray cliff lines lord over all. While working downstream you will pass the intersection with the Marks Branch Trail. This path cuts the loop in half, but if you take it you will also miss the rest of the highlights. Stay with the longer loop, as the vale of Marks Branch opens when nearing its mother stream, Rock Creek.

You are soon at a field near Rock Creek. The Sheltowee Trace then leads to the relatively faint but signed Gobblers Arch Trail. The path climbs to a cliff line and rock shelter, and a gentle rise takes you past a low-flow cataract spilling 15 feet. This tributary waterfall of Marks Branch can nearly dry up in autumn.

Beyond this waterfall you are in upland oaks and pines, circling the top of cliffs falling toward Rock Creek. Ahead, an outcrop on a spur trail leads to an overlook of the Rock Creek valley below. Here, Rock Creek courses through the bottom of a mountain gorge to meet the Big South Fork.

Past the overlook, the Gobblers Arch Trail takes you directly to and through Gobblers Arch. The stone bridge extends 50 feet wide and 12 feet high, a dry refuge with two sides. The hike leaves Gobblers Arch to pick up a forest road. From there the gravel track leads to Divide Road, which you follow a short distance to complete the rewarding waterfall circuit hike.

Miles and Directions

0.0 Leave Divide Road southbound on the Sheltowee Trace. Join a singletrack path among oaks and hickories. Come along a cliff line before descending toward Marks Branch.

0.5 Make your first crossing of Marks Branch. Follow the stream as it cuts the beginnings of a gorge.

0.7 Cross Marks Branch then come along the cliff line above Marks Branch Falls.

Marks Branch Falls creates a slender stream of beauty.

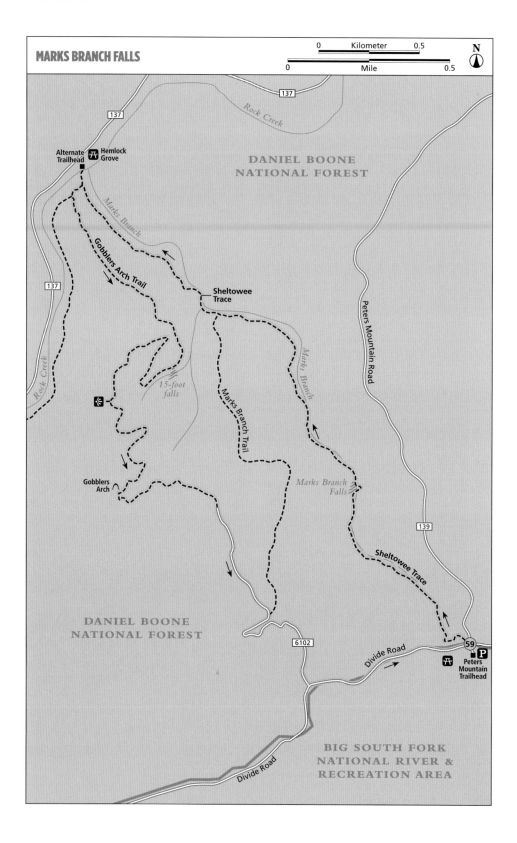

MARKS BRANCH FALLS

0 ——— Kilometer ——— 0.5
0 ——— Mile ——— 0.5

N

137

Rock Creek

137

Alternate
Trailhead

Hemlock
Grove

DANIEL BOONE
NATIONAL FOREST

Marks Branch

137

Gobblers Arch Trail

Sheltowee
Trace

Rock Creek

Peters Mountain Road

*15-foot
falls*

Marks Branch

Marks Branch Trail

Gobblers
Arch

*Marks Branch
Falls*

139

Sheltowee Trace

DANIEL BOONE
NATIONAL FOREST

6102

Divide Road

59

Peters
Mountain
Trailhead

P

Divide Road

BIG SOUTH FORK
NATIONAL RIVER &
RECREATION AREA

0.8 Reach the base of Marks Branch Falls, dropping 80 feet into a picturesque, primeval scene. Continue down Marks Branch, sometimes literally in the stream, repeatedly crossing the creek amid an implausible boulder garden.

1.2 Look for Marks Branch flowing under a house-size boulder. All the while regal cliff lines rise above the creek.

1.6 Pass the easily missed Marks Branch Trail leaving left. This intersection will occur when you are on the left bank of Marks Branch, heading downstream.

2.2 Walk around an equestrian barrier, then reach a trail intersection in a growing-over field. To your right, a signed trail leads 0.25 mile to the Hemlock Grove Picnic Area on FR 137. However, you must ford Rock Creek to reach the picnic area. Stay left, still on the Sheltowee Trace.

2.3 Head left on the less-used Gobblers Arch Trail and begin to climb.

2.7 Come to a cliff line and rock house.

3.0 Pass a low-flow tributary fall, pouring 15 feet into a narrow stone defile to the left of the trail.

3.7 A signed spur trail leads to a rock slab overlook where the Rock Creek valley opens below.

4.3 Hike through Gobblers Arch. Head left and hike through upland hardwoods to pick up an old doubletrack trail.

4.7 Reach FR 6102. Leave the dead end and head south on the gravel track.

5.1 Pass the south terminus of the Marks Branch Trail, coming in from your left.

5.6 Reach Divide Road and turn left, walking the boundary between the Daniel Boone National Forest to your left and Big South Fork National River and Recreation Area to your right.

6.1 Arrive back at the trailhead, completing the hike.

60 Seventy Six Falls

This high curtain fall swan-dives 45 feet into Lake Cumberland. The Army Corps of Engineers has developed a picnic area and a hiking trail to a view of the spiller, though it is best seen from a boat on the lake. However, don't let being boatless deter you, for a short trail leads from the developed overlook of the falls to the water's edge, and when the lake is down below full pool, you can enjoy a water-level vista of this tall and wide sheet cataract.

Waterfall height: 45 feet
Waterfall beauty: 4
Distance: 0.8-mile out-and-back
Difficulty: Easy
Hiking time: About 0.5 hour
Trail surface: Concrete and natural
Other trail users: None
Canine compatibility: Leashed pets allowed

Land status: Army Corps of Engineers property
Fees and permits: None
Maps: Lake Cumberland; USGS Wolf Creek Dam, Cumberland City
Trail contact: US Army Corps of Engineers, 855 Boat Dock Rd., Somerset 42501; (606) 679-6337; www.lrn.usace.army.mil/Locations/Lakes/Lake-Cumberland

Finding the trailhead: From downtown Burkesville, take Main Street/KY 90 east and stay on KY 90 for 14.5 miles, then turn left onto KY 734 north. Follow KY 734 a very short distance, then turn right onto KY 3062/Seventy Six Falls Road. Follow KY 3062 for 2 miles to the trailhead on your left. GPS: N36° 46.7158' / W85° 7.5865'

The Hike

Upon reaching and even after seeing Seventy Six Falls, most visitors assume the falls must be 76 feet high, but it is much less tall than that—at least nowadays. At one time Seventy Six Falls dropped over 80 feet! Now how does a waterfall get shorter? Glad you asked. Back in the 1950s, the Lake Cumberland project was under way, and after the dam was completed, the water rose to the current level, shortening the waterfall drop. Prior to the rising of the lake, Indian Creek—the stream of Seventy Six Falls—spilled off this ledge 80-plus feet then flowed onward into the Cumberland River. Today, it drops directly into the still waters of Lake Cumberland only 45 feet.

Therefore, the number 76 never had a thing to do with the height of the falls. But it had everything to do with the community named Seventy Six back in the early days of ol' Kentuck'. A hearty fellow named John Semple settled on the banks of Indian Creek back in 1806, using the stream's waterpower to run a gristmill. He followed that endeavor with a general store. Semple was dreaming big about the town he named Seventy Six, and platted off lots to sell for the soon-to-be boomtown. Problem was, the town never boomed, and Seventy Six faded from the annals of history, leaving a name to a waterfall and not much more.

The curtain drop of Seventy Six Falls can be appreciated by land and water.

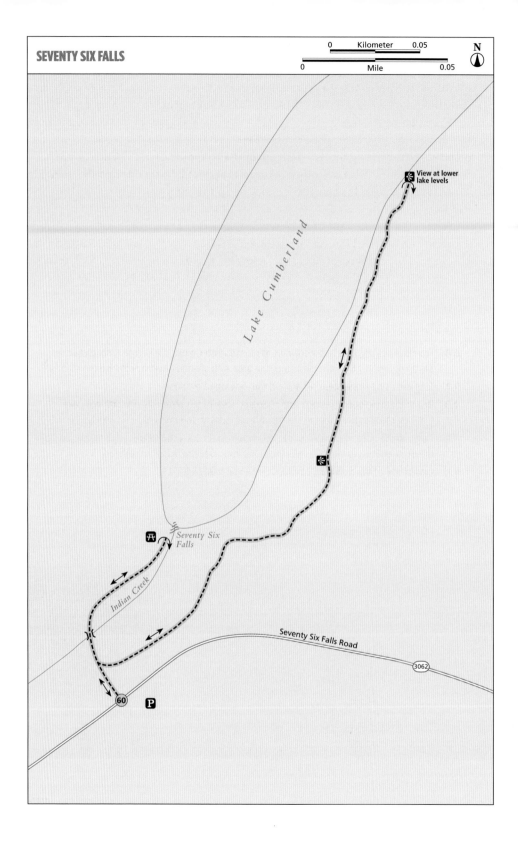

0   Kilometer   0.05

0   Mile   0.05

N

View at lower
lake levels

Lake Cumberland

*Seventy Six
Falls*

Indian Creek

Seventy Six Falls Road

3062

60

P

Indian Creek is a strange stream. The spring-fed waterway flows east from near the community of Ida, then goes underground, passing under a ridge. It then reemerges east of the ridge, flowing strong and dropping in a series of shoals before briefly flattening out just before the ledge dive into Lake Cumberland.

The walk to the falls is easy. The Army Corps of Engineers laid out a fine little trail system that first takes you over a bridge spanning Indian Creek, where you can observe the descending shoals before reaching a picnic area, with a shelter at the lip of the falls. The cliff is fenced. Many a person has perished diving off the falls—standing crosses testify to this. Furthermore, rumor has it that a few cars were pushed off the cliff long ago, creating an underwater hazard. Do not jump off here.

After enjoying the lip of the falls, make your way to the elevated vistas of Seventy Six Falls, accessed by concrete steps and walks. Here you can look down on the cascade, making a prototypical curtain dive. Finally, a dirt trail leads at a foot-friendly angle to the edge of the lakeshore, where you can see the falls by walking onto the rock outcrops exposed when the lake is below full pool, typically autumn.

Miles and Directions

0.0 From the parking area, walk downhill to cross Indian Creek on a bridge. A flat just above the lip of Seventy Six Falls avails a picnic area with shelter. Backtrack toward the trailhead.

0.1 Take the rising stone steps left toward the developed overlook.

0.3 Reach the developed overlook with a cleared view of the wide falls pitching into Lake Cumberland. Continue on the slender dirt trail beyond the overlook, descending.

0.4 Come to the edge of the lake. If the impoundment is below full pool, you can walk out on the exposed rock to view the falls from lake level. Backtrack to the trailhead.

0.8 Arrive back at the trailhead, completing the waterfall hike.

Johnny Molloy is a writer and adventurer based in Johnson City, Tennessee. He has been exploring and writing about waterfalls and the wilderness since the 1990s. Johnny has explored the splendor of Kentucky to hike, camp, paddle, fish, photograph, and explore the land from the Missouri border to the Virginia state line and from the Ohio River to Tennessee. He has penned several books about the outdoors of the Bluegrass State, including *A Falcon Guide to Mammoth Cave National Park*, *Best Tent Camping: Kentucky*, *Canoeing & Kayaking Guide to Kentucky* (with Bob Sehlinger), *Day & Overnight Hikes on Kentucky's Sheltowee Trace*, and *Land Between the Lakes Outdoor Handbook*.

Johnny's outdoor passion started on a backpacking trip in Great Smoky Mountains National Park while attending the University of Tennessee. That first foray unleashed a love of the outdoors that has led him to spend most of his time hiking, backpacking, canoe camping, and tent camping for the past three decades. Friends enjoyed his outdoor adventure stories; one even suggested he write a book. He pursued his friend's idea and soon parlayed his love of the outdoors into an occupation. The results of his efforts are over 65 guides. His writings include hiking guidebooks, camping guidebooks, paddling guidebooks, comprehensive guidebooks about specific areas, and true outdoor adventure books throughout the eastern United States.

Molloy writes for varied magazines and websites. He continues writing and traveling extensively throughout the United States, endeavoring in a variety of outdoor pursuits. His non-outdoor interests include serving God as a Gideon and University of Tennessee sports. For the latest on Johnny, please visit www.johnnymolloy.com.